MR. LINCOLN'S T-MAILS

MR. LINCOLN'S T-MAILS

The Untold Story of How Abraham Lincoln Used the Telegraph to Win the Civil War

Tom Wheeler

Collins

An Imprint of HarperCollins*Publishers*

HarperCollins books may be purchased for educational, business, or sales promotional use. For information, please write to: Special Markets Department, HarperCollins Publishers, 10 East 53rd Street, New York, NY 10022.

Designed by Ellen Cipriano

Library of Congress Cataloging-in-Publication Data has been applied for.

ISBN-10: 0-06-112978-X
ISBN-13: 978-0-06-112978-0

06 07 08 09 10 DIX/RRD 10 9 8 7 6 5 4 3 2

For Carol, Nicole, and Max

With Gratitude and Appreciation:

Jacob E. Davis, II
George W. Koch
Julian W. Scheer

CONTENTS

ACKNOWLEDGMENTS

If a young person is fortunate, he or she will be blessed with great mentors. Jacob "Jack" Davis, George Koch, and Julian Scheer were mine. Along with my father, Chuck Wheeler, these men had a major influence on my life. So many things I now take for granted would not exist without the mentoring friendship of these men.

Jack Davis took me under his wing as a young man in Columbus, Ohio. We shared a love of politics, and Jack opened doors to help me obtain seminal political experience and then to provide counsel along the way. When the time was right Jack staked his substantial credibility on his young friend, making it possible to follow my dreams to Washington, D.C.

Jack introduced me to George Koch who took a risk and hired the young kid. Working for George was my post-graduate education, and the most important professional education of my life. From George, I learned the ways of Washington as well as the discipline necessary to accomplish a task. George taught me that doing things the way they were done previously is just an excuse for not thinking. Most important, I sat in the shadow of and, I hope, learned from George's unbending honor.

One day George called me into his office where Julian Scheer was already present. "I'm hiring you to teach him everything you know" he told Julian. It was an amazing stroke of good fortune for me.

Imagine having as my public affairs instructor the man President Kennedy selected to help explain the space program to the American people. Julian was my first editor, starting with the basics of a press release; he taught me a new way to think about and analyze the positioning of policy issues. For 30 years, including after I moved on to my own leadership responsibilities, I always turned to Julian for his sage insight and counsel.

Jack, George, and Julian were my mentors. Carol Wheeler is my best friend. Carol is the wisest and most giving person I know. The gifts she has brought Nicole, Max, Michael Diggs, and me are limitless. Our gratitude is as boundless as our love for her. When one sets out to write a book in addition to holding a "day job," it is the family that first feels the pinch. Weekends, holidays, and vacations turn into research and writing periods. Somehow, Carol made it all seem normal. Her support was always there; she believed in the idea from the outset. Carol read and commented on multiple drafts with suggestions that improved the final product. Her genuine excitement over the small successes along the way was contagious. Without Carol, not only would there have been no book, but also there would not have been so many other good things in the lives of Nicole, Max, Michael, and me.

Rick Stamberger, business partner and friend, was the sounding board as the book went through multiple conceptual iterations. John Carlin, the former Archivist of the United States, heard the idea first and encouraged its development. Rick Peuser at the National Archives started me in the right direction and provided key initial thoughts. As the introduction discusses, it was while looking at Lincoln's telegrams with Governor Carlin and Rick Peuser that the term "T-Mails," a term I had first seen in a letter from a stranger named Jim Walker, came to mind.

Bob Barnett took up the cause of the book and made it into reality when others had poured cold water on the concept. Marion Maneker had the faith and vision to see the possibilities and to help find both the message and how to express it. Bob Willard, president of the Abraham Lincoln Institute, helped get the facts right and to pay the appropriate homage to this American Saint. Henry Rivera, who as a former Federal Communications Commissioner and Civil War expert understood both the network and historical components of the book, provided important review and comment, along with Luis Blandon.

The first "real author" I ever knew, Jane Stevens provided early suggestions on how to tell the story. Michael Beschloss provided his substantial historical insight, experience, and guidance; it was Michael who made the observation about how the telegraph made the Lincoln funeral the first national funeral. Ron Nessen is to blame for the fact that I would even try to write such a book. Bob Roche, in his own quietly thoughtful way, contributed early ideas and encouragement. Rob Mesirow helped me to understand that I am a "network guy" and to look for my voice in that area. Stan Sigman read an early draft and in his strong yet taciturn manner encouraged me to press on. Trevor Plante of the National Archives patiently plumbed the files to find the images of many of the telegrams that are republished herein. Jane Fitzgerald and Cynthia Cox helped in the archival retrieval. Barbara Grant, my right hand for so many years, kept me organized and running on multiple tracks. Karen Needles was invaluable as a researcher, diving into records in Washington and elsewhere to find the necessary documents to tell the story. Allen Weinstein, Archivist of the United States, provided his insights as a scholar as well as his support. John Lang helped me celebrate the joy of writing. Scott Steindorf encouraged me to push forward. Verne Newton helped me learn the ways of the electronic library. Philip Eliot stepped forward as both a volunteer researcher and technical consultant for graphics. John Hollar had faith in the concept early on and helped open doors. Daniel Ornstein shared his thesis on Civil War photography. Bill Grant, my high school history teacher who rediscovered his pupil after my last book, became "Mr. Grant" again to review his student's work.

Colonel Raleigh M. Edgar, my grandfather, was seminal to this project. "Pop" infected me with his love of history. He taught me to respect history's leaders and to discover and celebrate their stories. Many of the books from his library were used in the research for this book.

This book has only one name on the cover, but it belongs to all these people.

Tom Wheeler
Washington, D.C.
May, 2006

INTRODUCTION

The evening news video from the Iraq War showed a huge headquarters tent filled with soldiers and airmen sitting at computer terminals. They were sending electronic messages—some to the front lines to position troops and deliver intelligence, some to the rear to bring up the supplies necessary to keep the army advancing. "My goodness," I thought, "it's war by e-mail!"

Shortly thereafter I was standing with half a dozen other people amidst the miles of files in the vaults of the National Archives in Washington. Among the documents that Rick Peuser, an archivist of military records, was showing us was a book of glassine pages, each of which contained a handwritten telegram in the precise, forward-leaning cursive of Abraham Lincoln. As I turned the pages in awe, my vocation as a telecommunications executive and my avocation as an amateur historian collided; I was holding in my hands the physical record of the first time a national leader had ever used telecommunications as a regular part of his leadership. Remarking on the similarities between Lincoln's telegrams and the e-mails so common to us all, I turned to the Archivist of the United States, John Carlin, and said, "These are Mr. Lincoln's T-Mails."

Abraham Lincoln was the first national leader to project himself electronically. The command and control by e-mail that the evening news showed being employed in a 21st-century war traces its roots to the 19th-century American Civil War.

The Civil War was the first "modern" war, thanks to a troika of new technologies. On the field the rifled musket barrel extended the range and killing efficiency of the soldier's basic weapon. The railroad then expanded the area from which troops could be drawn to the killing field, replacing the trudging of men and animals with the speed of steam rolling on steel. The telegraph completed the collection by eliminating physical distance as a controlling factor in the exchange of information, thus allowing coordination among disparate forces and between the national leadership and those forces.

The application of the first two technologies, rifled weapons and rail transportation, evolved in the battlefield laboratory of men in blue and butternut gray. The outcome of the war's first major engagement, First Manassas (Bull Run), for instance, was determined by the arrival by rail of Confederate troops from a distance that in previous conflicts would have kept them out of the action. The Battle of Gettysburg was closed out by the ill-fated Pickett's Charge, in which the Confederates mounted a frontal assault using traditional tactics designed in the era of inaccurate smooth bore muskets against Federals who mowed them down with rifled weapons of increased range and accuracy.

The third new technology, the magnetic telegraph, may not have seemed as dramatic but it was equally, arguably even more, determinative in the outcome of the war. The Union army was electronically interconnected far more than their Rebel opponents. Perhaps even more important, however, at a time when the Union cause was faltering on the field was that Abraham Lincoln embraced the new electronic message capability and thus imposed his leadership in a manner and to a depth never before permitted any other leader in history. The telegraph changed the nature of national executive leadership and provided Abraham Lincoln with a tool that helped him win the Civil War.

Lincoln's telegrams have long been cited by historians looking at one aspect or another of the Civil War. As footnote fodder the telegrams are well mined. The process by which Lincoln learned to use electronic messaging and then implemented those lessons as an important part of his leadership, however, has been comparatively overlooked. It is a record to which we can all relate given the increasing role electronic messages play in our daily lives.

THERE WERE OVER 135 *billion* e-mails sent *every day* in 2005. Whether via laptop conveniently connected wirelessly at the local Starbucks, or thumbed in to a Blackberry from the back of a taxi, or from a headquarters tent in the sand, electronic messages have changed the character of communications. Because we are as we connect, this capability has, therefore, changed the patterns of our lives.

E-mail is the number-one application of the Internet. For all the many other applications the Net facilitates, the most common is the same one the telegraph made possible for Abraham Lincoln: the rapid delivery of text messages. We know how the acceleration in the flow of such information has sped up our lives and the pace of our decision making; the impact of such acceleration on Abraham Lincoln was even greater.

We have proudly proclaimed that we are at the dawn of the "information revolution." Despite our hype, however, this is not a revolution that began with the present generation. The birth of the information age was announced to the world by dots and dashes in the middle of the 19th century. The telegraph was the e-mail of the 1800s and its impact back then was even more profound than today's "information revolution."

Our present day use of electronic communications has over a century and a half of experience behind it, yet the changes it continues to deliver convince us we are in a "revolution." Contrasting these experiences with the last half of the 19th century, however, the true definition of a revolution comes into focus. The concept of messages instantaneously leaping great distances via electronic sparks on a wire—"lightning messages," some called it—was so revolutionary as to almost exceed human comprehension. This was a time, remember, when electricity was only an obtuse scientific concept to most Americans. It would be over a dozen years before Thomas Edison invented the light bulb (1879). In a world in which electricity was barely understood, sending messages via electric pulses surpassed the imagination.

Imaginable or not, the telegraph proceeded to destroy one of the pillar "truths" upon which the human experience had been based. Up until the telegraph, the history of mankind had been controlled by the absolute certainty that distance delayed the delivery of information. The telegraph upended that truth, and with it commerce and culture. It was a seminal change in the human experience, and it happened to occur at a seismic moment in American history.

Concurrent with the introduction of messages by lightning, the tensions between the northern and southern parts of the United States rose to a boil. The new technology helped to turn up the heat by rapidly delivering news from afar that engaged the population, both North and South, as never before. When the telegraph announced the news of Abraham Lincoln's election in 1860 it delivered what for many in the South was the last straw. The same instrument soon was delivering news of secession.

When Lincoln took office in 1861, it had been less than two decades since Samuel Morse's immortal "What hath God wrought!" first telegraph message. During the intervening period over 50,000 miles of telegraph wire had been strung, yet the technology's application was still in its infancy. The new president had seen his first telegraph device only three years before being elected. The White House into which he moved had no telegraph connection. While an interesting and growing technology, the telegraph's potential was still widely underappreciated and had certainly never been tested in a time of crisis.

The history of the telegraph was in many ways the prologue to what would happen over a century later with another electronic network, the Internet. Like the modern network that makes e-mails and the Worldwide Web possible, the telegraph got off to a slow start. Both technologies were developed with government grants and then rejected by those who stood to gain the most from their adoption. Morse offered his patent to the Post Office and was told that electronic messages would never replace the mail. The developer of the modern digital network, Paul Baran, tried to interest the monopoly phone company AT&T in his concept and was greeted with a similar self-preservation-laced, know-it-all attitude. As a result, the development of both the telegraph and the Internet became the domain of acolytes.

Among the telegraph's first acolytes were the railroads, newspapers, and financial markets. The acolytes for the 20th century's electronic digital network were in academic and research institutions where the technology was used to connect mainframe computers, while researchers hitch-hiked on that connection to exchange text messages. The first e-mail message, the test letters "QWERTYOP," was hardly as poetic as Morse's first message quoting the Bible's Book of Numbers, but it was the next step in the continuum of electronic messages that had began over 140 years earlier.

In 1988 Vinton Cerf connected the private electronic mail service, MCI Mail, to the Internet through the National Science Foundation computers. The following year the Internet computer at The Ohio State University provided access to a small company named CompuServe to make e-mails available to the general public (or at least to the computer hobbyists using CompuServe). We are today approximately the same distance on the calendar from those first commercial e-mails as Abraham Lincoln was from Morse's famous telegram in 1844.

When Lincoln became president he did not have the advantage we possess today of a century and a half of experience with electronic messages. The nation's leaders were flummoxed by what the new technology meant to government and the nature of leadership. In a few instances the government found new applications for the technology. The Weather Bureau, for instance, was formed to take advantage of the telegraph's ability to report the movement of storms faster than the wind could move the weather. For the most part, however, the nation's leaders were no different from the rest of America for whom the telegraph was a curiosity, not a common communicator. In this regard, Abraham Lincoln was just like his peers when he first entered the White House.

What set Lincoln apart, however, was the manner in which he grew to see the telegraph as an instrument of leadership. While there is no record through which we can watch Abraham Lincoln learn to read or write, the record of his telegrams allows us to observe Lincoln learning to use a communications capability that is basic to our lives today: the ability to send and receive electronic messages.

IN THE 20-20 HINDSIGHT OF history, the American Civil War often seems cut and dried. It was the last romantic war; a conflict with a seemingly pre-ordained outcome. The North's industrial might and a large troop-producing population triumphed over better generals leading barefoot but dedicated rebels. In reality, however, the Civil War was, as Wellington said of Waterloo, "a damn near thing." It was a hinge moment in American history that could have swung either way. That Lincoln used the telegraph to assure the hinge swung forward, not backward, makes his use of electronic messages even more important.

The story of Abraham Lincoln's use of the telegraph is a journey of discovery. During his first year in office the president infrequently availed himself of the electronic messenger. As times grew darker, however, Lincoln turned to the telegraph to project his leadership. When, in 1862, he began issuing direct orders to generals in the field, coordinating their movements and establishing expectations for their activities by telegraph, it was a turning point in the nature of national leadership.

The historical relationship between a leader in the political capital and his generals in the field was altered unilaterally by Abraham Lincoln. Never before had the commander in chief been able to issue orders and dialog with his generals in almost real time without leaving the capital. Lincoln also used his ability to read the telegraph traffic to and from his generals—even though it may have been addressed to others—as a keyhole through which he could eavesdrop on the headquarters tents of his armies. He felt free to inject himself into the conversation. When he finally found the general he and the nation deserved in Ulysses S. Grant, Lincoln continued to evolve his use of the telegraph, establishing a modern management structure.

Here is the amazing fact: Abraham Lincoln applied the telegraph's technology to create advantages for the Northern war effort entirely on his own. Because no national leader had ever had this technology, there was no guidance the president could rely upon in the experiences of historical figures. There was no text book on the application of electronic information; and certainly there was no tutor. Instinct alone was Lincoln's guide.

Reviewing the slightly fewer than a thousand telegrams Lincoln sent is a captivating experience. Through these messages it is possible to watch Lincoln's confidence grow and in turn, to observe his ongoing growth as a leader. It is also interesting to discover how his use of electronic messaging has echoes in our application of the derivative technology of e-mail. Mr. Lincoln's T-Mails are a chronicle of how one man, even while confronted by a civil war, applied new technology to define a new kind of electronic leadership.

The story of Abraham Lincoln and the telegraph is perhaps the greatest untold story about this great man. It is a story as current and relevant as your last e-mail.

MR. LINCOLN'S T-MAILS

CHAPTER ONE

ELECTRONIC LEADERSHIP

"WHAT BECAME OF OUR FORCES which held the bridge till twenty minutes ago, as you say?" the president of the United States telegraphed a Union army colonel during the 1862 Battle of Second Manassas (Bull Run).

For the second time in 13 months the Confederate army was thrashing Lincoln's troops on the ground around Manassas, Virginia, just outside the Federal capital. During the first battle the president followed the lead of his military advisors and patiently awaited the final news from the battlefield. It was different the second time around. Abraham Lincoln was fully engaged, making inquiries and receiving reports from the battlefield. The tool that allowed the president to become so engaged was the telegraph.

Like most of the people it represented, the U.S. government was slow in awakening to the opportunity presented by the telegraph. When Lincoln took office, if a government agency wished to send a telegram an employee was sent to queue up at the central telegraph office. At the outbreak of the war even an agency as essential as the War Department was not connected to the telegraph network.

Like his countrymen and his government, Abraham Lincoln had to learn how to use the telegraph. Lincoln's challenge, of course, was that his learning curve occurred amidst a military conflict to determine the fate of the national union.

The First Battle of Manassas (Bull Run) occurred four months into the Lincoln presidency. In the slightly more than a year between the first battle and the rematch on the same ground, Abraham Lincoln discovered the power of the telegraph to project his voice, as well as to extend his eyes and ears. As he grew in his role as a national leader, Lincoln simultaneously progressed in how he applied what he sometimes called "lightning messages" to extend that leadership.

First Manassas (Bull Run) was the first major battle of the Civil War. As the newspaper headlines cried "Forward to Richmond!" the new chief executive pushed his generals to take action. The route to the Confederate capital of Richmond ran through Manassas, Virginia, approximately 30 miles outside of Washington, a railroad junction at the mouth of a key pass through the Blue Ridge Mountains. There, on the plain beside a small, steep-sided stream named Bull Run, General Irvin McDowell planned to attack the Rebels, while another Union force on the opposite side of the Blue Ridge kept the Rebels in that area bottled up and out of the action.

The Union army's plan was based on the old realities of horse-mounted messengers and plodding troop marches. The new reality was an expanded battlefield made possible by two new civilian technologies: speedy telegraph messages and troops transported by rail. The application of these two technologies determined the outcome of the battle.

The telegraph summoned transport trains and Rebel troops to an historic event. It was the first time in the history of warfare that troops would be transported directly to the field of battle by train. After giving the slip to the Union force that was supposed to keep them caged, Confederate soldiers were loaded into boxcars. The troops moved faster than any army in history; one moment they were too far from the action to be decisive, the next moment they were on the battlefield. Their arrival turned the tide on July 21, 1861.

Lincoln and the other national leaders in Washington could hear the cannons' thunder on the horizon. Yet there was an almost unreal lack of involvement with the first engagement at Manassas. General-in-Chief Winfield Scott, hero of the Mexican War but now fighting a new war by the same old rules, was so accepting of the tradition of being unable to communicate rapidly with the front that he took a nap during the battle. The president had to awaken him as the battle raged.

Prior to First Manassas, Andrew Carnegie, who began his career as a telegraph operator for the Pennsylvania Railroad, was placed in charge of extending the telegraph lines across the Potomac into occupied Rebel territory. By the time of the battle, however, the line reached only as far as Fairfax Court House, about 10 miles from Bull Run. In a hybrid of the old and new, messengers galloped from the battlefield to the end of the telegraph line carrying news. "Lincoln hardly left his seat in our office and waited with deep anxiety for each succeeding despatch," recorded the telegraph office manager.*

Initial reports were of a Union victory. No doubt relieved, the president went for a stress-reducing carriage ride. When he returned half an hour later, the news was dramatically different. The rail-transported Rebel troops had arrived in the nick of time and routed the Union force. Lincoln's army was fleeing back to Washington in disarray. There was fear for the safety of the capital.

Thirteen months later, when the armies clashed again along Bull Run, it was a decidedly different Abraham Lincoln who took up residence in the War Department telegraph office. The telegraph office had become his Situation Room, where the president not only monitored events through incoming messages but also initiated communi-

* At the time "dispatch" was often spelled "despatch." This and other spellings, misspellings, and punctuation are henceforth used without notation.

cations directly to the field. Lincoln became so involved with the flow of information during Second Manassas that he did not return to the White House for sleep, preferring instead a cot that had been set up in the telegraph office.

Unable to communicate with his key generals because the Rebel movement had cut their telegraph lines, Lincoln opened a telegraphic dialog with a subordinate officer that continued over the next several days. The telegrams between Lincoln and Colonel Herman Haupt were at one point the national leadership's best source of information. It was another historic moment: a national leader electronically engaged in monitoring the activities of a battle at which he was not present.

Throughout the entire history of armed conflict, the ability to have a virtually instantaneous exchange between a national leader at the seat of government and his forces in the field had been impossible. As a result, field commanders had been the closest things to living gods. Cut off from the national leadership, the unilateral decisions of generals at the front determined not only the fate of individual lives, but also the future of nations. It was for this reason that heads of government, such as Henry V at Agincourt or Bonaparte in Russia, had remained in the field with their troops to combine both national and military leadership.

The American democratic experiment was different, however. American wars had always been fought with the head of government removed from the scene of battle, communicating primarily through messengers. When General Scott decided to march on Mexico City in 1847, for instance, the nation's leaders learned of the attack days after the event.

Had the traditional model of generals divorced from speedy interaction with the national leadership persisted during the Civil War the result could have been quite different. The Civil War, often referred to as "The First Modern War" because of the new technologies of the rifled musket, railroad, and telegraph, required its leaders to jetison large pieces of traditional military theory. Giving the benefit of the doubt to Lincoln's generals, they were having to adapt in the field in real time to the rifle's expanded killing power and the railroad's expansion of the battle space. Lincoln's early-adopter instincts, coupled with his being unburdened by the old dogmas, allowed him to outperform his generals in the ability to see change and harness it to his purposes. In no way was that instinct more apparent than in his embrace of the telegraph. Frustrated by his generals' reticence to act and inability to deliver victories, yet possessed of growing confidence in his own judgment, the telegraph became Lincoln's means to project leadership in a new manner.

At the heart of Abraham Lincoln's use of the telegraph was his natural receptivity to new technology. Lincoln's comfortable inclination toward innovative technological ideas was essential to his evolution as the first electronic leader.

The government that Lincoln took over had not been very adroit at embracing the management possibilities of the telegraph. The U.S. Army's major use of the telegraph, for instance, was for coordinating the ordering and shipment of supplies and personnel. The government was so unprepared for a greater application of the technology that when the war began the principal telegraph company serving the capital had to voluntarily pick up the tab for extending service to the War Department and other critical locations.

The most notable involvement Lincoln's predecessor had with the telegraph was a ceremonial message President Buchanan sent Queen Victoria in 1858 on the occasion of the completion of the trans-Atlantic cable. After having a telegraph station set up in the White House for the ceremony, Buchanan had it removed following the event.

That Lincoln mastered the leadership potential of the telegraph as rapidly and as well as he did is a manifestation of one of his unheralded traits. Far from a backwoods rail-splitter, Abraham Lincoln had a fascination with, and intuitive appreciation of, new technology. In the vernacular of today, Lincoln was an "early adopter."

Lincoln was so comfortable with technology that he is still the only president of the United States to hold a patent. That invention combined Lincoln's experience as a youth taking flatboats down river with a practical problem he encountered returning home halfway through his single term in Congress, when the boat on which he was a passenger became stuck on a sandbar. The device he conceived and patented would lift boats over such obstructions by means of adjustable buoyant chambers. While the invention was never manufactured, it speaks volumes about Lincoln's comfort with the application of new concepts to old problems.

As a lawyer in Illinois, Lincoln handled cases that sorted out the relationship between the first big technology shift of the 19th century, the steam railroad, and the economic and social realities upon which it was intruding. Described by one historian as "the completest change in human experience since the nomadic tribes became rooted in one spot to grow grain and raise cattle," the iron horse transformed the concept of geography as life's controlling force. People and products could now move great distances with dispatch, forcing the most significant economic and cultural changes the nation had ever seen.

Change of such magnitude triggered struggles between the new technology and the forces of tradition. Ultimately, many of these conflicts ended up in a court of law with Lincoln often arguing cases on behalf of technological innovation. When, for instance, rivermen whose livelihood was threatened by the first railroad bridge over the Mississippi "accidentally" crashed a boat into the bridge, thus "proving" it should be banned as a hazard to navigation, Lincoln defended the progress imposed by the railroad. If the rivermen's lawsuit had prevailed, it could have doomed the ability of railroads to cross navigable waters without putting railcars on ferries.

You can hear the early adopter in Lincoln's address to the court that was convened to decide the fate of the bridge. Embracing the issue with simple logic, he compared the rights of an east-west rail crossing to that of the north-south path of the river: "This [east-west] current of travel has its rights as well as that of north and south. This bridge must be treated with respect in this court and is not to be kicked about with contempt." Because of Lincoln's advocacy, the bridge stayed and the railroads continued westward.

Lincoln had a genuine intellectual curiosity about new technology. Two years before he was elected president, he set forth the fruits of that intellectual inquiry in a series of lectures on "Discoveries and Inventions." Beginning with the very first words of his remarks, Lincoln's love of technology shone through. "All creation is a mine, and every man, a miner," the text began. Technological innovation and its benefits, Lincoln expounded, were what separated "Young America" from "Old Fogey" other nations to the advantage of the new republic.

When he became president, Lincoln continued to look forward. He promoted and signed into law the Pacific Railway Act, an amazing act of faith in both technology and the national union. In the midst of a civil war, he dedicated the nation to the monumental technological challenge of building a transcontinental railroad.

Lincoln's technical curiosity also extended to the implements of war. On the lawn behind the White House he witnessed tests of new weapons whose development had caught his interest, sometimes even personally trying the devices. Joseph Henry, secretary of the Smithsonian Institution and America's foremost scientist, became his informal science advisor. Henry found a receptive audience to whom he could bring innovative technological concepts such as battlefield observation from a balloon. The president pushed for the adoption of such innovations despite the indifference of the army's leaders.

THOUGH PRESIDENT LINCOLN MAY have been an early adopter, his embrace of the telegraph was not instantaneous. Lincoln's use of electronic messages was more limited during his first year in office that it would be subsequently. This, perhaps, is attributable to the newness of his relationship with the device (he had seen his first telegraph key only three years before being elected president), his newness in the job, and to the fact that during most of this period military use of the telegraph was controlled by the army.

As telegraph technology was incorporated into government activity early in Lincoln's term, it was organized to favor serving the military, not the civilian, leadership. Lincoln learned early on how the party who controls the electronic conduit controls both its information and the application of that information. It was a lesson painfully realized as the result of yet another battlefield defeat; a battle that touched Lincoln personally.

Three months after the Union army lost its first major engagement along Bull Run, yet another debacle occurred—this time along the banks of the Potomac. Federal troops ferried across the river into Virginia were stacked up in an indefensible position atop a riverside escarpment known as Balls Bluff. When the Confederates attacked, it was a particularly ignominious defeat, driving the bluecoats back over the bluff and into the water where many were shot as they tried to retreat to the opposite shore. Killed leading his troops on the battlefield was Colonel Edward Baker, a former Illinois congressman and U.S. senator from Oregon—and an extremely close friend of the president's.

Telegraph dispatches reporting the disaster arrived at the headquarters of the commanding general, George McClellan, while the general was at the White House meeting with the president. Despite the fact that the message was rushed to him during the meeting, McClellan did not discuss its contents with his commander-in-chief.

Perhaps sensing something amiss, Lincoln later in the day wandered over to McClellan's headquarters a few blocks from the White House and inquired of the telegraph operator, Thomas Eckert, whether any dispatches had arrived from the front. Eckert, however, had been ordered to give dispatches only to the general. He slipped the Balls Bluff message under his desk blotter and told the president there was nothing new "in the file." Lincoln then walked into McClellan's office where he saw a copy of the report on the general's desk.

Returning to the telegrapher's office, a less-than-pleased commander-in-chief demanded to know why the clerk had withheld information. It was only then that the president learned of the standing orders to share such information only with McClellan. The telegraph operator argued he had told the truth while also following his orders; by slipping the offending telegram under his blotter, he had been technically truthful in telling the president there were no new messages "in the file."

It was an untenable situation. Secretary of War Simon Cameron had ceded control of electronic information to the military, even to the exclusion of the elected government. A growing number of such lapses in judgment convinced Lincoln to exile Cameron by making him minister to Russia. In January 1862, Edwin Stanton became the new secretary of war.

When Congress returned in January, 1862 it enacted legislation allowing the government to take control of the telegraph lines as necessary for military purposes. While the network continued to be owned by private companies and to carry civilian traffic, the new secretary of war assumed control for its military application under the supervision of a restructured U.S. Military Telegraph Corps (USMTC). The USMTC may have had "military" in its name, but it was a civilian operation answerable only to the secretary of war who, this time, understood that he worked for the president of the United States. Henceforth the telegraph was Lincoln's domain, operated by civilians who reported to civilians, independent from and immune to the orders of army officers.

Secretary Stanton's War Department, not McClellan's headquarters, became the hub for all telegraph traffic. Only enough equipment was left at army headquarters to handle the separate business of the commanding general. It was a decisive moment in the leadership of the war. Communication with the nation's military forces was now in civilian hands. The ability to review developments in the field on an ongoing basis was no longer the exclusive purview of men in uniform. Most important, moving the telegraph office from McClellan's headquarters to the War Department building next to the White House placed Abraham Lincoln in proximity to the technology and opened the door to his discovery of electronic leadership.

The cortex of the nation's electronic information network became a series of rooms adjoining Stanton's office in the War Department building, a nondescript four-story rectangular box next to the White House. On the second floor of this building, behind a small pillared portico appended in a none-too-successful effort to present an architectural façade to Pennsylvania Avenue, the department's former library had been pressed into service as the telegraph office.

The telegraph office became a center of Abraham Lincoln's activities. "His tall, homely form could be seen crossing the well-shaded lawn between the White House and the War Department day after day with unvaried regularity," wrote one observer.

One special room, between the instruments themselves and Secretary Stanton's office, became Lincoln's hideaway. "There only was he comparatively free from interruption and he would frequently remain for hours, and sometimes all night." Other than the Executive Mansion itself, the president spent more time in the telegraph office than in any other place during his term.

The president would set up shop at the desk of the chief of the operation, next to a window overlooking Pennsylvania Avenue. Sequestered in his hideaway Lincoln would "take his pen or pencil in hand, smooth out the sheet of paper carefully and write slowly and deliberately, stopping at times in thoughtful mood to look out of the window for a moment or two, and then resuming his writing." Thankfully, the procedure was for a message to be written out by hand before being given to the telegraph operator for transmission. Most of Lincoln's hand written messages still exist and examples are reproduced herein. To look at these documents in Lincoln's own hand brings the inanimate to life and links us with only one degree of separation to the living expression of Lincoln's electronic leadership.

IT WAS HIS FREQUENT presence in the telegraph office that opened the door to one of Lincoln's greatest electronic discoveries: the use of the telegraph as his personal news service. The more time the president spent in the telegraph office, the more he evolved his use of the technology from a tool for simply sending messages into a means of obtaining a bird's-eye overview of developments at distant points and a keyhole into his generals' thinking. "His thoughts by day and anxiety by night fed upon the intelligence which the telegraph brought," the president's two secretaries wrote in their recollections.

At times of breaking news, Lincoln would hover over the shoulder of the telegraph operator, reading the dispatch word by word as it was decoded. Most often, however, Lincoln's review of the online material consisted of the simple ritual of opening the telegraph clerk's desk drawer and reading all the dispatches that had been received since his last visit. Although a simple process, it was a revolutionary breakthrough that gave Lincoln an almost real-time understanding of activities for which previous national leaders would have waited days or weeks.

"Lincoln's habit was to go immediately to the drawer each time he came into our room, and read over the telegrams, beginning at the top, until he came to the one he had seen at his last previous visit," the manager of the office wrote. Upon reaching that previously read telegram Lincoln often proclaimed, "Well, boys, I am down to the raisins." It was an expression the president explained by spinning one of his folksy tales about the young girl who over-indulged in the food at her birthday party, topping it all off with raisins for dessert. During the night she became ill "casting up her accounts." When the doctor arrived he inspected the contents of the basin into which she had been discharging. Noticing the small black objects that had just appeared, he told the anxious parents that the danger was passed as the child was "down to the raisins." "So," Lincoln explained, "when I reach the message in this pile which I saw on my last visit, I know that I need go no further."

A personal news service is of limited value, however, unless something is done with the information. Lincoln acted on his discoveries in the desk drawer even if he was intruding into an exchange that had not included him. The telegraph was both his Big Ear, to eavesdrop on what was going on in the field, and his Long Arm for projecting his leadership now informed by the newly garnered information.

The late summer of 1864, for instance, was yet another dark hour. The war had been raging for over three years. The Union army's advance to Richmond had stalled and General-in-Chief Ulysses Grant was the target of mounting criticism. Confederate troops were advancing up the Shenandoah Valley, a well-worn path toward Washington and the northern states. The fall presidential election was only a few months away; unable to deliver either victory or peace, and facing draft riot upheaval in the cities, Lincoln anticipated electoral defeat. It was in this environment that the president read a telegram between Grant and the army chief of staff in which Grant fretted about the depletion of front line forces to quell the draft riots.

The telegraph clerk's drawer having provided a window into Grant's concerns, Lincoln used the same messenger to interpose himself, share his resolve, and allay the commanding general's conerns: "I have seen your despatch expressing your unwillingness to break your hold where you are. Neither am I willing. Hold on with a bull-dog grip, and chew and choke, as much as possible."

It was as good as walking into Grant's headquarters, sizing up the general's state of mind, and responding through conversation. The very phrase to hold on like a bull-dog even resembles a verbal repartee rather than a through-channels dispatch.

Grant's response proved the value of Lincoln's intercession. As he put down Lincoln's telegram, the general who had been beleaguered by criticism, including being called a "butcher" for pursuing strategies Lincoln endorsed, laughed out loud and exclaimed to those around him, "The President has more nerve than any of his advisers." Grant was correct in his observation, of course. More important, however, Grant had just held in his hands Lincoln's tool for reinforcing his resolve and making sure that neither distance nor intermediaries diffused Lincoln's leadership.

ABRAHAM LINCOLN USED THE telegraph to expand upon his leadership instincts, not to transform them. When conducting his business in Washington the president practiced what today is known as MBWA: Management-By-Walking-Around. Lincoln would walk among the government departments clustered near the White House, dropping into offices to catch up or to deliver messages in person. It was leadership at the retail level, face-to-face and one-on-one. The advantage of such face-to-face meetings was their ability to escalate beyond simple information delivery into a two-way conversation. Applying that concept to the telegraph, Lincoln discovered that beyond the lightning quick delivery of messages, the telegraph could create a virtual conversation in almost real time between parties separated by distance. As he grew to appreciate its capabilities, the telegraph became a surrogate for the transactional give and take of a face-to-face discussion. Lincoln could not physically walk into a general's tent the way he walked into Washington offices, so he used the telegraph to establish a virtual conversation.

While, for the most part, the president continued to transmit official orders through the chain of command, he used his own electronic messages to add color, substance, and animation to those orders. His telegrams to generals in the field added flesh to the bones of the official dispatches much as one would do in a one-on-one conversation.

As Robert E. Lee's Confederates maneuvered in the early summer of 1863 toward what ultimately would be the Battle of Gettysburg, Lincoln electronically dialogued with General Joseph Hooker commanding the Army of the Potomac. Only the month before, Hooker had been humiliated by Lee at the Battle of Chancellorsville. Now, on June 5, the general had telegraphed the president, ostensibly to clarify his overall orders but actually to float a trial balloon proposing that he attack the forces left behind by Lee. Lincoln quickly responded and spoke to Hooker in a colloquial manner that could leave no doubt as to the commander-in-chief's opinion about his general's proposal:

> *Yours of today received an hour ago . . . I have but one idea which I think worth suggesting to you, and that is in case you find Lee coming to the North of the Rappahannock, I would by no means cross to the South of it . . . In one word, I would not take any risk of being entangled upon the river, like an ox jumped half over a fence, and liable to be torn by dogs, front and rear, without a fair chance to gore one way and kick the other.*

Lincoln politely closed the telegram with the admonition, "these are mere suggestions," but Hooker, who had taken his job on the condition that he could deal directly with the president, surely must have gotten the message. Shortly thereafter General-in-Chief Henry Halleck delivered essentially the same message. Because of Hooker's ability to bypass him, the last line of Halleck's dispatch linked it with Lincoln's, "The foregoing views are approved by the President."

Five days later General Hooker again floated a new idea via telegram addressed to "His Excellency The President of the United States." This time he wanted to move south and attack the Confederate capital. Hooker's telegram, sent at 2:30 P.M. on June 10, was replied to by Lincoln at 6:40 the same day. Again, the president conversationally conveyed to Hooker what he felt were the errors in the general's judgment and reminded his commander as to the objective of the army:

> *If left to me, I would not go South of the Rappahannock, upon Lee's moving North of it . . . I think Lee's Army, and not Richmond, is your true objective point* [emphasis in original].

As before, Halleck followed up: "The President has just referred me to your telegram and his reply of yesterday, with directions to say to you whether or not I agreed with him. I do so fully."

The spirits of leaders past must have looked down on Abraham Lincoln with envy as he transposed the techniques of face-to-face dialog into electronic exchanges that imposed his will onto the decision-making of distant generals as though he was with them in the field. His leadership instincts unchanged, Lincoln continued to practice MBWA. Only this time the telegraph wire did the walking.

AFTER FOUR YEARS OF war, the spring of 1865 bloomed with the promise that the conflict could be drawing to a close. In April, with the fall of the Confederate capital in the offing, President Lincoln joined his Commanding General Ulysses Grant in the field outside Richmond. On April 3 he telegraphed the secretary of war, "This morning Gen. Grant reports Petersburg evacuated; and he is confident Richmond also is."

Secretary Edwin Stanton immediately replied, "I congratulate you and the nation on the glorious news in your telegram just recd." Then, the secretary of war went on to remind Lincoln that he was in Rebel territory and to express concern for the president's safety: "Allow me respectfully to ask you to consider whether you ought to expose the nation to the consequence of any disaster to yourself."

Lincoln, engaging in the kind of quick electronic exchange at which he had become adept, responded, "I will take care of myself."

Secretary Stanton's fears proved groundless. The president safely returned to Washington after having walked the streets of the fallen Confederate capital.

Abraham Lincoln, however, would send only 10 more telegrams in his life.

On April 15, 1865 the electronic messaging capability Abraham Lincoln had harnessed to save the nation delivered the news of his assassination.

The new technology was to play one more final role with Abraham Lincoln. Immediately following his death the telegraph permitted the organization of the first national funeral. Whereas news of the death of previous leaders, such as George Washington, had taken weeks to permeate the nation's geography, Lincoln's demise was known instantly throughout the land. The electronic messenger Lincoln used to preserve the union now became the organizing vehicle as Americans prepared to memorialize their lost leader. It was via telegraph that the circuitous rail path home to Springfield was arranged; via telegraph that citizens learned at what time to turn out to pay homage, and via telegraph that the nation kept abreast of the local honors and other news from the funeral train.

CHAPTER TWO

MESSAGES BY LIGHTNING

THREE MONTHS AFTER ASSUMING OFFICE Abraham Lincoln received a unique telegram: "I have the pleasure of sending you this first dispatch ever telegraphed from an aerial station," the message read. The telegram had been sent from a hot air balloon tethered above the site of the present day National Air and Space Museum on the National Mall in Washington.

Aerial reconnaissance by balloon was another of the technological innovations that confounded Civil War leaders by changing the rules of military conflict. Lincoln was a champion of the idea, thanks to the encouragement of Joseph Henry, secretary of the Smithsonian Institution, the president's informal scientific advisor and the foremost scientific mind of the day.

It was highly appropriate that the message came via telegraph, for Joseph Henry was the inventor of the first telegraph capable of sending messages over a significant distance. Samuel Morse, who successfully positioned himself as the inventor of the device, was, at best, the implementer of the breakthrough inventions of Henry and others.

As early as 1753 an article published in *Scots* magazine described how an electric current carried over a wire could mimic at the terminus commands entered at another point on the line. Over the intervening years, as the understanding of electricity expanded, the development of powerful batteries and electromagnets made the theory of electronic signals into a laboratory reality. Great Britain led the world in constructing demonstrations of electronic signaling.

The laws of physics, however, intervened to impede a practical telegraph. It was a physical fact that electrical current diminished in strength as it traveled down a wire. Over short distances electromagnetic signaling systems could work, but move the technology outside the lab and it had little useful application. Joseph Henry solved this problem by inventing the electromagnetic relay. With this breakthrough Henry transformed the magnetic telegraph from a lab demonstration into a technology with functional value.

At that point on the line where the electric current had attenuated to almost nothing, Henry installed an electromagnet. Receiving just enough of the dying current to activate it, the electromagnet closed a new circuit connected to a new power source. The resulting new and powerful signal, a perfect clone of the original, then continued down the line until it, too, weakened and was re-amplified by the next relay. With this development Joseph Henry vaulted the final core technical obstacle to a practical telegraph.

Using his relays, Henry built a mile-and-a-half demonstration line in 1831. Samuel Morse was in Europe at the time and had no idea either of Henry's relays, or the paper he wrote explaining the experiment. Joseph Henry's accomplishments have faded into historical obscurity compared to Morse, however, because of the different personal characteristics of the two men. Henry, unlike Morse, was not a publicity hound. Even more important, Joseph Henry wasn't greedy. It was Henry's belief that such scientific advancement should be available for the betterment of all rather than exploited for personal gain. Therefore Henry did not patent his breakthrough invention. Samuel Morse did not suffer from such selflessness.

When, in 1839, Morse was struggling to make his device functional, he made a pilgrimage to meet with Henry and solicit suggestions for improvements. Joseph Henry, practicing his belief in sharing knowledge for the benefit of all, helped Morse over his difficulties. Morse incorporated Henry's ideas into his experiments without as much as a nod of recognition. When it came time for Morse to patent "his" ideas, the patent included the technology that Henry had selflessly declined to claim for himself. Morse then went on to evangelize about the new technology he claimed *he* had developed without saying a word about Joseph Henry.

IN ADDITION TO BEING a self-promoter, Samuel Morse was a man of obsessively strong beliefs. Violently anti-immigrant and anti-Catholic, he would in later life turn his enormous prestige against Abraham Lincoln and emancipation. In the 1830s, however, Morse's obsession was electromagnetic telegraphy.

When, in 1837, the secretary of the treasury issued requests for a feasibility study for a chain of semaphore towers to carry messages between New Orleans and New York, Morse responded with a proposal to build an electronic signaling system. The following year he demonstrated his laboratory apparatus to members of Congress. The House Commerce Committee, so smitten by what it saw, reported a bill to authorize $30,000 to fund a test line for Morse's technology.

Morse's passion sometimes crossed the line of propriety. Unbeknownst to the public or Congress, the month before the 1837 legislation was reported from committee, he had given one quarter of his American patent rights to the chairman of the House committee to grease the skids. Even with this lubricant, however, the committee's bill died before being taken up by the full House of Representatives.

It wasn't until six years later that Congress would consider the matter again (four years before Lincoln would serve his single term in Congress). The Whig party had taken control of the Congress on a platform of government programs to foster internal improvements. The shifting political winds provided Morse with his opportunity. Once more he strung wires in the Capitol. Messages sent back and forth between committee rooms provided new impetus for legislation. Again the House Commerce Committee reported a bill to fund a demonstration project. This time the bill was considered by the full House.

Even with the push for new national infrastructure, however, the idea that a message could be delivered via sparks was beyond the capacity of many of the nation's leaders. It was easier for a member of Congress in the 1960s to comprehend placing a man on the moon than it was for his or her counterpart in the 1840s to grasp the concept of sending messages by electric sparks. When the Commerce Committee's bill came to the House floor it became the target of derisive jokes and amendments. Representative Cave Johnson of Tennessee led the mocking by proposing an amendment to spend half the authorized amount to support experiments in mesmerism (hypnotism). Another amendment was offered to support Millerism, a sect that predicted the second coming of Christ the next year.

While the House members laughed at Morse's expense, the bill squeaked through by a margin of 89 to 83. Seventy congressmen chose to abstain rather than have to make a decision one way or the other on the concept. In a telling precursor to the growing sectional difficulties, the victory margin was provided by Northern congressmen; their Southern colleagues' represented a way of life in which such innovations were less welcome.

It had been 11 years since what Morse immodestly described as his "flash of genius" onboard the packet ship *Sully* returning from France. Morse had departed the United States in 1829, a painter of moderate renown off to study the Masters of Europe and recover from his wife's death. Returning in 1832, the onboard dinner conversation turned to the relatively new phenomenon of electromagnetism. From that moment forward, Morse filled his sketchbook with ideas that his scientific ignorance led him to believe he was "discovering."

It was onboard the *Sully* that Morse came up with his only original technical contribution to telegraphy: a breathtakingly simple binary system of on/off signals that would become known as "dots and dashes." Morse's original plan was an apparatus in which a pencil attached to an electromagnet made long and short lines on a moving tape based on the signals it received. Those lines, in turn, would spell out numbers that could be looked up in a book where each word was assigned a specific number. The word "Wednesday," for instance, was coded as the number "4030."

There is debate as to whether Morse or his assistant, Alfred Vail, developed "Morse Code." The result, however, eliminated the numbered word reference book by applying the printing trade's concept that words are but an assembly of individual letters. By simply counting the number of each letter of type in a printer's type box it was possible to determine which letters were used more frequently than others. Then the simplest signal (a single dot) was assigned to the most frequently used letter ("e"), with increasingly complex combinations attributed to other letters based on their frequency of use.

With House passage of the funding legislation, only the United States Senate stood between the painter-turned-technology-entrepreneur and his dream. On March 3, 1843—the very last day of the congressional session—the Senate passed the appropriation with much less commotion than had the other body. President Tyler signed the measure into law the very same day. It was not a moment too soon, for Morse was for all practical purposes broke.

Fulfilling its Perils of Pauline legacy, the 40-mile line from Baltimore to Washington almost went bust after Morse had spent well over half of the appropriated funds. The plan had been to bury the cable alongside the Baltimore & Ohio Railroad track. The insulation for the wires, however, was inadequate to the task; once buried, the signal current kept grounding itself out.

Once again Morse was *en extremis.* Construction was halted. During the winter of 1843/44 the insulation was stripped from the cables and preparations were made for stringing the bare wires on poles. The problem remained, however, that the wires would ground against the poles absent proper insulation. The solution was discovered in the glass drawer pulls of a hotel room bureau. If the wires were held by a glass insulator the current could flow from pole to pole unimpeded. Once again, Morse had pulled victory from the jaws of defeat.

Cognizant of his sponsors, and ever the showman, Morse installed the Washington terminus of the line in the Capitol building where legislators could witness his accomplishment. The first official message, sent May 24, 1844, was, tradition has it, chosen by the daughter of the commissioner of patents (another shrewd political move) from the Bible's Book of Numbers (23:23).

"What hath God wrought!" Morse tapped out in dots and dashes. Common perception is that it was an interrogatory statement that closed with a question mark. That, however, is not the way it appears in Scripture. In the Bible the phrase closes a passage of exultation about Jacob and Israel. Certainly it was a similar exultation Morse felt—as well as what he sought to convey—about the miraculous nature of his demonstration. Samuel F. B. Morse was making an exclamatory statement about the future.

Morse, however, was one of the few who grasped that future. During its first year of operation the Washington-Baltimore line ran at only 15 percent of capacity. Chess matches with the opponents 40 miles apart were staged to demonstrate the potential of the technology. News from that summer's political conventions in Baltimore was delivered far faster than the previously fastest mode of communication, the railroad. But to a public for whom the concept of electricity was obscure, the thought of sending messages by lightning was beyond the grasp of credulity.

So revolutionary was the idea of electronic messages that some of the Baltimore clergy concluded it could only be Black Magic and promised hell, fire, and brimstone in retribution. Morse's operator in Baltimore, fearing the aroused faithful, suggested it might be wise to shut down the demonstration line until things cooled off.

Skepticism about electronic messages showed up in the till as well. The government began charging half a cent for every four words transmitted across the line, but people saw no need to purchase the service. During its first six months of operation the Morse line took in revenue of $413.44 against expenses of $2,594.02.

The solution, Morse determined, was to sell his patent to the U.S. Post Office. Having successfully petitioned Congress once before, Morse now proposed that it appropriate the funds necessary to buy his patent. As Morse's luck would have it, the new postmaster general was none other than Cave Johnson, the man who only two years earlier as a congressman had authored the mesmerism amendment to the original Morse-funding bill.

Postmaster Johnson was convinced the telegraph would never supplant the mail. Yet at the same time Johnson also believed the government should control the communications pathway. "The use of an instrument so powerful for good or evil cannot with safety to the people be left in the hands of private individuals uncontrolled by law," Johnson reported to Congress in 1845.

But control of Congress had once again changed hands. The majority Democrats were not as supportive of Federal development projects. Of even greater consequence, however, was Congress's embroilment in more pressing and divisive matters. All national politics seemed to revolve around the issue of whether new states should be slave or free. The North-South divisiveness percolated through the telegraph question. Just as they had held up the transcontinental railroad, and voted against the original Morse-funding bill, Southern congressmen opposed buying the Morse patent, a tool likely to be used to strengthen the industrial North, and of much less interest to the tradition-bound South.

Undaunted as always, Morse turned to private sources of capital. With Amos Kendall, former postmaster general under Andrew Jackson, as his business agent, Morse envisioned New York City as the hub from which wire spokes would radiate in all directions. Each line would be controlled by a separately capitalized company. Morse would contribute his patent rights for half ownership in each line, and the investors would own the other half.

Not unlike the Internet and e-mail a century and a half later, early adoption of the telegraph was slow, only to subsequently take off with a hockey-stick growth spurt. From 1844 to 1846, the 40 miles of the Washington-Baltimore test line constituted most of the telegraph capacity in the United States. By 1848 this had gradually expanded to over 2,000 miles of telegraph wire. The next two years saw that mileage increase six-fold to over 12,000 miles. By 1852 that amount had almost doubled. At the time of Lincoln's 1860 inauguration, 17 years after Morse's first official message, estimated telegraph mileage exceeded 50,000 miles.

"No invention of modern times has extended its influence so rapidly as that of the electric telegraph," observed *Scientific American* in 1852. "The spread of the telegraph is about as wonderful a thing as the noble invention itself."

Every new technology requires a "killer app" to turbo-charge its growth. In the case of the telegraph the breakthrough that ignited the

Growth in Telegraph Mileage (1844-1852)

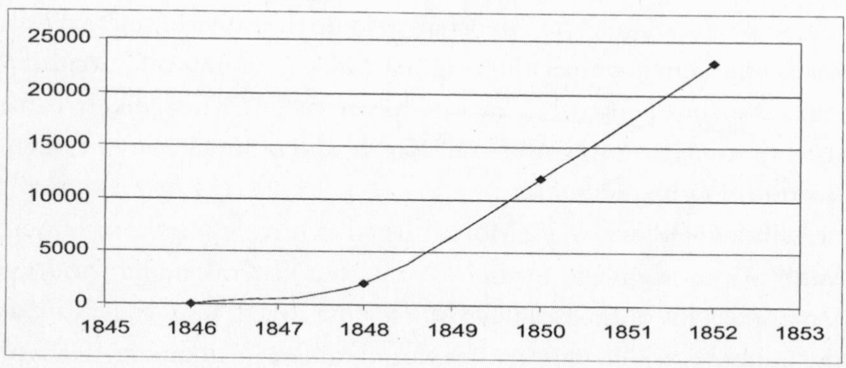

rapid growth was the marriage of the telegraph and the railroad. "Of all the innovations which entrepreneurs, great and small, brought to the development of the telegraph industry," one historian observed, "none is more important nor dramatic than the discovery of the symbiotic relationship between the telegraph and the railroad."

Amazingly, although the Morse test line ran along the B&O track, the railroad never considered using it to assist in the management of rail traffic. It was Charles Minot, superintendent of the New York & Erie Railroad, half a dozen years after the B&O passed on the opportunity, who demonstrated how rail traffic could be coordinated by the telegraph.

Minot was aboard a westbound express that was being held on a siding awaiting the passage of the eastbound express. When the other train did not appear as scheduled, Minot telegraphed the next station to inquire whether the train had passed. Receiving the answer that it had not, he told the stationmaster to hold the eastbound express so that his train could proceed up the track. The engineer on Minot's train, however, was less than enthusiastic about being such an innovator. He didn't care what the dots and dashes said; his train would not move until he could see the other train pass with his own two eyes. Minot overruled him and took the controls. The engineer retreated to the very last row of the very last car of his train, convinced it would soon go cannonballing head-on into the eastbound express.

When Minot successfully reached the next station the eastbound train had still not arrived. The process was repeated, telegraphing the next station down the line. The same was done at the station after that and, at the fourth station, Minot pulled in just as the eastbound train approached. Charles Minot had established the first electronic coordination of railroad movement. It was the dawn of a new era for both the rails and the wires. Railroads provided free rights of way along their tracks to telegraph companies that, in turn, carried railroad traffic as priority and for free. Railroad efficiency improved, as did the economics of building and operating a telegraph system.

• • •

THE TELEGRAPH BEGAN TO knit together a geographically disparate nation. In the process it accelerated the march to civil war.

From the beginning of the United States' existence as a national unit there had been concern about whether a democratic republic could survive across such a large geographic area. The only other attempts at a similar form of government had been in Swiss cantons and Greek states, both geographically smaller and thus easier to manage. America covered such a vast area and was so poorly interconnected that thoughtful people feared the democratic experiment might not be able to survive.

In the early years of the United States, it took so long to obtain information from afar that people lived their lives more in its absence than its presence. On average it took 22 days for news to travel between New York City and Charleston; and 26 days to reach Savannah. Founders such as Washington, Adams, Madison, and Hamilton favored a program to improve transportation routes over both land and water as a means of strengthening the bonds made weak by distance.

The result of such physical dispersion was economic and cultural diversity. Distance encouraged differences. When the Founding Fathers assembled to craft the new nation, for instance, one of their discoveries was not only the difference of ideas between sections of the country, but also the differing personal behavior of colleagues (some Southerners, for instance, considered the New Englanders crude). The government they created enshrined the opportunity for many of these regional differences to continue (including slavery). The Founders created as strong a union as was possible, but one that recognized that some states and regions had almost become nations unto themselves as a result of their physical insulation. This political reality affected even the English language. The proper verb usage prior to the Civil War was, "the United States *are,*" a conjugation that emphasized the individual states rather than their union.

During the second third of the 19th century, technology began to chew away at the geographic buffer that had allowed these differences to flourish. In the greatest technology-driven change in history, the age-old "truth" that distance delayed the delivery of information was dismantled. The result rewrote assumptions about commerce, culture, and community. It was the original information revolution.

First, the steam locomotive began pulling trains over ever-expanding rail networks. Since the beginning of time, land travel had been proscribed by animal muscle and stamina. The iron horse disposed of that tradition with seemingly inexhaustible speed and endurance. The railroad was the fastest mode of transportation and communication ever known in human history. The result mitigated the impact of distance and accelerated the internal migration of people, products, and ideas. The Northern states embraced the railroad and its potential to drive economic growth. The Southern states saw the opposite side of the development and, fearing its impact on their way of life, resisted the railroad.

For a brief period the longest rail line in the nation emanated from Charleston, South Carolina. Responding to the threat of the contamination of local customs and states rights by such high-speed intercourse, however, Southern state legislatures enacted laws prohibiting rail lines from crossing state borders. In contrast with the North, where trains sped across political boundaries, Southern interconnection was inhibited. It was a myopia that would return to haunt the region during the Civil War, as the lack of interconnection meant the Confederacy could not move men and supplies as rapidly as in the North.

The clash between isolated independence and technological interconnection affected the telegraph as well. The Morse–Kendall team sought funding for lines through the South in the same subscription process they had in the North, but with less success. With the Mexican War underway in 1846, a pitch was made once again to the Federal government to fund a line north from New Orleans to more rapidly bring news from that conflict. The proposal's rejection illustrated the continuing Southern antipathy to such new means of interconnection. One of the principal opponents of the telegraph line to New Orleans was states rights champion Senator John C. Calhoun of South Carolina, who challenged the constitutionality of the Federal government extending such communications through the South.

Half a dozen years later, the Census Report of 1852 featured a dozen pages heralding the expansion of the telegraph, including a map of all the existing telegraph lines. North of the Mason-Dixon Line it looked like a spider's web. South of that demarcation, however, were only two threads, one running down the east coast, and the other down the Mississippi Valley.

In many ways the census map was a blueprint for conflict, a picture of two different cultures driven by different economics and a different receptiveness to technological change. In the South, society held tightly to the ways of the past and support systems for that tradition such as slavery. In the North, technology-driven change was steaming forward on iron rails and buzzing over copper wires. These technology-induced differences further exacerbated an already-strained national division. The nation was not only "half slave and half free," as Lincoln would explain, but also divided between an economy looking forward to a new technology-driven industrial future, and a way of life clinging to the tradition of the good old days and institutions to perpetuate that tradition.

It was a situation discussed at the final Lincoln–Douglas debate during the 1858 U.S. Senate contest. In the debate at Alton, Illinois senator Stephen A. Douglas, in rebuttal to Lincoln, commented about the impact new technologies were having on the nation. Using inverse logic, Douglas argued that while there had been incredible improvements in interconnection, these changes did not alter the right of each state to follow its own isolated path.

"Mr. Lincoln says that when our fathers made this Government they did not look forward to the state of things now existing," Douglas rebutted. "They did not probably foresee the telegraph that transmits intelligence by lightning, nor did they foresee the railroads that now form the bonds of union between the different States. . . ." While such changes may, indeed, be occurring, Douglas argued, nothing had changed "the right of each State to do as it pleases in its own domestic affairs . . . and allow the people of each [state] to apply to every new change of circumstances such remedies as they may see fit."

In practice, however, new technologies were changing the character of the country. Innovations such as the telegraph and railroad were breaking down the geographic isolation that had permitted "the right of each State to do as it pleases." Technology was vaulting the geography that had shielded local idiosyncrasies. Significantly, it was also spreading the discourse on the national issues.

The national debate over slavery and federal versus states rights was current news both North and South, thanks to the telegraph. The debates between Lincoln and Douglas were news far beyond the boundaries of Illinois, thanks to wire reports sent to newspapers in all sections of the country. That flow of electronic news reports made the one-term congressman from the frontier into a national figure. When Lincoln journeyed to New York City in 1860 to speak at Cooper Union, the telegraph made his remarks into national news only a few months before the Republican convention would choose its standard bearer. In the campaign that followed, the new electronic envoy assured that the activities leading up to the election were more rapidly dispersed and the issues better understood across the population than at any time in the nation's history. The infrastructure for which

Washington, Adams, and others had longed for had become a reality. Instead of tying the nation together, however, the new infrastructure threatened the distance-driven disparity that, perversely, had permitted the continuance of the nation they created.

Thanks to news via the telegraph, the South had become a tinder box. When electric sparks delivered the news of the election of Abraham Lincoln, the kindling ignited. As soon as the election results were known, the wires helped organize the rebellion. As one state after another enacted ordinances of secession, their rebellion was electronically delivered to others, deliberating similar activity, thus further fueling the clamor for disunion.

The telegraph, along with its handmaiden in interconnection, the railroad, had simultaneously drawn the nation together and torn it apart. To Abraham Lincoln fell the awesome task of leading the country through the fires that would reforge it from "the United States *are*" to "the United States *is*." The telegraph technology that had helped to create the crisis became a tool available to Lincoln to manage the emergency. Ultimately, electronic messages became a new and potent tool of presidential leadership. However, just as the nation was struggling to learn how to deal with the new technology, so would Abraham Lincoln need time to learn how to use the new electronic leadership tool.

CHAPTER THREE

THE TELEGRAPH CREATES A PRESIDENT

THE FIRST RECORDED INSTANCE OF Abraham Lincoln laying eyes on a telegraph device was in 1857, only three years before he was elected president of the United States. On a March day, while riding the legal circuit trying cases in local court rooms, Lincoln checked into the Tazewell House hotel in Pekin, Illinois. The hotel was also the site of one of the state's early telegraph offices. While he had no doubt been aware of telegraph service, it was at Tazewell House that Lincoln witnessed for the first time the phenomenon of electronic messages to and from distant points.

Watching as the key clicked messages from afar animated Lincoln. He asked the operator, Charles Tinker, for an explanation of the technology. Only a few years later, Tinker reentered Lincoln's life as a telegraph clerk in the War Department where he recounted for colleagues the president's telegraph tutorial. The presentation began with a discussion of the flow of electric energy from the batteries and continued through a review of electromagnetism. Lincoln kept pace with the high-tech description and in his cross-examination of Tinker, "asked pertinent questions showing . . . that he comprehended quite readily the operation of the telegraph."

Three years later, electronic messages informed Lincoln of his nomination and subsequent election. In many ways, it was the telegraph that made Lincoln's election possible. The man from the frontier became well known across the nation as a result of telegraphic news reports carried in local newspapers. As the *New York Times* observed on its front page in 1859, "The telegraph gives the speaker in the furthest West an audience as wide as the Union. He is talking to all America . . . immediately, and literally, with the emphasis of lightning." Such telegraphic reports kept the nation up to date on Lincoln and the issues in which he was an increasingly principal player.

The 1858 debates with Stephen A. Douglas during the Illinois U.S. Senate campaign—seven in total—had made Lincoln's position opposing the extension of slavery a national news story and raised the country's awareness of the former one-term congressman. Although Lincoln lost the senate election (for the second time) in the state legislature (where such decisions were made at the time) the Lincoln–Douglas debates had permanently conjoined the man from Illinois with *the* over-riding national issue and lifted him out of regional obscurity.

In the fall of 1859, Lincoln was handed a telegram written on the form of the Illinois & Mississippi Telegraph Company inviting him to bring his message to New York City. East coasters had only read of the man from the prairie. Now New York's political elite would have the opportunity to hear him in the flesh. Equally important, so would the oracles of the press because, thanks to the telegraph, New York was the media capital of the nation.

By all appearances Lincoln fully appreciated the power of the telegraph to spread his ideas. His quest for the presidency was not a media campaign in the sense of today's media-obsessed political contests, but it was a campaign in which Lincoln relied on the new electronic media to expose him and his message to the nation at large. The New York speech fit snuggly with this strategy. On February 27, 1860 Abraham Lincoln delivered an address that "proved so thrilling to its listeners, so irresistible to contemporary journalists," as to propel his candidacy forward only three months before the Republican convention was to meet to select its candidate. The venue for the address was Copper Union, a free educational institution founded by industrialist Peter Cooper. Half a dozen years earlier, Cooper had helped found one of the telegraph companies that would carry reports of Lincoln's presentation across the nation.

In his insightful *Lincoln at Cooper Union,* Harold Holzer observed that the power of the electronically-delivered press was not lost on Lincoln as he crafted his New York remarks. Since he had gone to New York both for the exposure to its political powers, as well as to its media, his message had to be crafted for both audiences. "Lincoln became wise not only in the ways of enthralling crowds, but in creating prose that could also be usefully reprinted in party-affiliated newspapers," Holzer wrote. "Lincoln would want his Cooper Union speech to resound in print as effectively as it did in person, helping to magnify its impact and increase its influence."

One audience member who had known Lincoln's oratory from back home picked up on the speaker's attentiveness to the press even in the midst of his remarks. In a letter reporting on the event, he described Lincoln as "casting at each finished period, a timid, sidelong glance at the formidable array of Reporters who surrounded the table close at his elbow, as if conscious, that after all the world was his audience, on whose ear his words would fall from the thousand multiplying tongues of the Press." The last line of the speech (capitalized in the text that Lincoln reviewed and approved for publication) furnished what today would be called a sound bite. "LET US HAVE FAITH THAT RIGHT MAKES MIGHT, AND IN THAT FAITH, LET US, TO THE END, DARE TO DO OUR DUTY AS WE UNDERSTAND IT." Powerful, crisp, and direct, the line bears all the hallmarks of a carefully designed effort to have an effect both in the hall and in print.

The strategy proved perfect. The New York audience leapt to its feet and cheered. The sound bite "right makes might" sped across the nation bringing others, figuratively, to their feet.

As he continued a post–New York speaking tour, Lincoln reflected on the effects of his successful media strategy in a letter to his wife. The subsequent addresses, he lamented, could not just reiterate what he said in New York because the audiences had already read that news. "The difficulty was to make nine others [speeches], before reading audiences who had already seen all my ideas in print."

Lincoln's media strategy was successful. The telegraph-driven national media, which had brought the lanky Westerner to the country's consciousness in the first place, began reporting that Abraham Lincoln of Illinois was a serious contender for his party's presidential nomination.

Lincoln did not attend the 1860 Republican convention in Chicago that nominated him, but the telegraph allowed the candidate to stay in touch with his delegate hunters. It was a foreshadowing of the remote, yet rapid relationship with distant subordinates that he would perfect during the war, yet it was a rudimentary application that used the telegraph as little more than a speedy messenger. His supporters in Chicago would report in with updates via wire, and occasionally the candidate would respond with directives such as, "I authorize no bargains and will be bound by none" (a vain admonition since his agents were at full pace with their political logrolling).

The Lincoln forces trailed on the convention's first ballot. Senator William Seward of New York, the vote leader, however, could not muster a majority. As the balloting continued, the candidate monitored the results via telegraph from his hometown, Springfield, Illinois. After waiting in the telegraph office for the first ballot's results, Lincoln moved to the office of the *Illinois State Journal* where he could follow the news wire reports. On the third ballot the convention chose the Illinois rail-splitter. A telegraphed news dispatch announced the decision to both the candidate and the nation.

"Vote just announced," the wire report to newspapers read, "whole no 466–necessary to choice 234–Lincoln 354 votes–on motion of Mr. Evarts of NY the nomination made unanimous amid intense excitement." On the heels of the news report there arrived a telegram from his supporters in Chicago: "We did it, Glory to God."

Six months later Abraham Lincoln once again sat in the Springfield telegraph office awaiting results. In a precursor to the late nights he would spend at the telegraph office adjacent to the White House, it wasn't until around 2:00 A.M. that the wires brought word that he had carried New York and was victorious. "I went home, but not to get much sleep," he later recalled, "for I then felt as I never had before, the responsibility that was upon me."

For all his awareness of the role of the electronically-driven media, Abraham Lincoln remained limited in his use of the telegraph. When time was of the essence, such as during the Chicago convention, the telegraph was his speedy messenger. Absent the press of time, however, Lincoln still relied on letters for long-distance dialog.

Upon becoming president-elect, Lincoln *wrote* to his prospective cabinet choices. He *wrote* vice president-elect Hannibal Hamlin to meet him in Chicago (where the two met each other for the first time). The letter to Hamlin illustrated how the president-elect related to the telegraph. After asking the vice president-elect to name a date he could be in Chicago, Lincoln requested Hamlin to "telegraph me; unless there be sufficient time, before the day named, to communicate by mail."

Lincoln *wrote* his rival for the nomination, William Seward, two letters (one formal and one more personal) regarding a nomination as secretary of state; both were sent via Hamlin. He *wrote* Simon Cameron several times: first offering a cabinet post, then withdrawing it. The latter letter, in keeping with Lincoln's operational thesis that the telegraph was only for bursts of speedily delivered information and not discourses, was preceded by a telegram informing Cameron that a letter was coming. While Lincoln could have put the contents of the letter into the body of the telegram, he chose instead to send an electronic message to the effect that the slower message was on its way.

The second letter to Cameron further reinforced the Lincoln perception that telegrams were only for the speedy delivery of simple messages. After the body of the letter delivered the necessary message, and after Lincoln's signature, was the following P.S.: "Telegraph, me instantly, on receipt of this, saying 'All right.' " [Despite this on-again, off-again courtship, Lincoln ended up appointing Cameron secretary of war.]

Taking office on March 4, 1861, Lincoln continued to use the telegraph sparingly. Fewer than 20 telegrams were sent by the president during 1861. Even during the crisis surrounding Fort Sumter, he eschewed electronic messages.

The American Telegraph Company line still ran directly from Washington to Charleston, the capital of seceded South Carolina, in whose harbor the stars and stripes still flew over Fort Sumter. Using that wire, the Confederate commissioners, who had been sent to Washington to resolve the details of secession, communicated with their government in Montgomery, Alabama, as well as with the governor of South Carolina, F.W. Pickens.

In early April the president also had something important to communicate with Governor Pickens: that he intended to resupply the fort with nonmilitary provisions. The telegraph line between the two capitals could have functioned like the Cold War Hotline would years later, avoiding intermediaries and putting the two leaders directly in communication. The president did not put the wire to such use, however.

Lincoln wanted the Confederate leadership to know his intention to resupply Fort Sumter, as well as memorialize that if the fort were fired upon it would be an act of aggression against the peaceful act of humanitarian aid to hungry men. Both purposes could have been served by a telegram, but instead the president sent a clerk from the State Department to read a message to the governor. The clerk was instructed to depart without awaiting a reply.

"I am directed by the President of the United States," the messenger began, "to notify you to expect an attempt will be made to supply Fort-Sumter with provisions only; and that, if such attempt be not resisted, no effort to throw in men, arms, or ammunition, will be made, without further notice, or in case of an attack upon the Fort."

The president may have eschewed the telegraph, but a Rebel spy in Washington used it to communicate the same information to Charleston. "Positively determined not to withdraw Anderson [the fort commander]. Supplies go immediately, supported by naval force under Stringham if their landing is resisted," wired the spy, a South Carolina newspaper correspondent, from Washington's central telegraph office.

Governor Pickens also did not share Lincoln's inhibition about using the telegraph. The president's message had established the predicate that if Sumter were fired upon, the first shots of the war would come from Rebel cannon. Immediately Governor Pickens got on the telegraph to Confederate president Jefferson Davis in Montgomery. By return telegram Davis, former U.S. senator and secretary of war, conveyed the decision to attack the fort.

Fort Sumter was fired upon, rendered helpless, and its defenders withdrawn on the supply ships. The following day, April 15, 1861, President Lincoln issued a call for 75,000 troops from the state militias to suppress the rebellion.

It fell to Secretary of War Cameron to implement a plan that would turn the telegraph into an implement of war. To accomplish this purpose, and lead both the railroad and telegraph mobilization, Cameron tapped Thomas Scott, vice president of the Pennsylvania Railroad. Scott, in turn, assigned Andrew Carnegie, a young superintendent of the railroad's Pittsburgh division, to oversee the initial telegraph activities. The U.S. Military Telegraph Corps (USMTC) was organized for the purpose of securing the lines around the capital.

Such key government facilities as the War Department and Navy Yard had not yet been connected to the telegraph because the technology was still so alien to those in charge. The president of the American Telegraph Company, Washington's service provider, recognized that it made little sense to force officials to come to the company's central telegraph office to use the medium; he ordered essential government facilities connected to the network. But there were no government funds to pay for the line extensions. The Congress was in recess and unavailable for the necessary appropriation. So American Telegraph built the new infrastructure at its own expense. It was an extraordinarily patriotic act, especially considering that a large amount of the company's lines were in the South, thus inviting retaliation. When the Congress returned, an appropriation was passed to reimburse the company.

In a decision that speaks volumes about the prevailing mindset, the expansion of telegraph connectivity to government facilities did not include a line to the White House. The need for the military to access the telegraph without having to go to the city's central telegraph office was understood. The thought that the technology might become an executive tool with relevance far beyond relaying orders and directing supplies, however, lay in the future.

One of the few individuals in a position of leadership who could conceptualize the role of the telegraph in wartime was General George B. McClellan. Half a dozen years earlier the army had sent the young West Point graduate to observe the Crimean War (1854–56). There McClellan witnessed the premiere of the telegraph in a military conflict. It was a limited application, used principally to connect the headquarters of the European allies with one another and with their capitals, but it was nonetheless the instrument's first battlefield engagement. McClellan resigned his commission in 1857 to become a railroad executive, where he was again exposed to the power of electronic messages. When the war brought George McClellan back into uniform, he made the telegraph an integral part of his operations.

McClellan's embrace of electronic messages was atypical of the army and was questioned by many of his subordinate officers. Nevertheless, as the commander of the Department of the Ohio (Ohio, Indiana, Illinois, and Western Virginia), he enlisted a Western Union official, Anton Stager, to organize a field telegraph operation. When McClellan advanced his troops into Western Virginia in late May 1861, the telegraph moved with him. With a sense of pride he wrote, ". . . the first field telegraph that ever advanced with an army in America kept pace with this one."

General McClellan soon proved his telegraph critics wrong. Here was a railroad man who was comfortable expressing his leadership electronically. To General Jacob Cox, one of his subordinates, he challenged, "Win your spurs by capturing Wise & occupying Gauley Bridge. I impatiently wait to hear from you that my expectations are justified." Two days later the wire reached out to metaphorically shake General Charles Hill: "I think you should have attacked the enemy on Sunday . . . I can see no good result likely to follow your present movement which . . . is not in the spirit of your instructions."

At one point in the campaign McClellan's unprecendented tactical communication with his command allowed him to change battle plans three times in as many days. As one historian noted, this was "probably an unprecedented event in military history." By mid-July, what McClellan immodestly described in his report as a "brief but brilliant campaign" was over. "Our success is complete, and secession is killed in this country," he crowed by telegraph to his superiors in Washington.

The telegraph carried more than McClellan's orders and triumphal dispatches, however. Also moving over the wires were the newspaper stories being filed by reporters who were advancing with the army. To a nation hungry for victory and searching for heroes, these reporters delivered stories singing McClellan's praises and dubbing him the "Young Napoleon." The technology that had helped make George McClellan victorious also made him famous. It was no surprise, therefore, that after the disaster at First Manassas (Bull Run), President Lincoln's search for someone to head his army led him to George B. McClellan.

When he came to Washington, General McClellan imported his appreciation for the power of electronic messages. Soon the commanding general's headquarters was festooned with wires connecting him to all the fronts and making McClellan the hub of military information. While McClellan was burning up the wires in 1861, the president was using the technology sparingly. Lincoln sent no telegrams in June and July, four in August, five in September, three in October, none in November, and one in December. It was a study in contrasts: the commanding general sitting at the core of an electronic nervous system that he used to expand his command and control, and the commander-in-chief, isolated from the medium and using it sparingly.

OF THE 13 TELEGRAMS Lincoln sent in the last half of 1861, nine were to or about the Western Theater of operations and its commander, John C. Frémont. General Frémont was a certified national figure, the famous Pathfinder of the West. Frémont's prewar exploration of the trails to the Pacific and his role establishing California as a state propelled him to fame, fortune, a seat in the U.S. Senate, and nomination as the first Republican candidate for president in 1856 (Lincoln lost the nomination to be his running mate). As befitting the Pathfinder's geographic orientation, Lincoln made him commander of the Department of the West, an area running roughly from Missouri to the Rockies.

Hostilities were already at a fever pitch when Frémont took command. In Missouri, "The secession question had long since passed the political stage" and disintegrated into guerilla war, bushwhacking, and the training ground for Jesse James and his ilk. The Confederate army was on the march as well. In early August 1861, Rebel forces advanced on St. Louis in two columns from the southwestern and southeastern borders of the state.

When it came to giving battle, Frémont had an affliction that would become all-too-common among Union generals: he continually overestimated the size of Confederate forces and, as a result, was reluctant to engage his own. As the Rebels advanced, the Pathfinder beseeched, "Will the President read my urgent dispatch to the Secretary of War?" Lincoln, in his first telegram since May, replied that the War Department had been responding. "Been answering your messages ever day [*sic*] since before yesterday. Do you receive the answers? The War Department has notified all the governors you designate to forward all available force. So telegraphed you. Have you received these messages? Answer immediately."

The same day as his telegram to Frémont, the president telegraphed the governor of Indiana, "Start your regiments to Saint Louis at the earliest moment possible . . . Do not delay a single regiment." A little over a week later, Lincoln was still moving troops around. This time, however, he was countermanding Frémont. "Intelligent gentlemen at Louisville say the presence of Rousseau's regiment is needed there," the president wired, adding deferentially, "Pardon us for countermanding your order to him to join your department."

Lincoln had broken his electronic hiatus, but the telegrams bear little resemblance to those he would begin sending the following year. The Frémont-related telegrams have more of a political than a military feel to them. Assuring Frémont that troops were coming and communicating with those responsible for raising those troops was a part of the president's political responsibilities. Nevertheless, a glimmer of what was to happen eight months later, when Lincoln had his electronic breakout, can be seen in these early telegrams. The president was not hesitant to use the telegraph to issue instructions regarding the disposition of forces. Yet his "Pardon us for countermanding your order" solicitude illustrated a continued deference to those who supposedly knew better on matters military.

Most significantly, however, after this brief flurry of messages the president once again disengaged from sending telegrams. In the last three months of 1861 Lincoln sent only four—and one of those was simply a congratulatory telegram to the governor of Utah on the occasion of the extension of the telegraph line to Salt Lake City.

Five weeks to the day after the fall of Fort Sumter, May 21, 1861, the men of the American Telegraph Company met on the Long Bridge across the Potomac River and severed the North-South connection. The Southern assets became the Confederate Telegraph Company (generally referred to as the Southern Telegraph Company) and the backbone of Rebel communications.

Lacking the wherewithal to produce battery acid, glass insulators, and wire in necessary quantity, the South's electronic infrastructure grew only slightly during the war. While the USMTC constructed and operated about 15,000 new miles of telegraph lines during the hostilities, the Confederates were able to construct fewer than 500 miles of new lines.

It was not just the shortages of materials that constrained the Confederacy's use of the telegraph, however; it was also a lack of coordinated vision. Early in the conflict the Rebels had access to the supplies that were left in stock by the prewar companies. They could have used the inventory to extend the wires from the main lines, even following the armies to the front, but the Confederacy lacked the purpose-driven leadership that characterized the North's communications. The Confederate Congress had authorized the seizure of all telegraph lines in July 1861 and provided for a supervisor of telegraph activities, but the Confederate government did not establish an organization equivalent to the USMTC that was charged with the single-minded focus of extending communications to the army wherever it may be.

In part, no doubt, the Confederacy's lack of a coordinated program to take advantage of the new technology was ideological. In a war they felt was about states rights, the idea of a strong central authority was an anathema. And without a planned and centralized strategy to exploit the technology, including line extensions allowing for its tactical application, the telegraph could never play the kind of role it played in the North.

The Civil War was the first "modern" war. But the Confederacy's limited application of one of the most modern technologies would have major implications and leave it without the electronic command and control of its Northern opponent.

As a result, Confederate president Jefferson Davis' ability to use the telegraph was different from Abraham Lincoln's. Davis used the telegraph principally for strategic purposes—some would say meddling purposes. A West Point graduate, Mexican War veteran, and former U.S. secretary of war, Davis considered himself professionally proficient to guide military activities. He used the telegraph to constantly remind his generals of this fact. The juxtaposition with Lincoln in this regard is revealing. The Union leader had little military experience and was cursed with lesser military leaders. Davis had the military experience and was blessed with a better pool of generals. Lincoln grew into his relationship with his generals and the telegraph played a major part in that growth. Davis, characterized by the editor of one newspaper as treating "all men as if they were idiotic insects," used the telegraph to tell his commanders how smart he was.

At the end of 1861 Lincoln's growth as an electronic leader was still a work in progress. Only four telegrams sent during the entire last quarter of the year were signed by Lincoln.

One of those few late-1861 telegrams illustrated the president's willingness to turn to the telegraph to get his own answers. It was the first time the commander-in-chief had bypassed his general officers and communicated directly with a field grade officer. The telegram was sent at 10:00 p.m. the evening the president discovered the defeat at Balls Bluff, the death of his close friend Colonel Edward Baker, and of General McClellan's program to withhold information from him.

The president wanted direct answers, not responses filtered through the commanding general. Lincoln did not know whom he was addressing; the message was simply addressed to "Officer in Command at Poolesville," an encampment close to the scene of the action. "Send a mounted messenger to the battle-ground and bring me information from General Stone," the president ordered, "I want the particulars as to result of engagement and the relative position of the forces for the night, their numbers, and such other information as will give me a correct understanding of affairs."

Wounded by the loss of his friend and the deception of his general-in-chief, Abraham Lincoln took it upon himself to discover the "correct understanding of affairs." The telegraph gave him the capability to quickly bypass those who had been attempting to manipulate him. General Charles Stone replied 35 minutes later, "It is impossible to give full particulars of what is yet inexplicable to me. Our troops under Colonel Baker were reported in good condition and position until fifteen minutes of the death of Colonel Baker."

There is, of course, no way of knowing what was going through Lincoln's mind at this time; however, the Balls Bluff experience appears to have been an electronic Rubicon. The incident at McClellan's headquarters in which the president discovered the official policy of withholding information was a distasteful affront, but probably not a surprise; Lincoln already knew of McClellan's arrogant distain and distrust. It is hard to imagine that someone as astute as Abraham Lincoln wasn't at least already contemplating the new electronic medium's ability to pierce the military's control of information. As a man fascinated by technology, Lincoln's early-adopter instincts must have been churning. Surely he recognized how McClellan used the telegraph to achieve a level of tactical control in Western Virginia that had been unseen in the history of war. Likewise, Lincoln observed how, as the general-in-chief, McClellan was using the telegraph to expand the scope of strategic command and control. One can only assume that there must have been a growing awareness that the telegraph was more than a passive instrument; that Lincoln was awakening to how he might apply the technology to his own leadership purposes.

Consciously or subconsciously, the pieces on the board were moving into place in late 1861 and early 1862 in a manner that would allow Lincoln's electronic breakout. The Congress gave military oversight of all telegraph lines to the civilian-controlled U.S. Military Telegraph Corps. Simon Cameron, the secretary of war who had authorized withholding telegraphic information from the president, was replaced. The new secretary, Edwin Stanton, a prewar telegraph company director, knew of the medium's power and moved immediately to assure its civilian, rather than military, control. Most important, the hub of the telegraph network was moved from McClellan's headquarters to the civilian-run War Department next to the White House where Lincoln, inevitably, would be in frequent contact with its unfiltered messages.

CHAPTER FOUR

ELECTRONIC BREAKOUT

As the last day of 1861 was torn from the calendar, Abraham Lincoln's forces in both the Eastern and Western Theaters remained in a stalemate; Union generals continued to amass a long list of reasons why they could not change the *status quo*. To add to the president's burden, his general-in-chief was in bed with typhoid fever.

McClellan's illness created a void. On New Years Day, 1862, Lincoln carefully stepped into it. He telegraphed both General Henry Halleck, who had replaced Frémont in command of the west, and General Don Carlos Buell, commanding in Tennessee. McClellan was sick, he told them, and "should not yet be disturbed with business." Rather, they should coordinate activities with each other. Once again demonstrating his continued preference for letters over telegrams, the president's message to each general stated, "I write you tonight." In those slower messages Lincoln urged an advance against the Rebels. His letter closed with, "Please do not lose time in this matter."

Three days later Lincoln was back to the telegraph. To Buell he sent a message inquiring, "Have arms gone forward for East-Tennessee? Please tell me the progress and condition of the movement in that direction." The general rapidly wired back excuses as to why there had not been an advance. Lincoln's reply was lengthy, so he once again fell back upon the same kind of written communication that had characterized the dialog between a leader and his commanders in the field since the beginning of warfare. The letter explained the basis for his suggestions while bookending those observations with deference. Early in the letter the president wrote "I am not competent to criticize your views," and closed with "I do not intend this to be an order in any sense."

Such subtlety is the hallmark of a political environment. However, it wasn't getting the job done in this military situation. Thus, on January 7 the president returned to the telegraph to communicate with both Halleck and Buell. The subtlety was gone; the imperative of the message was conveyed both by its means of speedy delivery and its lack of deference. The identical messages read, "Please name as early a day as you safely can, on, or before which, you can be ready to move Southward in concert with General Buell [Halleck]. Delay is ruining us; and it is indispensable for me to have something definite. I send a like despatch to Buell [Halleck]."

It was the early rumblings of an awakening. McClellan's incapacitation had opened the door for the president to interject himself directly with his military commanders. And the telegraph provided the means. In a matter of a week the president's involvement had advanced from "I am not competent to criticize your views" to a command that a date for an advance be named. It was the first time that Abraham Lincoln used the telegraph to communicate a direct order.

It did not become a habit. General McClellan, "fearful that his command was being undermined," got out of his sickbed to make a surprise visit to the White House on January 12. A planned strategy session was put off until the following day when the general-in-chief could be present. For the remainder of January the president sent only one telegram. He then remained silent for the entire month of February 1862, sending not a single telegram. In March his telegraphic output totaled only three messages.

Events were beginning to determine a strategic plan for the Eastern Theater. McClellan unveiled a grand vision for an assault on the

Confederate capital. While Lincoln had been advocating an advance back through Manassas and then overland to Richmond, McClellan had a more strategically innovative concept. The Union Army of the Potomac would be loaded onto ships, sailed down the Potomac, through the Chesapeake Bay, and put ashore below Richmond at the southern tip of the peninsula between the James and York Rivers. When the troops landed they would be only about 60 miles as the crow flies from the seat of the Rebel government. Lincoln approved the plan, provided that "in and about Washington" there would remain sufficient forces so as to "leave said city entirely secure."

McClellan's imminent departure from Washington provided the rationale to remove him as general-in-chief, ostensibly so that he could concentrate on his campaign. Lincoln named no replacement. In so doing he created a situation not unlike when McClellan was sick earlier in the year. There would be no general in overall command of all theaters. The president and Secretary of War Stanton would hold that responsibility.

As April 1862 began, George McClellan was landing on the thinly defended Virginia peninsula. The largest armed force yet seen in North America was only a few days' march from the Confederate capital. It was a brilliant plan and well executed. Sixty-seven thousand men (soon to swell to over 100,000) had moved to the soft underbelly of the Richmond defenses. With only a few days of marching they could be walking the streets of the enemy capital.

Coordinating Confederate military affairs as President Jefferson Davis's military advisor was Robert E. Lee. Lee had already tangled with the Young Napoleon in the western Virginia campaign and had come out with the short end of the stick. The Confederate field commander was Joseph Johnston; strategically, however, it was Lee vs. McClellan again.

The Union landing south of their capital came as a surprise to the Rebels. In anticipation of an overland advance, Confederate forces were out of position between Washington and Richmond. With only a badly outnumbered force between the Union troops and his capital, Lee devised a two-pronged strategy: he would try to stall McClellan on the peninsula long enough to move his men to confront the bluecoats; at the same time he would try to slow the flow of men to McClellan by giving Lincoln cause to keep them around Washington. It was typical Lee: audacity coupled with an expansive view of the scope of the engagement.

Lee's most important advantage was George McClellan's lack of equivalent leadership qualities. General John Magruder commanded a small Rebel force of only 13,000 men in the face of McClellan's huge army. Magruder, an amateur thespian, produced a show for McClellan.

First Magruder extended the Rebel line across the peninsula at its narrowest point near the Revolutionary War battlefield of Yorktown. There his men erected earthworks, flooded fields, placed black-painted logs on wagon wheels to make them appear to be cannon, and marched back and forth in a manner that suggested a larger force than was actually present.

George McClellan bought the ruse. Instead of advancing his mighty force, McClellan decided the Confederates were too strong and the only solution was to lay siege. McClellan allowed his huge force to be stopped by a Confederate charade.

It was a stunning failure of military initiative. As Confederate field commander general Joseph Johnston later observed, "No one but McClellan could have hesitated to attack." Lee's first goal of delaying the Union advance had worked.

At the same time McClellan was settling in on the peninsula, Lee was playing his other strategic card: "Stonewall" Jackson.

Thomas Jonathan Jackson had been the hero of First Manassas (Bull Run) when his brigade of Virginians stood "as a stone wall" against the Union attack. Now a major general, Jackson was loose in the Shenandoah Valley, the pathway between the two belligerents' capitals. Lincoln began to fear that, while his army was concentrated on the peninsula to attack the Confederate seat of government, his own capital had been left vulnerable to Jackson.

Part of the president's concern was a result of good, old-fashioned politics. Lincoln was struggling not only with the Rebels in his front, but also with the politicians in the rear. Leaders in his own Republican party complained, among other things, that McClellan, a Democrat, was delaying victory on the peninsula while putting the nation's capital (and its leaders lodged there) in jeopardy. The breaking point came when Lincoln discovered that the number of troops that McClellan had assured him had been left behind to defend Washington had been manipulated by double-counting and other inflationary assumptions. This misrepresentation gave credence to the "McClellan has left Washington exposed" case. With congressional Republicans nipping at his heels, Lincoln rescinded the order sending General Irwin McDowell and his 38,000 men to the peninsula; they would remain in the proximity of the capital, ready to spring to its defense. Lee's second strategic goal had been achieved.

The stage was now set for a dramatic change in the manner in which Abraham Lincoln exercised his leadership. McClellan was immobile on the peninsula. Jackson was moving in a manner that could threaten Washington. The politicians were in full cry. There was no general-in-chief.

Trapped in this strategic failure with no one to fall back on, Lincoln relied on his instincts and natural skill as a leader. He had to project his personal authority into the field and the only way was to use the long arm of the telegraph.

ON MAY 1 THE president telegraphed McClellan, who was still encamped before the Confederate "army." He had been reading the general's telegrams to the War Department and feared that "indefinite procrastination" was the general's plan. Frustrated, he asked, "Is anything to be done?"

Two days later the Confederates withdrew from Yorktown. Magruder's audacious theater had served its purpose; McClellan had been delayed for a month while the Rebel forces had regrouped between the Union army and Richmond. McClellan completely misread what had happened: "Our success is brilliant" he immodestly crowed in a telegram to the secretary of war. Nothing could have been further from reality. Whereas once he had faced a small force, McClellan now had before him (or on the way) the bulk of the Rebel army in Virginia.

The day after McClellan's telegram about brilliant success, the president, accompanied by War Secretary Stanton and Treasury Secretary Chase, boarded ships in Washington and retraced McClellan's path to the James and York Rivers. While McClellan was crowing, the president, in keeping with his Management-By-Walking-Around philosophy, sailed to the peninsula. The traveling White House became Fort Monroe on the peninsula's tip. The president was now at McClellan's starting point, only 30 or so miles behind the advancing Union army.

Fort Monroe looked out on Hampton Roads, the body of water that joined the Chesapeake Bay to the two rivers. On the other side of Hampton Roads was Norfolk, still in Confederate hands and home of the Confederate ironclad *Merrimac* (officially the *C.S.S. Virginia*). The new-style warship had been threatening McClellan's supply lines and harassing Federal naval operations, including being the co-star of the famous battle with the Union ironclad *Monitor* less than two months earlier.

When he arrived at Fort Monroe, the president discovered that during the month that McClellan had sat before Yorktown he had done nothing to silence the seemingly invincible ironclad by attacking its base of operations. Lincoln was livid. He took off his stovepipe hat and slammed it to the ground. The next day he took matters into his own hands.

The commander-in-chief, now at the front, ordered the shelling of Rebel positions around Norfolk. The bombardment drew the *Merrimac* out of her berthing, but she did not engage. The following day, May 9, 1862, the president of the United States boarded a tugboat to personally reconnoiter the far side of Hampton Roads in search of a landing site for Union troops. Putting ashore on enemy soil, Lincoln was unaware that the Confederates were already in the process of abandoning the city. The next day the president was at the landing point as troops disembarked for the advance on Norfolk that he had ordered. The city was quickly occupied. The *Merrimac,* once the scourge of the waters, was sunk below them, destroyed by her defenders lest she fall into Union hands.

Lincoln sailed back to Washington on May 11. It had to be heady times for a man who had been so often frustrated by the inactivity of his generals. As commander-in-chief he had been to the front, ordered action, and seen its victorious result. "So has ended a brilliant week's campaign of the President," wrote Secretary Chase; "for I think it quite certain that if we had not come down, Norfolk would still have been in possession of the enemy, and the *Merrimac* as grim and defiant and as much a terror as ever."

Having tasted the fruits of decisive action, Lincoln's return to Washington could only have been a disappointment. The back-and-forth struggle over troops to protect the Union capital versus those necessary to assault the Confederate capital continued. From the Congress came cries of concern over the safety of Washington. From the peninsula came calls for more troops.

McClellan used the telegraph to press his case. In a lengthy message to the president, the general estimated that his army, now swollen to 80,000, was opposed by "a much larger force, perhaps double my number." After expounding on how the Rebels might abandon Richmond and force him to pursue "some place in Virginia," McClellan whined, "I beg that you will cause this Army to be reinforced without delay by all the disposable troops of the Government."

In his reply the president couldn't resist commenting on his general's verbosity, "Your long despatch of yesterday is just received," Lincoln's wire began. Assuring McClellan that he had seen the previous dispatches, the president reiterated, "Have done and shall do, all I could and can to sustain you." Lincoln then reiterated his position that, "I am still unwilling to take all of our force off the direct line between Richmond and here."

Lincoln may have considered McClellan's May 14 telegram to be long, but exactly a week later the Young Napoleon sent him a *10-page* screed. For page after page McClellan carried on about being outnumbered, yet promised to "advance steadily & carefully & attack." The majority of the general's telegram, however, was about bureaucratic issues regarding the organization of the army, including whether McDowell remained under his command.

The president again began his response by commenting on McClellan's wordiness, "Your long despatch of yesterday just received." Then Lincoln required only three more sentences to reply to the general's essay. McDowell would stay where he was. From that position he could move to protect Washington, or, if necessary, "can reach you by land sooner than he could get aboard boats . . . unless his march shall be resisted, in which case, the force resisting him, will certainly not be confronting you." The tension between Lincoln and McClellan was coming to a head.

At that very moment, in the Shenandoah Valley, Stonewall Jackson was cooking up reasons for the president to be concerned. His force now swelled to 16,000 by the addition of General Richard Ewell's command, Jackson began one of the most audacious and well-managed military campaigns in history.

Lee's instructions to Jackson were concise: "Whatever movement you make against [Union general] Banks do it speedily, and if successful drive him back toward the Potomac, and create the impression, as far as practicable, that you design threatening that line."

While McClellan dawdled, Lee played the Jackson card to make it seem as though Washington was threatened.

And what a magnificent card Jackson was in this campaign! Demanding more of his troops than other generals, he marched them so fast from one engagement to another that they earned the nickname "foot cavalry." On May 23 Jackson defeated the Union force at Front Royal, Virginia, about the same distance from Washington as McClellan's peninsula landing had been from Richmond. It was a small engagement, but it positioned the foot cavalry to get between the Union forces and their capital.

The breakout moment had arrived for Abraham Lincoln. Frustrated by his main force's inability to advance; heartened by his field command success at Fort Monroe; worn by the bickering as to the safety of Washington and the disposition of troops for that purpose; and responding just as Robert E. Lee had hoped, the president turned to the telegraph to take command.

The next day, May 24, 1862, Lincoln sent nine telegrams, more messages than he had sent in a single day since becoming president. This time his use of the telegraph wasn't a flash in the pan; during the last week of May, Lincoln sent more telegrams than the sum total of his output since taking the Oath of Office. From May 24 forward, through the remainder of his presidency, the telegraph was an integral part of Abraham Lincoln's leadership.

In an eerie historical coincidence, Abraham Lincoln's May 24 electronic breakout occurred 18 years *to the day* from Samuel F. B. Morse's "What hath God wrought!" first telegraph message.

THE COMMANDER-IN-CHIEF's telegrams gave explicit and direct commands to his generals. His immediate plan was to smash Stonewall.

To General Frémont (removed from command in the west but given a small command in western Virginia): "The exposed position of General Banks make his immediate relief a point of paramount importance. You are therefore directed by the President to move against

Jackson at Harrisonberg . . . this movement must be made immediately." Gone was the "pardon us" tone of the telegrams to Frémont the previous August; in its place was, "You will acknowledge the receipt of this order and specify the hour it is received by you."

General McDowell, the subject of the recent bickering with McClellan, was near Fredericksburg, across the Blue Ridge Mountains from the Shenandoah Valley. The telegram he received from Lincoln was equally commanding. "Gen Fremont has been ordered by Telegraph to move from Franklin on Harrisonberg to relieve Gen Banks and capture or destroy Jackson & Ewell's force. You are instructed . . . to put twenty thousand men (20000) in motion at once for the Shenandoah . . . Your object will be to capture the forces of Jackson & Ewell."

McDowell telegraphed back to express his disappointment at not going to Richmond, as well as his doubt that Lincoln's strategy would work. Nonetheless, he saluted and complied. "I have ordered General Shields to commence the movement by tomorrow morning." The president replied with appreciation, but also made his expectations clear: "I am highly gratified by your alacrity in obeying my order. The change was as painful to me as it can possibly be to you or to any one. Every thing now dependes [*sic*] upon the celerity and vigor of your movement."

Lincoln used the telegraph to tell McClellan, "We have so thinned our line to get troops for other places [*i.e.,* for you] that it was broken yesterday at Front-Royal with a probable loss to us of a Regiment infantry, two companies of cavalry, putting Banks in some peril." Another wire told his general on the peninsula, "In consequence of Gen. Banks' critical position I have been compelled to suspend Gen. McDowell's movement to join you. The enemy are making a desperate push upon Harper's Ferry, and we are trying to throw Fremont's force & part of McDowell's in their rear."

Electronic messages may have put the president in touch with his generals, but it did not eliminate the fog of war that often left commanders guessing as to what their opponent was doing. In an attempt to penetrate the fog Lincoln turned again to the telegraph. This time he reached further down the chain of command. A summary of what was known went out to General Rufus Saxton at Harper's Ferry, accompanied by a query: "Please inform us, if possible, what has become of the force which pursued Banks yesterday. Also, any other information you may have." Bypassing the general staff altogether, Lincoln wired Colonel Dixon Miles, commanding the Railroad Brigade at Harper's Ferry, "Could you send scouts from Winchester, who would tell whether enemy are North of Banks, moving on Winchester? What is the latest you have?"

Abraham Lincoln had Stonewall Jackson in his sites. If the Rebels moved toward Washington, Lincoln's troops would come upon them from the rear. If Jackson withdrew, the same forces would cut him off. Like the long-distance chess matches Morse had staged to promote the telegraph, Lincoln was using the technology to move his pieces on the chessboard.

On May 25 Jackson attacked Banks at Winchester. With a two-to-one numerical superiority, Stonewall was victorious. Banks's retreat was so hasty that he left his supplies behind. Grateful for the windfall, the hungry and ill-equipped Rebels anointed their opponent "Commissary Banks."

Stonewall was now less than 40 miles from the Potomac, the moat that separated the Union from the Confederacy. As Shelby Foote eloquently explained, Lincoln had "once more swung around to find the Shenandoah shotgun loaded and leveled at his head."

"The enemy is moving North in sufficient force to drive Banks before him," Lincoln telegraphed McClellan. "I think the movement is a general and concerted one, such as could not be if he were acting upon the purpose of a very desperate defence of Richmond." Then the president, vexed by McClellan's inaction, became very direct with his general: "I think the time is near when you must either attack

Richmond or give up the job and come to the defence of Washington. Let me hear from you instantly."

The Young Napoleon's reply reminded the president just who was making the decisions on the peninsula. "Telegram received. Independently of it the time is very near when I shall attack Richmond." Then McClellan reminded Lincoln, "The object of the Enemys movements is probably to prevent reinforcements being sent to me."

If McClellan was finally getting ready to move, perhaps he could give the Rebels a taste of their own medicine. Lincoln wired, "Can you get near enough [to Richmond] to throw some shells into the city?" The general once again replied that he was operating on his own schedule: "Hope very soon to be within shelling distance."

The president's focus remained on Jackson. At some point in time, Lincoln assumed, Jackson was going to have to fall back. He could not continue to advance such a relatively small force forever northward. Frémont was coming from the west, and McDowell was coming from the east. The president had arranged a vise to close on Stonewall.

On May 27 a telegram was received from General Frémont that sent Lincoln into a rage. The president's telegram to Frémont of three days earlier had been a very precise order "to move against Jackson at Harrisonberg" so as to become one jaw in a closing vise. Lincoln's order left little doubt as to the importance of timing: "this movement must be made immediately." Frémont's response had also been specific: "will move as ordered & operate against the Enemy in such way as to afford prompt relief of genl Banks." Perhaps recalling his earlier experience with the Pathfinder, Lincoln replied with yet another reinforcement of the importance of alacrity: "Much—perhaps all—depends upon the celerity with which you can execute it [the order]. Put the utmost speed into it. Do not lose a minute."

Now, three precious days later, the Pathfinder was way off course.

Far from moving "to afford prompt relief," his force was more than twice as far from Harrisonberg as it should have been. Secretary of War Stanton penned a hot telegram to Frémont; the signature, however, was in Lincoln's hand. "I see you are at Moorefield. You were expressly ordered to march to Harrisonberg. What does this mean?"

Frémont replied that he had taken a detour because of bad weather, bad roads, and the need to feed his men.

While the commander-in-chief was frustrated by the performance of Frémont and Banks, McClellan kept up his telegraphic drumbeat from the peninsula. After indicating he would try to cut off any Rebel support moving to Jackson, "but am doubtful whether I can," McClellan put more heat under the same old message. "It is the policy and duty of the Government to send me by water all the well-drilled troops available," he lectured. "I am confident that Washington is in no danger . . . The real issue is in the battle about to be fought in front of Richmond . . . If any regiments of good troops remain unemployed it will be an irreparable fault committed."

On March 28 Lincoln's wire countered his general's hyperbole with logic. "That the whole force of the enemy is concentrating in Richmond, I think can not be certainly known to you or me. Saxton, at Harper's Ferry, informs us that a large force (supposed to be Jackson's and Ewell's) forced his advance from Charlestown today. Gen. King telegraphs us from Frederick'sburg that contrabands give certain information that fifteen thousand left Hanover Junction monday morning to re-inforce Jackson. I am painfully impressed with the importance of the struggle before you; and I shall aid you all I can consistently with my view of due regard to all points."

It was a measure of just how close he was to reaching the end of the rope with the Young Napoleon that the president penned and subsequently excised a last clause reminding McClellan as to who was in charge: "and last I must be the Judge as to the *duty,* of the government in this respect."

• • •

THE PRESIDENT'S SEEMINGLY DAILY jousting with McClellan did not keep him from focusing on the Jackson strategy. Four telegrams went to General McDowell bringing him up to date on developments in front of Richmond as well as passing on reports of Jackson's movements. Just before dinner on May 28 he told McDowell, "I think the evidence now preponderates that Ewell and Jackson are still about Winchester. Assuming this, it is, for you a question of legs. Put on all the speed you can. I have told Fremont as much, and directed him to drive at them as fast as possible."

The following day Jackson was near Harper's Ferry. Intelligence reports had told him of the converging Union forces in his rear, yet he continued skirmishing along the Potomac, just as Lee had requested. Lincoln, in the meantime, was in electronic communications with the three forces he hoped would put an end to Stonewall. To General Banks, who remained closest to the Rebels: "Gen. McDowell's advance should & probably will be at or near Front Royal at 12 M to-morrow. Gen. Fremont will be at or near Strasburg as soon. Please watch the enemy closely, and follow & harass and detain him, if he attempts to retire." To Frémont and McDowell the president reiterated their expected noon arrival at Front Royal.

Lincoln continued to increase the intensity of the campaign against Jackson. The morning of May 30, the sixth day of his active telegraphic command, he wired General Banks that the Rebels could be about to collide with Frémont or McDowell and that Banks should stand ready to assist either one. Just before noon, when Frémont was supposed to be showing up in the valley, a telegram from the president asked, "Where *is* your force? It ought this minute to be near Strasburg. Answer at once." Once again, however, the Pathfinder had proven his shortcomings. Frémont telegraphed he had stopped his march due to the fatigue of his men. His troops would be back on the road the next day and at Strasburg by 5:00 P.M., May 31, Frémont promised. That, of course, was over a day behind an already-delayed plan.

"I somewhat apprehend that Fremont's force, in it's [*sic*] present condition, may not be quite strong enough in case it comes in collision with the enemy," the president wired McDowell. "For this additional reason, I wish you to push forward your columns as rapidly as possible." As the day wore on, Lincoln kept feeding information to McDowell as to the status of the other jaw of the vise. Finally, the evening of May 30, Lincoln forwarded to both Frémont and McDowell a dispatch from Harper's Ferry that Jackson had not yet begun his return to the valley. "It seems the game is before you," the president told his two generals.

As Lincoln described it in a telegram to General McClellan, Jackson was penned within "A circle of circumference [that] shall pass through Harper's Ferry, Front-Royal, and Strasburg." The president fully expected the circle to close and Stonewall to be trapped between the Union forces.

To avoid just such an outcome, Jackson, once again, put his foot cavalry in overdrive.

At the top of the valley the Shenandoah River divides into two forks to flow around a ridge grandiosely named Massanutton Mountain. Front Royal was on the eastern side of the fork and Strasburg on the western. Frémont was advancing from the west and McDowell from the east. Their joining up would close the top of the valley and block Jackson's path.

The plan seemed to be working. McDowell's forces under General James Shields occupied Fort Royal. Keeping McClellan informed, Lincoln telegraphed on June 1, that "Shield's advance came in collision with part of the enemy yesterday evening six miles from Front-Royal . . . Firing in that direction to-day, heard both from Harper's Ferry and Front Royal, indicate a probability that Fremont has met the enemy."

Frémont had, indeed, made contact with the Rebels, but had not given battle. The other side of the valley saw a similar reticence: Shields was sticking close to Front Royal and not pushing forward to connect with the force from the west.

Jackson's force slipped through the gap in the vise.

Lincoln's grand plan had been thwarted. The president of the United States had exercised his commander-in-chief authority to an extent unparalleled in history. From the political capital he had devised a strategy and commanded the maneuvering of armies in the field in almost real time. At the end of the wire, however, the president's generals lacked the drive of their opponent and his foot cavalry. While Frémont, for instance, advanced his troops 70 miles in seven days (admittedly over challenging terrain and in bad weather), Jackson had driven his troops into legend. In the final burst to escape the closing vise, Stonewall's men had marched 35 miles in a single day.

Only five days previously the president had told General McDowell, "it is, for you a question of legs." The legs had failed.

Lincoln's forces, having lost the race to the mouth of the valley, now chased Jackson down its length. But the reticence of Lincoln's generals continued. "Terrible storms of thunder and hail now passing over," Frémont telegraphed Lincoln, explaining that he was stopping his march.

Jackson, operating under the same sky, pressed on.

Lincoln's subsequent use of the telegraph manifested how the air was seeping out of his strategic balloon. Prior to Jackson's slipping through, the president had been coordinating movements by shooting wires back and forth to the valley—sometimes multiple messages in a single day. After Jackson escaped it was two days before the president's next wire to any of his generals in the valley. That telegram simply asked McDowell, "Anxious to know whether Shields can head or flank Jackson. Please tell about where Shields and Jackson respectfully are, at the time this reaches you."

The opportunity for a second shot at Jackson was slipping away.

Stonewall was making good time advancing down the macadamized road on the western side of the valley, while Shields was slogging a path along a poorer road on the other side of Massanutton Mountain.

It was just possible, however, that there could be one more chance to smash Stonewall. While Shields was on the eastern side of the ridge, Frémont was in pursuit on the good road on the western side of the valley. At the end of Massanutton Mountain there remained the possibility they could join up and engage Stonewall.

Jackson saw that possibility as well. His solution was to go on the offensive and attack the two forces serially. On June 8 he defeated Frémont at Cross Keys. Then Jackson turned eastward the following day to welcome Shields at Port Republic. He left with the same result.

The Shenandoah Valley Campaign was over. On June 9, Lincoln telegrammed General Frémont: "Halt at Harrisonberg, pursuing Jackson no farther . . . stand on the defensive . . . and await further orders which will soon be sent to you." The Confederates would make a few feints that kept the Union forces edgy, but the campaigning was concluded. Stonewall Jackson, having brilliantly accomplished his assignment, was soon marching his men out of the valley to join in the defense of Richmond.

LINCOLN, TOO, TURNED HIS attention to the Confederate capital. While McClellan prevaricated the Confederates had determined that the best defense of Richmond was a good offense. On May 31 the rebels attacked McClellan at the Battle of Seven Pines (Fair Oaks). Little was decided in the two-day battle except that Confederate general Johnston was seriously wounded. His successor as field commander was Robert E. Lee.

In the valley of the Shenandoah, Lincoln's generals had at least moved (albeit slowly). In front of Richmond, things were *status quo ante;* McClellan was standing still, continuing to lament how he was facing a superior force. McClellan had defined his goal as preserving his magnificent force, rather than destroying the enemy. The job of a military leader being to give battle and defeat the enemy, the Young Napoleon had failed miserably in this goal. Such shortcomings, nonetheless, did not stop McClellan from presuming he alone possessed the critical insights as to what must be done, even in those areas where he had no authority.

The telegraph, while having many important advantages for Lincoln, also had a drawback: at a time when McClellan should have been worrying about the job assigned to him, he had the speedy ability to tell the chief executive how he should do his job. On June 20 McClellan telegraphed Lincoln, "I would be glad to have permission to lay before your Excellency by letter or telegram my views as to the present state of military affairs throughout the whole country." It was a quizzical message; the man who commanded the largest army in the history of the continent, but could not bring it to the purpose for which it was assembled, was reasserting that he still deserved to be listened to as if he were general-in-chief. Lincoln politely responded, "I would be glad to have your views . . ."

Before the general could share his wisdom, however, the old back and forth about reinforcements resumed. In a remarkable telegram to Secretary Stanton, McClellan complained, "I regret my great inferiority in numbers but feel that I am in no way responsible for it as I have not failed to represent repeatedly the necessity of reinforcements . . . I will do what I can with the splendid Army I have the honor to command & if it is destroyed by overwhelming numbers can at least die with it & share its fate . . . But if the result of the action which will probably occur tomorrow or within a short time is a disaster the responsibility cannot be thrown on my shoulders—it must rest where it belongs."

It was a breathtaking message from a commanding officer. McClellan was already preparing for defeat and allocating blame!

The message may have been to Secretary Stanton, but it was the president who replied. Lincoln chose to accentuate the positive in other McClellan dispatches of the day, but then got to the heart of his general's complaint. "[T]he probability of your being overwhelmed by 200,000, and talking of where the responsibility will belong, pains me very much. I give you all I can, and act on the presumption that you will do the best you can with what you have, while you continue, ungenerously I think, to assume that I could give you more if I would."

The Battle for Richmond, however, was now underway. The jockeying by telegram was over. Complaints were irrelevant. The time had come for McClellan to command.

On June 25 McClellan tested the supposedly overwhelming Confederate position by advancing his picket lines. It was the first of seven days of fighting, appropriately named the Battles of the Seven Days. Robert E. Lee, as was his wont, went on the offensive the following day. Lee continued to attack through July 1. In all but one of those engagements McClellan was victorious. Yet following each victory the Young Napoleon retreated.

There were no telegrams sent by Lincoln during the Seven Days. McClellan stayed in touch with Secretary Stanton, reporting on the activities and adding his editorial comment. The president anxiously monitored each report, sometimes standing over the telegraph clerk's shoulder to read each word as it was deciphered. On June 28, after another attack from Lee's forces drove McClellan to retreat, the general resumed delivering his favorite message. He wired Secretary Stanton that he could take Richmond if he only had 20,000 or so fresh troops. "If we have lost the day . . . I have lost this battle because my force was too small." Just in case his first broadside had not been appreciated, McClellan added, "I again repeat that I am not responsible for this . . ."

It was unbelievable and unconscionable behavior. George McClellan outnumbered Robert E. Lee by two-to-one; he was winning the majority of his engagements with the enemy; yet after every victory he was withdrawing, moving further away from his objective.

On top of it all, McClellan had the temerity to blame Lincoln. "I know that a few thousand men more would have changed this battle from a defeat to a victory—as it is the Govt must not & cannot hold me responsible for the result . . . the Govt has not sustained this Army. If you do not do so now the game is lost."

McClellan's rhetoric was on a rampage. The general who hesitated to give battle to the enemy was nevertheless engaged against his superiors. After whining that "the game is lost" because of the lack of reinforcements, McClellan closed his telegram with, "If I save this Army now I tell you plainly that I owe no thanks to you or any other persons in Washington—you have done your best to sacrifice this Army." Secretary Stanton and President Lincoln, however, never saw this last sentence. The supervisor of the telegraph office was so taken aback by its insubordination that he deleted it from the copies reviewed by the president and secretary.

A general who goes into battle anticipating the result will be "a disaster" will normally have his expectations fulfilled. For seven days Robert E. Lee's smaller force drove the Union Army back down the Virginia peninsula. The same day as McClellan's "I am not responsible for this" message, Lincoln telegraphed McClellan: "Save your Army at all events."

By July 2 the Seven Days' battles were over, and the Peninsula Campaign would soon be as well. McClellan pulled his troops back to the James River. Six weeks later the greatest fighting force the nation had ever possessed began loading on ships for transit north.

THE TELEGRAPH HAD GIVEN Abraham Lincoln a power not possessed by any other leader in history: to converse with his military leaders in the field as though he were in the tent with them. Accompanying this was the ability to assume the role of commander-in-chief in more than a titular sense.

That Abraham Lincoln would have turned to the telegraph in

such an electronic breakout should not be surprising. The interesting consideration is why it was so long in coming. Part of the reason, undoubtedly, can be attributed to the military's domination of the medium until early 1862. Part, also, goes to Lincoln's growth in the job; the man who never before had played on such a huge stage got better with each performance. Regardless of the rationale, however, the man who for 14 months had only toyed with the telegraph technology fully embraced its power in May 1862.

And it is no wonder that Lincoln embraced the electronic messenger as he did. Union field leadership was not up to the task before it. McClellan, the commander of the largest army, had done little but complain about why he could not act and had dissembled about the number of troops protecting Washington. Frémont, who had failed as commander in the west, but for political purposes had been given a smaller command, was again unable to rise to the moment. Banks and Shields were political generals, neither of whom had distinguished themselves in the field. McDowell had been the loser at First Manassas (Bull Run). In short, the president had a weak General Staff, especially when compared to that of his opponents.

Historians have argued over whether Lincoln's direct involvement—some would say intervention—was at fault for McClellan's defeat on the peninsula. On one hand, the president did take the bait put in front of him by Robert E. Lee. On the other hand, nothing in McClellan's *modus operandi* suggests the general suddenly would have become a tiger with a few thousand additional troops.

The fact of the matter is that in late May 1862 the ability to send and receive T-mails effectively put the president of the United States into the field with his generals.

In the case of McClellan, Lincoln's telegrams did not begin until after the campaign was well under way. He could cajole and affect the disposition of troops, but he did not issue direct orders to the Young Napoleon.

In the case of Banks, Frémont, and McDowell, however, the president was the father of the strategic plan. He issued the orders and oversaw their execution.

That the result of Abraham Lincoln's electronic breakout was not a success is important to history. For this analysis, however, what is more important is that Lincoln *acted;* that he turned to the new telecommunications technology to help him take command. The president also learned lessons that would pay off later. Primary among those lessons was that moving troops was not the same as moving pieces on the chessboard; that even the best plans can falter without the best hands for their implementation.

CHAPTER FIVE

AFTER THE BREAKOUT

"ANY NEWS FROM THE FRONT?" Lincoln telegraphed George McClellan at 4:00 P.M. the afternoon of August 27, 1862. This time, however, the general was not at the front, nor did he command a large force. Having withdrawn from the peninsula earlier in the month, McClellan's army had been parceled out to General John Pope's newly created Army of Virginia. McClellan was in Alexandria, across the river from Washington. The run up to the Second Battle of Manassas had begun, but it would not be McClellan's fight.

Even before the Union troop withdrawal from the peninsula, Robert E. Lee had determined to go on the offensive. He sent Stonewall Jackson North to lead the way. The Confederates captured Manassas and its rail and telegraph lines on August 26. Soon the citizens of Washington were experiencing what the residents of Richmond had experienced only a few weeks previously: the thunder of cannons on their doorstep.

A consequence of the Confederate advance was the severing of telegraph connections between Washington and General Pope. President Lincoln, now more comfortable in his use of the telegraph to interact with the battlefield, found himself cut off. He was back in the same situation as during First Manassas, waiting for word from the action. Unlike 13 months earlier, however, Lincoln did not wait around patiently. He turned to his new electronic ally in search of answers.

Thirty minutes after his "Any news" message to McClellan, the president telegraphed General Ambrose Burnside, commanding on the other side of Manassas at Falmouth, Virginia, "Do you hear anything from Pope?"

The following day, at about the same time, Lincoln again asked General Burnside for information. "Any news from Gen. Pope?"

Neither McClellan nor Burnside was of much help. They, too, were cut off. Pope's forces were on the wrong side of almost half of the Confederate Army, which was now between the Union troops and Washington. A principal source of information became a colonel, Herman Haupt, chief of military railroads, who had been carrying on an electronic conversation with the War Department for several days. "I was cut off from communications, and the only information that could be received in Washington was through operators and assistants connected with my department, who were directed to advance as far as possible under cover of brush, climb trees, and report observations," Haupt wrote afterward.

The day before Lincoln's queries of McClellan and Burnside, Colonel Haupt had leapt the chain of command and telegraphed the president directly.

August 26, 1862

President Lincoln: Two operators from Manassas have gone up the Gap road towards Gainesville, with instruments, to get as near as possible to the scene of action, make connection with the wire and report. You are probably advised of this fact, but if you are, there is no harm in repeating, and if you are not, it will be of interest to you.

H. Haupt

It most certainly was of interest to the president. The "instruments" Haupt's telegram had referenced were portable telegraph devices that would allow the national leadership, otherwise cutoff from the action, to understand what was going on at the front.

The next day Haupt again reached out to the president. There had been multiple engagements around Manassas, including a fight for the railroad bridge over Bull Run. Haupt reported to the president on the bridge action:

August 27, 1862, 4:25 P.M.

A. Lincoln, President: Intelligence received within twenty minutes informs me that the enemy are advancing and have crossed Bull Run bridge; if it is not destroyed, it probably will be. The forces sent by us last night held it until that time.

H. Haupt

Lincoln, who was in the telegraph office for just this purpose of receiving such timely reports, rapidly penned a quick response.

August 27, 1862

Colonel Haupt: What became of our forces which held the bridge till twenty minutes ago, as you say?

A. Lincoln

Haupt responded just as rapidly, telling the president:

Alexandria, Aug 27, 5 P.M.

A. Lincoln, President: Our latest information is "The Eleventh Ohio was covering the retreat had held the Bridge some time and was retreating."

H. Haupt

The president continued his inquiries:

War Department, August 27, 1862

Colonel Haupt: Is the railroad bridge over Bull Run destroyed?

A. Lincoln

Haupt, however, was unable to reply quickly. His hands were full. Earlier in the day Colonel Haupt had proposed to General McClellan, who had just arrived from the peninsula, that a rail-borne expedition be mounted to advance as many men as possible as close as practicable to Bull Run. When he proposed this plan to McClellan, the general "listened, and, when I ceased, remarked that he could not approve the plan; that it 'would be attended with risk.' " Haupt, a West Point graduate, was taken aback: "I reminded the General that military operations were usually attended with risk, but that I did not consider the risk in this case excessive." The Young Napoleon, however, remained true to form, avoiding risk and in the process avoiding opportunity.

McClellan did, however, repackage the news he had received from Colonel Haupt and send it to the new general-in-chief Henry Halleck. "After sending this telegram, General McClellan mounted his horse and rode off, leaving me in a condition of great dissatisfaction and uncertainty," Haupt wrote. "I had been directed to consult with him, and the consultation had resulted in no decision whatever."

Colonel Haupt went ahead with his plan, however. That evening (August 27) he telegraphed McClellan that he was starting a train forward to the battlefield at around 4:00 A.M. the following morning. McClellan remained silent.

It wasn't until just before 1:00 P.M. on the day following his query about the bridge over Bull Run that the president received a reply.

August 28, 1862, 12:50 P.M.

President Lincoln: I am much gratified to be able to inform you that Colonel Scammon is safe and has returned to Alexandria. I went out on an engine to meet him and bring him in. He held Bull Run bridge a long time against a very superior force, retired at last in perfect order, eluded the efforts of the enemy to surround him, and brought off his whole command with but little loss. I have advised General McClellan of his presence; he has important information to communicate.

The rebel forces at Manassas are large and several of their best Generals were in command. I have sent out a reconnoitering party of 200 sharpshooters by rail, with operators and wire to repair telegraph, make communications and report observations.

H. Haupt

Recalling the situation afterward, Haupt wrote: "The President was in a state of great anxiety, and frequently telegraphed to know if any further information had been received."

The next set of telegrams between the two men was almost as if they were facing each other in the same room.

War Department, Aug. 28, 1862, 2:40 P.M.

Col. Haupt: Yours received. How do you learn that the rebel forces at Manassas are large and commanded by several of their best generals?

A. Lincoln

August 28, 1862, 3:15 P.M.

President Lincoln: One of Colonel Scammon's surgeons was captured and released; he communicated the information. One of our firemen was captured and escaped; he confirms it, and gives important details. General McClellan has just seen him; also Colonel Scammon.

H. Haupt

Ninety minutes later Colonel Haupt had further news:

August 28, 1862, 4:40 P.M.

President Lincoln: The latest news is that our men are busy reconstructing bridges beyond Bull Run . . . Major Fifield has this moment arrived on a return train, and gives it as his opinion, from the position of affairs when he left, that Jackson has by this time surrendered; this is doubtful, as we can still hear firing.

H. Haupt

Colonel Haupt's skepticism regarding the report of Jackson's surrender was appropriate. Stonewall, far from surrendering, had moved his men into a strategic position and attacked an advancing Union force.

The following day Lincoln again turned to his observer:

August 29, 1862

Colonel Haupt: What news from direction of Manassas Junction? What generally?

A. Lincoln

August 29, 1862

President Lincoln and General Halleck: General Pope was at Centreville this morning at 6 o'clock; seemed to be in good spirits;

Hooker driving the enemy before him, McDowell and Siegel cutting off his retreat; army out of forage and subsistence; force of enemy 60,000. This is the substance of information communicated by two ambulance drivers who came from Centreville, and who also gave many particulars confirming previous statements . . ."

H. Haupt

The day was not going well for Lincoln's men. Instead of "driving the enemy," the bluecoats were unsuccessfully flailing at the Confederates. Jackson had dug his troops in behind an unused railroad embankment and was cutting the Union troops to shreds.

As Pope was throwing men against the Rebels, the president telegraphed General McClellan, "What news from direction of Manassas Junction?" The capability of the telegraph for quasi-real time dialog was amply demonstrated when McClellan responded only 15 minutes later. The speedy response, however, was more about McClellan's positioning for his own purposes than it was about meeting the needs of Lincoln and the nation.

After rehashing the news he had learned from Haupt, McClellan launched, uninvited, into providing strategic advice. "I am clear that one of two courses should be adopted—1st To concentrate all our available forces to open communication with Pope—2nd To leave Pope to get out of his scrape & at once use all our means to make the Capital perfectly safe." The Young Napoleon then made a bid to get back into command: "Tell me what you want me to do and I will do all in my power to accomplish it. I wish to know what my orders and authority are . . ."

While McClellan was pledging fidelity, his actions were far from his "I will do all in my power" soliloquy. Unbeknownst to anyone in Washington, McClellan had unilaterally initiated his second option to "leave Pope to get out of his scrape" alone. General-in-Chief Halleck had ordered an army corps, approximately 20,000 men, forward from Alexandria to aid Pope. McClellan countermanded the order and stopped the movement after it was under way.

The president did not know of this insubordination. Reading Lincoln's telegram in response to McClellan's undesired counsel, one can imagine the president taking a deep breath before smoothing the paper on which to write his tempered reply. "I think your first alternative, towit, [*sic*] 'to open communications with Pope,' is the right one." The president simply chose to ignore the "get out of his scrape" comment. He also chose not to become further embroiled with McClellan, adding, "But I wish not to control. That I now leave to Gen. Halleck, aided by your counsels."

But, of course, Lincoln was involved. "The President was never so wrathful as last night against George," the Washington bureau chief of the *New York Tribune* wrote to his editor. That one general officer would, uninvited, recommend that the commander on the field be left "to get out of his scrape" alone was contemptuous to Lincoln. "The President was very outspoken in regard to McClellan's present conduct," Lincoln's secretary John Hay recorded in his diary. "He said it really seemed to him that McC wanted Pope defeated."

The following morning the president was back on the telegraph, inquiring of Haupt again:

August 30, 1862, 9 A.M.

Colonel Haupt: What news?

A. Lincoln

August 30, 1862

President Lincoln: Firing this morning is heard in direction of Centreville . . . I have also sent wire, operator and instrument . . . and a force of 200 riflemen, with directions to . . . send out scouts and report everything.

The intelligence last evening was that Hooker and Pope were pushing the enemy towards the Gaps in the mountains through which they had advanced, and that McDowell and Siegel were heading them off. This morning the direction of the firing seemed to be changing, and it is not impossible that the enemy's forces may be changing direction and trying to escape towards Fredericksburg . . . I await intelligence with some anxiety, and will communicate anything of importance that I hear.

H. Haupt

Later in the day the president once more interrogated Haupt.

August 30, 1862, 3:50 P.M.

Colonel Haupt: Please send me the latest news.

A. Lincoln

August 30, 1862

A. Lincoln, President: Our operator has reached Manassas; hears no firing of importance. I have directed part of 200 riflemen to go out as scouts, make observations and report constantly. Two or three flashes just seen from Manassas in direction of Centreville . . . We have re-established telegraphic communications with Manassas . . .

H. Haupt

Information was now reaching the capital by many sources; little of it was encouraging. That evening the president walked into John Hay's room in the White House. "Well, John we are whipped again, I am afraid." The Federals had been soundly beaten on the same ground as their ignominious defeat a year earlier.

Early the following morning Lincoln, still unable to communicate with his field general, once again turned to Colonel Haupt.

August 31, 1862, 7:10 A.M.

Colonel Haupt: What news? Did you hear any firing this morning?

A. Lincoln

August 31, 1862

President Lincoln: No news received yet this morning; firing heard distinctly in direction of Bristoe at 6 o'clock.

H. Haupt

The battlefield outcome was the same as the last time the armies had clashed along Bull Run. Abraham Lincoln's role during the second engagement, however, was much different than during the first. There was no patient, disengaged waiting. The president was involved, keeping in touch with developments in the field. Lincoln's connection to the telegraph went so far that he ordered a cot installed in the telegraph office so that he could remain in proximity to the wires and not return to the White House to sleep.

"It is due in great measure to his indomitable will, that army movements have been characterized by such energy and celerity for the last few days," John Hay wrote in his diary about the president's activities during the battle. Confronted with an enemy advance outside his capital, burdened by McClellan's unwillingness to help Pope, unaided by General-in-Chief Halleck who seemed incapable of decisiveness, Abraham Lincoln and his army had again been humiliated.

This time, as Hay's diary makes clear, the president was a part of doing whatever could be done from Washington to aid at the front.

While Lincoln's generals once again let him down, one person emerged from the battle holding the president's esteem: Herman Haupt. "There is one man who seems thoroughly to reflect and satisfy him in everything he undertakes," wrote Hay. "This is Haupt the Rail Road man at Alexandria. He has as [Treasury Secretary] Chase says a Major General's head on his shoulders. The President is particularly struck with the businesslike character of his despatch, telling in the fewest words the information most sought for, which contrasted so strongly with the weak whining vague and incorrect despatches of the whilom General-in-chief [McClellan]."

A few days later Colonel Haupt presented himself at the War Department. It happened that the president and most of the cabinet were in the secretary's office at the time. "I was received with much cordiality, [and] addressed as General Haupt," he later wrote. The president thanked Haupt "for what he was pleased to consider the important service rendered." The next day Haupt received an appointment as Brigadier General of Volunteers, "for meritorious services in the recent operations against the enemy near Manassas."

NOT ALL THE PRESIDENT'S appointments were so well received. With the Rebels once again at the gates of the capital, and with no general having distinguished himself at Manassas, Lincoln put George McClellan back in command. "We must use what tools we have," he told John Hay. The defense of Washington was the priority and, while McClellan was wanting in offensive instincts, there was no doubt he was superb on the defensive. General John Pope was sent to Minnesota to worry about Indians.

Robert E. Lee had no intention of attacking Washington, however. After the Manassas repeat, Lee pushed through Virginia to the Potomac. Less than a week after victory along the stream called Bull

Run, the Confederate Army of Northern Virginia was crossing the Potomac into the Union state of Maryland.

The Union Army of the Potomac, once again under the command of George McClellan, slowly followed Lee north, shielding Washington and Baltimore.

Telegraph traffic reminded the president, however, that he was fighting a two-front war. At the same time that Lee was moving north into Maryland, Confederate General Braxton Bragg was pushing north through Tennessee, with the border state of Kentucky in his sites.

Or was he? The telegraph helped spread the rumors that forces from the west were joining Lee in the east. Union general John Wool, commanding in Baltimore, telegraphed General Halleck the morning of September 7, with a report "from undoubted authority" that General Bragg had moved operations from Tennessee and was "advancing up the Shenandoah Valley for Pennsylvania, with 40,000 troops."

To General Jeremiah Boyle, military governor of Kentucky, Lincoln telegraphed that same day, "Where is Gen. Bragg? What do you know of the subject?" Boyle responded that evening, "I do not know . . . but believe he is in Tennessee threatening [Union] Genl Buell . . ." The following day, however, Boyle was feeding the rumor machine: "There is some conjecture that Bragg may have joined the forces near Washington."

The president wired General Don Carlos Buell (interestingly, Confederate General Bragg's brother-in-law) who was in Louisville, "What degree of certainty have you, that Bragg with his command, is now in the valley of the Shenandoah, Virginia?" The same day he telegraphed General Wool, "How certain is your information about Bragg being in the valley of the Shenandoah?"

The president was using lightning messages to scramble for hard information. To General Horatio Wright, that same day: "Do you know, to any certainty, where Gen. Bragg is? May he be in Virginia?"

Turning back and forth between the two fronts, Lincoln wired McClellan late in the afternoon of September 8, "How does it look now?" McClellan responded 30 minutes later, reporting only small skirmishes. "I will inform you of everything of importance that occurs," he promised.

Two days later, at 10:15 in the morning, Lincoln sent the same message again: "How does it look now?" McClellan replied shortly after noon with a detailed situation analysis. The president's electronic interrogatories may have been repetitive, but the commanding general was treating them with the respect they warranted.

It looked like events would come to a head in the east first. McClellan sent a peninsula-like telegram to Halleck for "all the troops you can spare from Washington." This time Lincoln responded with what the general wanted to hear, sending General Fitz John Porter, a McClellan favorite, and 21,000 men on their way.

The wires also brought a message from Pennsylvania governor Andrew Curtin the evening of September 11 asking for 80,000 troops to be sent to defend his state. The president dealt with this political problem in a telegram that patiently explained, "Please consider. We have not to exceed eighty thousand disciplined troops . . . this side of the mountains, and most of them . . . are now in the rear of the enemy supposed to be invading Pennsylvania." Then the president gave a little military strategy lesson: "Start half of them to Harrisburg, and the enemy will turn upon and beat the remaining half, and then reach Harrisburg before the part going there, and beat it too when it comes. The best possible security for Pennsylvania is putting the strongest force into the enemies rear." Governor Curtin saw the light: "Your message received. Reasons for not sending force entirely satisfactory. We are doing all that is possible in this direction."

In keeping with his newfound willingness to use the telegraph proactively, rather than waiting for reports, the president again queried McClellan on September 12. It was the third iteration of an identical message: "How does it look now?" Less than two hours later

Lincoln answered his own question, reporting to McClellan, "I have advices that Jackson is crossing the Potomac at Williamsport . . . Receiving nothing from Harpers Ferry or Martinsburg to-day." Lincoln closed the telegram with a plea: "Please do not let him [Jackson] get off without being hurt."

The following day a windfall of incalculable magnitude fell into George McClellan's hands. A copy of Lee's orders to his corps commanders was, inexplicably, discovered by some Indiana troops near Fredericksburg, Maryland, camping in a field recently occupied by Confederate forces. The Union leader now knew Lee's plan, his objective, the disposition of his troops, their routes of travel, and their timetable for battle. The information revealed that the Confederates had split their forces into five separate parts, each capable of being dealt with serially before they could regroup. Here was the opportunity to destroy the Rebel army once and for all.

At noon on September 13 McClellan telegraphed Lincoln: "I have the whole rebel force in front of me . . . Lee has made a gross mistake and that he will be severely punished for it . . . I have all the plans of the Rebels and will catch them in their own trap . . . Will send you trophies."

Then the Young Napoleon squandered his intelligence coup. At least seven hours of daylight remained, the gaps in South Mountain, a spur of the Blue Ridge Mountains through which the Federals would have to pass to catch up with Lee's troops, could be reached by dark. But McClellan decided he wouldn't put his troops in motion until morning the next day! The first Union troops finally began their march to engage the Rebels a full 18 hours after McClellan knew every detail of Lee's plans.

Robert E. Lee was not as slow to respond to intelligence, however. The minute he heard that Union forces were in pursuit, he countermarched his men to meet the Yankees at the passes of South Mountain. After a day of heavy fighting, the Rebels withdrew. McClellan wired Halleck the next morning: "the Enemy . . . in a perfect panic &

Gen Lee last night stated publicly that he must admit they had been shockingly whipped."

At last! The kind of news the president had been wishing the wires would deliver. He responded to McClellan, "God bless you, and all with you." Then, perhaps remembering the proclivities of his general, the president reminded him that small victories weren't enough, that his job was to "Destroy the rebel army, if possible."

The following day, the president hung around the telegraph office awaiting news. In Maryland, however, McClellan passed up the opportunity to deliver the kind of devastating blow Lincoln had been requesting. The Confederates sat exposed with their forces split outside of Sharpsburg. Fifteen thousand graybacks faced 90,000 bluecoats. It was the kind of opportunity for which Lincoln had been hoping. Once again, however, George McClellan squandered the moment by not giving battle.

The following day, September 17, 1862, was the Battle of Antietam (Sharpsburg), the bloodiest day of the Civil War. Lee's forces had mostly regrouped, but were still outnumbered, when McClellan attacked. Continuing to be parsimonious in his actions, McClellan fed his men piecemeal against Lee's line. While the young Napoleon held back 25,000 men as a precaution in case they might be needed after a Union defeat, Lee used every man he had, moving them from hot spot to hot spot, a force-multiplying luxury McClellan had given him by the failure to give battle on a broad front.

At the end of a horrific day both armies remained on the field. The battle had not been clear-cut enough to cause one of the forces to retreat. The following day McClellan, once again, demurred. This hesitation allowed Lee to begin an orderly withdrawal back across the Potomac. General McClellan crowed in a telegram to General Halleck the following day, "I have the honor to report that Maryland is entirely freed from the presence of the enemy, who has been driven across the Potomac."

There was no congratulatory telegram from the president of the United States. The Rebels had escaped.

For the remainder of September and the first week of October the president went electronically silent, sending no telegrams. While Lincoln continued to conduct his typical daily activities, these three weeks bring into sharp focus the formidable burdens and isolation that history had visited upon Abraham Lincoln.

In the army there was talk of marching on Washington to put things right. From his Minnesota purgatory, General John Pope wrote the governor of Illinois, "Already this Potomac Army clique talk openly of Lincoln's weakness and the necessity of replacing him by some stronger man . . . You would be surprised and alarmed to see how openly these things are talked of . . ."

Adding to the mood of the army was a rumor circulating among officers that the reason McClellan had not chased and destroyed the Rebels after Antietam was because it was "not the game"; that the controlling military strategy was for the armies to engage but not extinguish the other. By wearing down both the troops and the public, the story went, it would become possible to have a political compromise that ended the war yet allowed for the continuation of slavery. The rumor was traced to Major John Key, a member of the staff of General McClellan. That McClellan was a Democrat who had supported slavery made the rumor all the more heinous. To send the message that the war was not a "game," the Major was called to the White House, interrogated by the president, and summarily dismissed on September 27.

The pressures of his responsibilities amidst challenges both military and political were weighing on the president. Earlier in the month Attorney General Bates recorded in his cabinet meeting notes that the president "seemed wrung by the bitterest anguish—said he felt almost ready to hang himself." Pouring that anguish onto a piece of paper, Abraham Lincoln sought to discover the rationale for the circumstances confronting the nation and his leadership.

"The will of God prevails," Lincoln's lonely thoughts began. "In great contests each party claims to act in accordance with the will of God. Both *may* be, and one *must* be wrong. God can not be *for,* and *against* the same thing at the same time. In the present civil war it is quite possible that God's purpose is something different from the purpose of either party—and yet the human instrumentalities, working just as they do, are of the best adaptation to effect His purpose. I am almost ready to say this is probably true—that God wills this contest, and wills that it shall not end yet. By his mere quiet power, on the minds of the now contestants, He could have either *saved* or *destroyed* the Union without a human contest. Yet the contest began. And having begun He could give the final victory to either side any day. Yet the contest proceeds."

It was in this darkest of hours, however, that Abraham Lincoln took the brightest step of his presidency. During his quiet time at the desk by the window in the War Department telegraph office the president had been writing the Emancipation Proclamation. Previously, on July 22, Lincoln had read the document's first draft to his cabinet. Secretary of State Seward had urged that any issuance be delayed until after a military victory lest it be viewed as an act of desperation. On September 22, Lincoln determined the battle of Antietam had been enough of a victory to obviate that risk. He released the Preliminary Emancipation Proclamation, a final version to take effect the first day of the following year.

> *That on the first day of January in the year of our Lord, one thousand eight hundred and sixty-three, all persons held as slaves within any state, or designated part of a state, the people whereof shall then be in rebellion against the United States shall be then, thenceforward, and forever free . . .*

"What I did, I did after very full deliberation, and under a very heavy and solemn sense of responsibility. I can only trust in God I have made no mistake," Lincoln told a crowd that assembled at the White House.

The general of his largest army, George McClellan, indeed did believe the Emancipation Proclamation was a mistake. Earlier—only two weeks before Lincoln had shared the draft with his cabinet—McClellan had written the president that if the war was defined as being about the abolition of slavery, he doubted his army would fight. Such an action "would rapidly disintegrate our present Armies," McClellan warned.

Now, with the Proclamation set to take effect in a few months, Lincoln decided it was time to assess the mood of the army and engage McClellan one-to-one. The president traveled to the site of the recent engagements and the headquarters of the Army of the Potomac.

It was classic Lincoln leadership. While he and General McClellan had maintained an ongoing telegraphic correspondence, the president extended his Management-By-Walking-Around technique into the field so that he could take the measure of both his general and his army. How that measurement was shaping up was revealed one morning during his visit. At sunrise the president walked to a hilltop from which he could see the broad landscape. Spread before him was the awesome sight of thousands of tents and the materials of war running to the horizon. Turning to a friend from Springfield who had accompanied him, O. M. Hatch, Lincoln asked rhetorically, "Hatch—Hatch, what is all this?" The response, "this is the Army of the Potomac," was greeted with the rejoinder, "No, Hatch, no. This is General McClellan's bodyguard." The following day the president returned to Washington.

As the first full week of October began, Lincoln told General-in-Chief Halleck to order McClellan to break camp and put his army in motion. "I am instructed to telegraph you as follows: The President directs that you cross the Potomac and give battle to the enemy or drive him south. Your army must move now while the roads are good."

THE PRESIDENT ENDED HIS three-week hiatus from the telegraph the day after Halleck's order to McClellan. Lincoln's eyes had turned westward once more; there he found victory. The Confederates had been repulsed at Corinth, Mississippi, by troops under the overall command of General Ulysses S. Grant. In his first-ever telegram to Grant, the president wired, "I congratulate you and all concerned on your recent battles and victories. How does it all sum up?"

The taciturn Grant's "sum up" response gave a vivid image of the horror of battle. After reporting on those paroled and the number of wounded Rebels being held in Union camps, Grant explained, "Cannot tell the number of dead yet. About Eight hundred Rebels already buried. Their loss in Killed about Nine to one of ours. The ground is not yet cleared of their unburied dead."

Amidst such gruesome reports, the telegraph sometimes provided access to the president that was frivolous or unwarranted. Such was the case on October 8, the same day that Lincoln wired Grant. Thomas Clay, son of the famous Kentuckian Henry Clay, wired from Cincinnati that he had been visited by a group of refugee Kentuckians requesting that the president order General G. W. Morgan's division into the bluegrass state because "this division has done so much and suffered so much in their late march from Cumberland Gap to Greenupsburg that they are entitled to this favor."

Lincoln's response illustrated both his candor, as well as his frustrations. "You cannot have reflected seriously when you ask that I shall order General Morgan's command to Kentucky as a favor." Noting that General Buell's troops might, at that very moment, be confronting the Rebels, the president added, "I sincerely wish war was an easier and pleasanter business than it is, but it does not admit of holidays."

There were, in fact, no such holidays in central Kentucky at that moment. On the very day of Lincoln's response to Clay, Union forces under General Buell had stopped the Rebel advance at the Battle of Perryville. On October 10, General Boyle wired General Halleck from Louisville: "Terrible battle yesterday [*sic*] near Perryville. Buell drove Bragg 8 miles, with great slaughter on both sides." Now, if the generals in the west would only do what McClellan had not: chase the Rebels and finish them off.

Lincoln telegraphed General Boyle to find out whether Buell was pursuing. "Please send any news you have from Gen. Buell to-day." When he didn't hear back, another message went out 24 hours later: "We are very anxious to hear from Gen. Buell's Army. We have heard nothing since day-before yesterday. Have you any-thing?" Boyle replied that he had received both messages, but had no reliable information: "Battle was fought on Wednesday . . . Our loss estimated at 1,500 to 2,000 killed and wounded. The enemy's loss is great, and believed to be greater . . . My understanding is that Buell is pressing the enemy. Heavy fighting reported at Harrodsburg. Expect to receive news by courier tonight. Will send it to you."

Back in the east, General McClellan kept sending out reconnaissance forces but was hardly fulfilling Lincoln's order to "give battle to the enemy." A week after Halleck's telegram, the president communicated directly with George McClellan. As was his style when there was something heavy to convey, or when he wanted to fully develop his thoughts, he wrote a letter that was hand delivered, instead of sending a wire. The letter began with Lincoln reminding McClellan of their conversation only a few weeks earlier when the president had visited the Army of the Potomac: "You remember my speaking to you of what I called your over-cautiousness. Are you not over-cautious when you assume that you can not do what the enemy is constantly doing? Should you not claim to be at least his equal in prowess, and act upon the claim?" The president then went on for six more long paragraphs to spell out exactly what he meant.

General McClellan replied via the president's courier on October 17, "I have been unable to give Your Excellency's letter that full and respectful consideration which it merits at my hands." Then the general gave the president the back of his hand: "I do not wish to detain Colonel Perkins [the messenger] beyond the morning's train; I therefore think it best to send him back with this simple acknowledgement of receipt of Your Excellency's letter . . . I promise you that I will give your views the fullest and most unprejudiced consideration . . ."

McClellan followed his sophistry with more of the same: little action, and more calls for support before he could move. The president, having heard all this before, was coming to the end of his rope. It had now been five months since his electronic breakout; Lincoln now dealt with McClellan in a manner that was more direct and less deferential than when the army had been on the peninsula.

When McClellan, seeking to bolster the rationale for his lack of offense, wired General Halleck a verbatim report from a cavalry colonel complaining about the condition of his horses, Lincoln stepped between his generals and fired back. "I have just read your despatch about sore tongued and fatiegued [*sic*] horses—Will you pardon me for asking what the horses of your army have done since the battle of Antietam that fatigue anything?"

Reinforcing his assertiveness, Lincoln telegrammed McClellan the following day, October 26, after receiving the general's reponses explaining how hard his troops had been working chasing General J. E. B. Stuart's Confederate cavalry that was still in Maryland. "Yours in reply to mine about horses received," Lincoln replied. "Of course you know the facts better than I, still two considerations remain. Stuart's cavalry outmarched ours, having certainly done more marked service on the Peninsula, and everywhere else since. Secondly, will not a movement of our army be a relief to the cavalry, compelling the enemy to concentrate, instead of 'foraging' in squads everywhere?" After taking the shot, the president ended the wire on a positive note that also indicated how closely he was monitoring the War Department's telegraph traffic: "But I am so rejoiced to learn from your despatch to Gen. Halleck, that you begin crossing the river this morning."

The commander-in-chief and his field general were engaged in their own electronic equivalent of a long-range artillery exchange. McClellan lobbed a telegram back at the president defending his cavalry and observing, "I cannot resist the strength of my own conviction that some one has conveyed to your mind an erroneous impression in regard to the service of our cavalry."

Lincoln fired back, "Most certainly I intended no injustice to any; and if I have done any, I deeply regret it. To be told after more than five weeks total inaction of the Army, and during which period we had sent to that Army every fresh horse we possibly could, amounting in the whole to 7918 that the cavalry horses were too much fatiegued to move, presented a very cheerless, almost hopeless, prospect for the future; and it may have forced something of impatience into my despatches. If not recruited and rested then, when could they ever be?"

Having been out-pointed on the battle of the horses, McClellan opened a new line of debate. Casualties had reduced his units; he reminded the president of "how necessary it is to fill up these skeletons before taking them again into action." Thus, "I have the honor to request that the order to fill up the old regiments with drafted men may at once be issued." Availing himself of the speed of the telegraph, it took the president only 25 minutes to reply, promising that "the request therein shall be complied with as far as practicable." Then the former litigator began his cross examination, focusing on the general's comment about having to fill out the units before engaging the enemy: "And now I ask a distinct answer to the question, Is it your purpose not to go into action again until the men now being drafted in the States are incorporated into the old regiments?"

George McClellan beat a retreat in a telegram four hours later. He blamed the "before taking them again into action" language on the officer who had been instructed to draft a reply, but who sent it "without first submitting it to me." Then the general threw in the news that he knew the president wanted to hear: "I commenced crossing the Army into Virginia yesterday and shall push forward as rapidly as possible to endeavor to meet the enemy."

Lincoln, ever the gracious victor, replied, "I am much pleased with the movement of the Army." Having seen the evaporation of similar assurances from McClellan before, the president indicated his intention to stay abreast of McClellan's movements: "When you get entirely across the river let me know."

The play had run its course, however. The president's cabinet, along with the Republican congressional leadership, had long ago determined the Young Napoleon had to go. That McClellan stayed as long as he did was a testament to Lincoln's patience as well as his political shrewdness. With state and congressional elections slated for November 4, Lincoln did not want to create a preelection firestorm by sacking Democrat McClellan. The day after the election (in which the Democrats made gains but the Republicans still controlled Congress), the president ordered General Halleck to relieve General McClellan of command. General Ambrose Burnside was named to head the Army of the Potomac.

THE MCCLELLAN ERA WAS over. This time it was for real; there would be no return to rival his resurrection after Second Manassas (Bull Run). In two years George McClellan would be the Democratic standard bearer in the race for the White House. For now, however, the man who had been so good at organizing the army, and so poor at using it, was on his way home.

Now with Burnside in command, the president sent fewer telegrams to the Army of the Potomac. Once again demonstrating his hierarchy of communications in which face-to-face meetings were on the top rung, the president used the speedy messenger to suggest that he and General Burnside meet. On November 25 the president wired, "If I should be in a Boat off Aquia-Creek, at dark to-morrow (wednesday) evening, could you, without inconvenience, meet me & pass an hour or two with me?" At that meeting Lincoln presented his strategic thoughts: the army should develop a three-pronged attack around Fredericksburg, Virginia, midway between the belligerents' capitals. Burnside agreed with the strategic objective, but rejected Lincoln's tripartite plan.

As the Confederates entrenched themselves on the heights behind Fredericksburg, Burnside prepared for his army to cross the Rappahannock River, capture the town, and assault the heights. George McClellan had been sacked for his failure to attack; Ambrose Burnside would be damned if the same would be said of him, even if the wisdom of his planned frontal assault was suspect. Three weeks after his meeting with Lincoln, on December 13, Burnside's army attacked the Confederates head-on.

During the battle Lincoln was at his usual post in the telegraph office. Around midday the messages started pouring in. In one message the telegraph operator's editorial comment captured the intensity of the fight: "The wounded & killed is immense. The battle rages furiously. Can hardly hear my Instrument."

Burnside had ordered his troops into a devastating slaughter. As he watched wave after wave of men in blue bravely march as if on parade into the murderous crossfire of his cannons, Robert E. Lee remarked of the spectacle, "It is well that war is so terrible. We should grow too fond of it."

Once again, Lee's Rebels had beaten Lincoln's army. The president had sought a general who would be aggressive. Burnside had responded with monstrously inept implementation.

On December 30 the president reasserted himself with General Burnside: "I have good reason for saying you must not make a general movement of the army without letting me know." Burnside wired his compliance.

The year 1862 had been *annus horribilis* for Lincoln's army. Nevertheless, in responding to these awful events, he had discovered a new outlet for his leadership instincts. Abraham Lincoln found his electronic voice in 1862.

As the year progressed Lincoln's approach to the war began to evolve, as had his use of the telegraph. During the first year of his presidency, Lincoln approached the war in a cautious manner, not wanting to upset what he hoped was the silent majority in the seceded states who would soon come to their senses and cease supporting the rebellion. His use of the telegraph had been equally cautious: he sent only slightly more than a dozen electronic messages in 1861, none of which imposed his will on military affairs.

In 1862, however, Lincoln's approach to the war changed significantly. The silent majority did not materialize. The president's strategy evolved. Increasingly the goal became to destroy the Rebel army. The telegraph became the vehicle by which he remained informed, provided direction, and prodded.

Yet the telegraph remained a learning experience for Abraham Lincoln in 1862. The primary lesson, in which he received high marks, was to extend his reach to the front. Once Lincoln had his electronic breakout, the telegraph became an integral part of his leadership. Exactly how to use the lightning messages, however, remained in development; while he could move men around the chessboard, even the best-laid plans required a field commander who shared his intensity. It would be another year before the president had assembled the team of battlefield leaders necessary to win the war.

CHAPTER SIX

NEW ELECTRONIC CHALLENGES

LET'S PAUSE AT THIS POINT in the narrative—almost at the midpoint of the Lincoln presidency—to investigate some of the collateral changes brought on by lightning messages. The telegraph was an instrument that presented the president with challenges that had no precedent.

News Media

"Have you any news?" was the second message sent over Samuel Morse's test line, immediately following "What hath God wrought!" It began a relationship between the telegraph and the rapid delivery of news that transformed both American journalism and politics. "Washington is as near to us now as our up-town wards. We can almost hear through the Telegraph, members of Congress as they speak," wrote the *New York Express* in 1846. President Lincoln was buffeted by the political realities created by this new medium. His government responded by using the telegraph to affect public opinion.

At the time of the Civil War, the United States was the most newspaper-rich nation in the world. The over three thousand American newspapers constituted one-third of the total number of newspapers on the entire planet. These were partisan publications. Today we assume the press is nonpartisan, without an axe to grind, but in Lincoln's day, newspapers' editors and owners were often political powerhouses in their own right. Their ownership of the media provided an unabashed bully pulpit.

Prior to the arrival of the telegraph, local newspapers had focused on hometown events and politics. News from afar (including newspapers from afar) arrived by mail or rail; individuals had access to the news as quickly as the local newspapers did. Naturally, the press focused on those activities where they could beat the mail, chiefly local news and political commentary. But with the telegraph newspapers became a source of breaking news from afar, not just a commentator on events, and the papers pressed their advantage.

Collecting such information from afar, was expensive. The newspaper not only had to pay for the reporter and his expenses in the field, but also the high cost of transmitting his stories back by telegraph. During the war, for instance, a telegram from Washington to New York cost five cents per word.

Only four years after Morse's test, six New York City newspapers banded together to share the costs of keeping correspondents in the field and paying the tariff on their telegraphed reports. They called it the New York Associated Press. Within a few years the coop was providing telegraph-delivered news reports for a fee to newspapers across the nation. The Associated Press wire service allowed even those newspapers that could not afford field reporters to give their subscribers breaking news delivered with instantaneous speed.

When war brought a surge in the public's desire for fresh news, the Associated Press was not enough to quench the thirst. In response to this demand, the leading dailies expanded their newsgathering, as well as increased their prices. Publications that had begun the war as the "penny press" typically added another penny annually. Part of this new revenue was spent to expand information collection. The Associated Press may have provided a common information feed, yet there were still over 300 special war correspondents assigned by individual newspapers to travel with the troops. The *New York Herald* alone had 63 field reporters, including one with every division of the army.

It was the original embedded reporting, but they were called "specials" in the Civil War. They traveled with the troops, collecting both camp stories and battle reports for their readers back home. While the mail, delivered via horseback or rail, was sometimes used for delivering their stories, the speediest reporting found the specials bringing their reports to the nearest telegraph office.

"We must have something to eat, and the newspapers to read," opined Oliver Wendell Holmes, Sr. "Everything else we can do without . . . Only bread and the newspaper we must have." The most compelling content of each day's newspaper was in the columns headed "News By Magnetic Telegraph" or similar variations. Before the war, newspapers had constrained their telegraphic reports because of the high cost; with a war to decide the nation's future raging, however, major papers were printing several pages of electronically delivered news from both their own correspondents as well as the Associated Press.

The telegraph, which had given Abraham Lincoln unprecedented capability for a chief magistrate, also brought to the American people an unprecedented awareness of and vicarious participation in both battlefield events and political intrigue. This, in turn, created new challenges for the president for which, once again, he was without precedent for guidance.

Two years prior to his presidential campaign, in the first of the Lincoln–Douglas debates, Lincoln had observed, "public sentiment in this country is everything. With public sentiment, nothing can fail; without it nothing can succeed." The development of public opinion meant that "he who moulds public sentiment, goes deeper than he who enacts statutes or pronounces decisions." To prevail in the rebellion, the president knew he needed to mold public sentiment.

How Lincoln dealt with the wartime press was a political priority. It was also a perilous undertaking as the right of a free press was at the core of the Constitution that Lincoln was fighting to preserve.

Fresh news from the front created a new triangle trade in information, which helped define political reality. In the first leg, the stories from the front, formed and fanned by accompanying editorial commentary, had an impact on local opinion. As that opinion ripened into political significance, it was transmitted on its second leg to Washington where it influenced the national debate. In the final leg of the triangle, the political realities of Washington were reflected in the telegrams to the front from Lincoln and his lieutenants.

It was the first time that a government, let alone a government at war, was confronted by such a well-informed constituency. Such speedy news held the possibility of divulging sensitive strategic and tactical information. In addition, the spotlight of the press and its natural second-guessing did not sit comfortably with those in positions of leadership. The result was America's first exposure to widespread and systematic censorship.

When General George McClellan first arrived in Washington, he embarked on what today would be called a "charm offensive" with the press. Assembling the leading reporters at his headquarters, McClellan sought their cooperation. He had known such a relationship with the reporters who had covered his western Virginia operations, he told the group, and saw no reason why it would not work for those covering the Army of the Potomac as well. It was a time of national crisis, he reminded the reporters, and he would rely on their common sense and patriotism to control what they put in their dispatches. As a result, on August 2, 1861, the Washington reporters of America's major newspapers signed an agreement with General McClellan in which they voluntarily agreed to "refrain from publishing . . . any matter that may furnish aid or comfort to the enemy."

The self-regulation plan lasted less than a week. By August 7 the secretary of war ordered all telegrams containing military information to be cleared with the officer in charge of the particular activity. A short while later, management authority for censorship was transferred to Assistant Secretary of State Frederick Seward (the secretary's son). In February of 1862, pursuant to an Act of Congress, the War Department took "military possession of all telegraph lines in the United States." From that point forward Secretary of War Edwin Stanton assumed censorship responsibility.

During the period leading up to "military possession," the former manager of the Philadelphia American Telegraph Corporation office, H. Emmons Thayer, was brought in to be the government's chief censor. Thayer and his assistants read every one of the hundreds of messages that were sent daily from the Washington telegraph office. Their instructions expanded on McClellan's voluntary code for the censorship of military information to include non-military affairs. "[A]ll telegraphic dispatches from Washington, intended for publication, which relate to the civil or military operations of the government" were, henceforth, prohibited.

The engagement at Balls Bluff that had opened Lincoln's eyes to McClellan's control of the telegraph also exposed the extent to which the government was controlling what was sent out over the wires. McClellan, who had withheld the news from the president, sought to do the same with the public. The general ordered that nothing pass over the wire until the official report of the battle was finally ready, and then only that report would be allowed to be disseminated. Correspondents seeking to do their own reporting about this latest military debacle were denied the benefits of the telegraph to share their discoveries. This restriction prompted many reporters to become creative in their dispatches, trying to signal their news editors that things had not gone well at Balls Bluff without really saying it in so many words. One clever reporter, for instance, sent the message, "the Gov't wd not permit me to telegraph the facts," hoping that his editor would read between the lines that if the facts weren't allowed to be sent then they must be bad.

The administration may have been imposing censorship, but the press still had friends on Capitol Hill. The House of Representatives passed a resolution in December 1861 instructing the Judiciary Committee to investigate the censorship allegations. Its report, issued the following March, concluded, "A telegraphic censorship of the press has been established in this city . . . Despatches, almost numberless, of a political, personal, and general character have been suppressed by the censor, and correspondents have been deterred from preparing others because they knew they could not send them to their papers by telegraph."

The control of nonmilitary information was relaxed when the War Department took over censorship responsibilities in February 1862. Yet, as the House Report indicated, censorship did not have to spike a story to be effective. The mere threat of censorship influenced the message the reporters delivered. As the House Report observed, that threat had a chilling effect; as reporters crafted their messages to avoid the censor's wrath, the content of those messages was subtly influenced. A reporter, under pressure to deliver news to his editor had every incentive to conform his story to the censor's expectations.

Apart from restricting the press, the Lincoln administration also proactively sought to use the medium; this included the government's first systematic program of news releases. In the early days of the war these amounted to little more than releasing the official reports from the field (like the aforementioned official report on Balls Bluff). As the war progressed, however, the Lincoln administration became more adept at issuing and spinning information. In so doing, its official mouthpiece became the Associated Press. An understanding was reached with the wire service: the administration would favor it as the outlet of choice, but with the expectation that it would report the story just as the administration wanted.

The AP was also given preferential access to the telegraph lines themselves. While most reporters would have to queue up to send a message over an increasingly crowded telegraph network, the AP reports went to the head of the line. Ostensibly this was because the AP reports were for the broadest distribution; the reality was that the administration got its story out first.

Beyond preference in the use of the wires, the news association was such a handmaiden to the Lincoln administration that it was immune from censorship. The early standards for the censors stated they were "to prohibit all telegraphic despatches from Washington, intended for publication, which relate to the civil or military operations of the government, *with the exception of the despatches of the regular agent of the associated press*" [emphasis added].

Censor Thayer further established the AP as the government's preferred voice by making its dispatches the standard by which all other reporting was judged as to its suitability for distribution. "I take the associated press as my guide in all cases," Thayer explained. Those reporters whose stories became ensnared on the censor's spike complained that the AP delivered the government's propaganda while their more factual reports were stopped at the telegraph office.

As a part of the administration's proactive public relations efforts, Secretary Stanton developed his own spin machine that leveraged both the telegraph and the symbiotic relationship with the AP. Stanton and his staff would draft their version of events, then bypass the reporters in Washington by telegraphing the information to General John Dix, commanding in New York, who would then have the material delivered directly to the headquarters of the Associated Press.

Lincoln not only approved the spin efforts, but also made himself available to further its activities. The president, too, could go on a "charm offensive." By granting private sessions to journalism's powerhouses, Lincoln exploited the prestige of the presidency to explain his policies and influence their coverage without ever having to withstand a press conference-like event. According to one historian, "almost every Northern journalist of prominence" was invited to the White House for a one-on-one with the president.

Abraham Lincoln had run the first modern media campaign to

win the presidency. Recognizing that "With public sentiment, nothing can fail; without it nothing can succeed," he also developed the rudiments of modern media theory to feed as well as control the beast.

Wiretapping and Ciphers

The telegraph was speedy, but sometimes unreliable. Messages were intercepted, or false messages were sent altogether.

As the nation tried to piece together the events at Fort Sumter, the *New York Times* report of April 14, 1861, included this caveat: "as the telegraph is known to have been constantly tampered with by the secession authorities, it is feared that even private dispatches may have been mutilated for the purpose of cutting the Government off from all possible means of correct information."

Intercepting a telegraph message was not a difficult task. It simply required splicing into the official line and attaching that new feed to a telegraph key. It was possible, then, not only to listen to the traffic, but also to insert bogus messages.

Confederate raiders would frequently tap into the lines to gather intelligence. Occasionally they also engaged in electronic frivolity, as when Rebel general J.E.B. Stuart raided a Union supply base in Burke, Virginia, in 1862. Installing his own telegraph operator at the base's key, Stuart sent a signed message to the U.S. Army's quartermaster-general, the notoriously nonhumorous Montgomery Meigs, complaining about "the bad quality of the mules lately furnished, which interfered seriously with our moving the captured wagons."

In order to safeguard important transmissions, both sides developed cipher codes that turned important messages into gibberish. Because complex codes required time for encoding and decoding, some messages moved without code, others with a simple code, but the most important transmissions were encrypted with a complex code.

The decision not to code, even for the most basic messages, had its risks. In 1864, as Union forces were laying siege to Petersburg, for instance, Confederate wiretappers listened to the Federal telegraph traffic for six weeks. While the significant messages were indecipherable, one message reporting on the shipment of 2,536 head of cattle to feed the Union army was sent in the clear. The hungry Rebels sent troops to intercept the shipment and dined on Union beef for over a month.

President Lincoln developed his own simple code that he used for messages that weren't of the utmost security. Here is the transcript of a Lincoln-encoded telegram that he sent from the front in 1865:

Headquarters Armies of the U.S., City Point,
8:30 A.M., April 3, 1865

To Charles A. Tinker, War Department, Washington, D.C.— A. Lincoln its in fume a in hymn to start I army treating there possible if of cut too forward pushing is he is so all Richmond aunt confide is Andy evacuated Petersburg reports Grant morning this Washington Sec'y War. (Signed) S.H. Beckwith

Reading this message backward rapidly, phonetically, and understanding that S. H. Beckwith was General Grant's telegraph operator, the true text of the president's message emerges:

Headquarters Armies of the U.S., City Point,
8:30 A.M., April 3, 1865

Washington Sec'y War: This morning Grant reports Petersburg evacuated and is confident Richmond also. He is pushing forward to cut off if possible their retreating army. I start to him in a few minutes. (Signed) A. Lincoln

Important messages were sent in a cipher that was never broken by the Confederates. This unbreakable code was known as the Route Code, so called because the message contained within it instructions for the "route" to be used to piece it together.

To use the Route System the operators followed several steps. First the number of words in the original message was counted. That count was then looked up in the cipher book where it corresponded to a code word. A 32-word message, for instance, was signaled by the cover name "Guard." The cover word was sent first, telling the operator at the other end that the next 32 words were the message and that the route corresponding to the code word "Guard" should be used to decode the message. In the case of the "Guard" code word, it told the receiver that the original encoder had broken the message into a grid with five columns across and seven rows down. In each cell created by the column/row intersection there was one word. The "Guard" cipher told both the coder and the decoder which "route" to follow through that matrix (e.g., up column 1, down column 3, up column 5, down column 2, etc.).

At the top of many of Abraham Lincoln's telegrams can be seen, in the president's hand, the word "cypher," indicating that the message was to be encoded using the Route System. So frustrated did the Rebels become with the Route System code that ciphered messages were published in Southern newspapers with a plea that readers try to decrypt the text. Despite these efforts, however, a Route System message was never successfully deciphered.

Interestingly, beginning a message with a code such as "Guard" is a concept similar to the data "header" used in the modern digital packets that carry e-mails. Just as the code word "Guard" told the recipient how to reassemble the gibberish, the digital header tells the receiving computer how to reassemble the message that has been broken up into digital packets.

Oversight of Justice

The largest single topic of President Lincoln's telegrams concerned wires that were literally a matter of life and death. "Let execution of the death sentence upon William Jeffries, of Co. A. Sixth Indiana Volunteers, be suspended until further order from here," the president telegraphed on January 12, 1864. Unsure of who had custody of the convicted, Lincoln sent the telegram to both General Grant and General George Thomas.

Lincoln sent more telegrams dealing with the appeal of military court martial decisions than any other specific topic by far. It was another challenge without precedent brought on by the new electronic technology, and another area in which the telegraph allowed Lincoln to inject himself into affairs of an army in the field.

Military discipline was enforced by courts martial in which a panel of higher-ranking individuals (it was forbidden for a trial court to contain men of subordinate rank to the accused) was assembled to review the facts and pass judgment. Offenses such as cowardice and desertion were punishable by being "shot to death." The very term "shot to death" illustrated the depth of the issue Lincoln faced. A convicted soldier, standing before a firing squad, was not always facing a swift and merciful execution. The imprecision of Civil War weapons, coupled with the nerves of the soldiers ordered to execute a comrade, often meant that the first volley failed to do the task. As the condemned lay writhing on the ground, the execution squad would reload and fire again until the victim was "shot to death."

The principal purpose of courts martial was to maintain discipline in a harsh environment. When not being ordered to march into a hail of bullets, the soldiers were crammed into camps with nothing but time on their hands. Drawing the troops together to witness the extermination of a transgressor from their ranks was deemed a forceful tool for maintaining discipline and, some believed, morale.

The courts martial were governed by strict procedural regulations. After the verdict was rendered, the decision and accompanying testimony was sent to the general who had established the court in the first place. In most cases (but not always) the general affirmed the decision and passed it up the chain of command to his superior. In the case of death sentences, the file was sent for review by the judge advocate general in Washington. As commander-in-chief, Abraham Lincoln had the final word.

Joseph Holt was Lincoln's judge advocate general. A Democrat, Holt had served as secretary of war in the previous administration of James Buchanan. Holt and his staff received the courts martial reports, wrote their commentary, and sent the case on to the president. "Today we spent 6 hours deciding on Courtmartials, the President, Judge Holt & I," wrote John Hay in his diary on Saturday, July 18, 1863. "I was amused at the eagerness with which the President caught at any fact which would justify him in saving the life of a condemned soldier."

As Hay recorded, the president actively sought reasons for clemency. Carl Sandburg retold the story of a visitor to the White House, John Eaton. Upon hearing the sound of muskets firing from the Union camps just across the Potomac in Virginia, Lincoln walked to the window. "This is the day when they shoot deserters." As the president uttered those words, Eaton reported, tears were running down his cheeks.

A statistical analysis of Lincoln's clemency decisions by Dr. Thomas P. Lowry found a pattern to the president's judicial review. He was forgiving in relation to human frailty, but unforgiving when it came to disloyalty or to acts against women. There was a 100-percent record of reversing the sentences of sentries found sleeping at their post and a 95-percent reversal of the death sentences of deserters. Those who deserted for the purpose of going over to the enemy, however, were shot. Soldiers convicted of rape were also executed.

Judge Holt told the story of the day when he was reviewing appeals with the president. One of the cases involved a soldier who had pled guilty to throwing down his weapon and cowering behind a stump during battle. "[Y]ou call [these cases] 'cowardice in the face of the enemy,' " Lincoln said, "but I call them, for short, my 'leg cases.' But I put it to you, and I leave it for you to decide for yourself: if Almighty God gives a man a cowardly pair of legs how can he help their running away with him?"

It was argued at the time that Lincoln's tendency toward clemency was costing the army victories because of its impact on discipline and morale. "I pray you do not interfere with the courts-martial of the army," General Benjamin Butler telegraphed the president. "You will destroy all of the discipline among our soldiers." When General Sherman was asked how it was that so many of the sentences of his courts martial escaped Lincoln's pardons, he simply replied, "I shot them first."

Lincoln's rationale for his decisions was simple. "I don't believe it will make a man any better to shoot him, while if we keep him alive, we just may get some work out of him." It also wasn't bad politics to issue the reprieves, especially when their advocates were congressmen and senators looking for a way to curry favor back home. "With pardons as with patronage, there were political foes to be appeased, political friends to be rewarded," one historian observed. The reprieve for William Jeffries, cited at the beginning of this section, was apparently at the behest of Indiana governor O. P. Morton. After sending the reprieve telegrams to Generals Grant and Thomas, Lincoln telegraphed Governor Morton, "I have telegraphed to Chattanooga suspending the execution of William Jeffries until further order from me."

The language in the Jeffries reprieve was typical. Lincoln did not pardon the soldier, but rather stayed his execution "until further order." One father who had advocated his son's case directly to the president was disappointed to see that Lincoln's respite was only "until further order." "I thought it was to be a pardon," the father said, "but you say, 'not to be shot till further orders,' and you may order him shot next week." Lincoln reportedly smiled and explained, "I see you are not very well acquainted with me. If your son never looks on death until further orders come from me to shoot him, he will live to be a great deal older than Methuselah."

For those facing the ultimate penalty, however, the speedy messenger was often the angel of mercy with the president's reprieve arriving at the last minute. And the president was not averse to letting the condemned stew in his own juices until the eleventh hour. Typical of such last-minute telegrams was a December 8, 1864 dispatch from Lincoln to General Rosecrans in St. Louis: "Let execution in case of John Berry & James Berry be suspended until further order." Attached to the draft was a note to the head of the Telegraph Office from the president's secretary: "Will you please hurry off the above Tomorrow is the day of execution."

Husband and Father

Amidst the anguish of war, Abraham Lincoln was also a husband and father. "The draft will go to you. Tell Tad the goats and father are very well—especially the goats," Lincoln wired his wife on April 28, 1864. Mrs. Lincoln traveled frequently. In this case the First Lady was with her 11-year-old son in New York City.

The "draft" Lincoln spoke of was a check. Mrs. Lincoln had telegraphed earlier in the day, "We reached here in safety. Hope you are well." Having dispensed with the obligatory comments, she immediately settled down to business: "Please send me by mail to-day a check for $50 directed to me, care of Mr. Warren Leland, Metropolitan Hotel, Tad says are the goats well."

He may have been president of the United States, but Mrs. Lincoln's husband immediately snapped to attention. His reply telegram, sent the same day, contained the requisite assurance that the check was in the mail, along with a twinkling of humor as to the pressures of his job.

While few spouses in the 1860s could telegraph messages back and forth, the messages between the Lincolns are so typically the correspondence between a married couple. Their telegrams are not unlike the e-mails that spouses would send each other 140 years later.

During the hot Washington summers, the Lincoln family took refuge in a cottage on the grounds of the Soldiers' Home in the cooler outskirts of the city. On November 9, 1862—two days after firing George McClellan and the day that Ambrose Burnside took command of the Army of the Potomac—a telegram went to Mrs. Lincoln who was in Boston. "Mrs. Cuthbert & Aunt Mary want to move to the White House, because it has grown so cold at the Soldiers Home. Shall they?" Mrs. Cuthbert was a seamstress and "Aunt" Mary Dines was a Negro nurse who helped with the boys. It was a simple domestic matter, yet Abraham Lincoln, president of the United States and commander-in-chief of the largest army assembled in the history of the world, covered his bases like any husband.

In July 1863 the newspapers reported that Mrs. Lincoln had been hurt in a fall during a carriage runaway while returning to the White House from the Soldiers' Home. Knowing his son Robert, then at Harvard, would see the news, Lincoln sent a telegram, "Dont be uneasy. Your mother very slightly hurt by her fall." Only 10 days later, Lincoln wired Robert again. This time the son was in New York City. You can hear the message's terse fatherly tone: "Come to Washington. A. Lincoln" was all it said. When the response wasn't immediately forthcoming, the father returned to the telegraph. "Why do I hear no more of you?" Fortunately for Robert, he was already *en route* to Washington.

Shortly after this exchange, Mrs. Lincoln departed for New York herself. Via telegraph she stayed in touch with her husband. It was a time when the Union army had just suffered a major defeat at the Battle of Chickamauga. The entire Western Campaign was in jeopardy, and the pressure was again mounting on the president. No doubt a visit from his spouse and young son would be a welcome respite. "The air is so clear and cool, and apparently healthy, that I would be glad for you to come," Lincoln wired on September 21, 1863. "Nothing very particular, but I would be glad [to] see you and Tad." Mrs. Lincoln replied by telegraph to the White House doorman telling him to go to the head of military railroads and "ask him to send the green car on to Philadelphia for me and make arrangements for a special car from New York to Philadelphia. Send me a reply immediately."

Throughout Lincoln's presidency, the husband and the peripatetic wife stayed in touch electronically.

To Mrs. Lincoln in New York on December 5, 1863: "All is going well, A. Lincoln." She replied the next day, "Do let me know immediately how Taddie and yourself are. I will be home by Tuesday without fail; sooner if needed." On the following day the president responded, "All doing well. Tad confidently expects you tonight. When will you come?" Back came the message from New York, "Will leave positively at 8 a.m. Tuesday morning. Have carriage waiting at depot in Washington at 6 p.m. Did Tad receive his book? Please answer." Lincoln replied, "Tad has received his book. The carriage shall be ready at 6 PM. tomorrow."

The following month Mrs. Lincoln was back on the road, this time in Philadelphia. The president wired his common report, "All is very well." Then, two days later, "We are all well, and have not been otherwise." Mrs. Lincoln traveled on to Cambridge, Massachusetts, to see Robert at school. The president's January 11 telegram returned to matters monetary: "I sent your draft to-day. How are you now? Answer by telegraph at once."

While the First Lady was on another trip to Boston in June of 1864, the president wired a piece of news that was far more than his typical report: "All well, and very warm. Tad and I have been to Gen. Grant's army. Returned yesterday safe and sound." A few days later, when his wife was back in New York, the president's message once again reported, "All is well." Then reporting on how a member of the White House service staff was moving some of their effects to the cooler Soldiers' Home, Lincoln added, "Tom is moving things out."

And so it went. Typical exchanges between a husband and wife delivered atypically for the time.

The last telegram Abraham Lincoln ever sent Mary Todd Lincoln was April 2, 1865. About a week earlier she had accompanied the president to General Grant's headquarters in anticipation of the fall of Richmond (see Chapter Ten). While there, Mrs. Lincoln exhibited some of her frailties. Early in their stay she was to ride with the president as he reviewed troops of General Edward Ord's Army of the James. Arriving late, she discovered the review underway and the attractive Mrs. Ord riding in her position with the president. That evening she publicly scolded the president about the prominence Mrs. Ord had received and accused him of flirting with her. Shortly thereafter Mrs. Lincoln returned to Washington. Nevertheless, the president kept her informed via the Military Telegraph, including a bit of matrimonial fence-mending that invited her back:

> *Mrs. Lincoln: At 4:30 p.m. to-day General Grant telegraphs that he has Petersburg completely enveloped from river below to river above, and has captured, since he started last Wednesday, about 12,000 prisoners and 50 guns. He suggests that I should go and see him in the morning, which I think I will do. Tad and I are both well, and will be glad to see you and your party here at the time you name.*
>
> A. Lincoln

CHAPTER SEVEN

COMMANDING THROUGH THE INBOX

Abraham Lincoln continued to explore the optimal application of the telegraph during the war's third year, 1863. It was a year that would prove momentous for the president's armies. Small sleepy crossroads such as Chancellorsville and Gettysburg became immortal by summer, while seeming defeats at Vicksburg and Chattanooga became victories. From the crow's nest of the telegraph office, the president observed and participated in it all.

The prior year had witnessed Lincoln's embrace of the telegraph. As he sought to discover his electronic voice that year, the nature of the president's telegrams had pivoted from the direct command of troops during Jackson's Shenandoah Valley Campaign to frustrated exchanges with General McClellan about troop numbers on the peninsula and sore-tongued horses after Antietam. In 1862 Lincoln had discovered the telegraph's ability to project his voice; in 1863 he expanded on the telegraph's ability to also be his eyes and ears.

It was a rudimentary step toward the modern command structure where strategic policy is centrally decided, decentralized for tactical implementation, yet closely monitored by the central authority. Only 15 years earlier, in the conflict that trained many of the Civil War's leaders, General Winfield Scott had embarked for Mexico with only broad instructions. His orders explicitly stated, "It is not proposed to control your operations by definite and positive instructions, but you are left to prosecute them as your judgment, under a full review of the circumstances, shall dictate." Both Scott and his superiors knew there would be no timely exchanges with the civilian authorities to whom he reported, thus making his decisions in the field supreme. That all changed in the Civil War as the telegraph made the miles that separated the national authority from troops in the field almost irrelevant.

Amidst this communications change a strategic change was occurring as well. From the outset of the war, Lincoln had a strategic plan to surround the Confederacy, cut it off from the rest of the world by naval blockade, and engage its armies. For two years, however, the strategy had failed to deliver the desired results. In 1863, implementation of this plan began to change. Whereas George McClellan had emphasized maneuvers with the goal of occupying real estate with minimal combat, the new policy recognized that the rebellion would not be put down until the armies that maintained it were put down. McClellan's 1862 Peninsula Campaign had been designed to take Richmond by the tactical movement of troops in preference to pitched battles. Similarly, at Antietam, McClellan's effort had been to block Lee's advance into the north, not annihilate his army. As it became clear that allowing the Rebel army to live to fight another day only prolonged the war, strategic thinking began to focus on the destruction of the Rebel army.

President Lincoln became increasingly deft in the uses to which he put the telegraph. Through his consistent review of the telegraph traffic in and out of the War Department, he gained an insight into the attitudes of his armies and the thinking of his generals. By interjecting himself into those activities, whether invited or not, Lincoln maintained his virtual presence in the headquarters of his generals. Electronic messages clipped the wings of commanders in the field and strengthened the role of the national political leadership.

When Lincoln remarked, "Well, boys, I am down to the raisins" and recounted the story of the young girl who had overindulged, it exemplified how he used the telegraph as a means of gathering information. By far the preponderance of the messages received at the telegraph office were not addressed to the president. Reviewing each of the incoming messages "down to the raisins," however, gave Lincoln a timely depth of awareness across a broad scope of activity. It was perhaps his greatest application of electronic messages.

It wasn't just during battles that the president relied on the telegraph to stay informed. Every day, sometimes multiple times a day, Lincoln would repair to the telegraph office for his information bath. We can envision the lanky figure walking the short distance westward from the White House to the War Department. Entering the telegraph office, Lincoln would greet the clerks while heading to the drawer containing copies of all the dispatches. Taking that stack to the large flat-topped desk next to the window overlooking Pennsylvania Avenue, he would read the dispatches "down to the raisins" and sort them by priority. Having set aside the important messages for further review, the president would then settle in for more detailed contemplation of the picture painted by dots and dashes. It was a simple act, but revolutionary, because it was a capability that no chief executive had ever before possessed.

Beyond reading the incoming traffic, Lincoln actively solicited information. Frequently telegrams to field generals simply stated, "Tell me all you know," or "What news this morning?" The president was not just the passive observer, reading the telegrams addressed to someone else on topics determined by someone else; he was also a reporter, collecting news on topics in which he was interested, especially at times when he felt anxious or ill-informed.

While Lincoln was embracing the changed reality resulting from the telegraph, his new general-in-chief, Henry Halleck, was less adaptive. General Halleck, dubbed "Old Brains" because he had written the basic text on military theory, was not converting well to the new electronic world. The general-in-chief was still fighting the

18th-century wars described in the pages of his book (basically an adaptation of the texts of Antoine Henri Jomini, a general on Napoleon's staff) in which the general in the field was supreme.

Lincoln had reinstated the position of general-in-chief in the period between McClellan's failure on the peninsula and Pope's defeat at Second Manassas. It was during the absence of a general-in-chief, it will be recalled, that Lincoln had his electronic epiphany. From personal experience—especially during Jackson's Shenandoah Valley Campaign—the president had grasped the power of electronic messages and incorporated them into his leadership. General Halleck, however, had never experienced that growth. It wasn't that Halleck hadn't used the telegraph; he had been promoted from command of the Western Theater and had experience with the technology. It was simply that, unlike the president, Halleck had failed to internalize the transformational impact electronic messages had on the nature of command.

Halleck's view of leadership was best summed up in his December 15, 1862, telegram to General Burnside immediately following the Fredericksburg disaster. Burnside had turned to Old Brains for counsel after an excruciating defeat resulting from a suicidal plan (on which Halleck had refused to provide guidance). The general-in-chief used the telegraph to reply, but failed to comprehend how that ability had changed his role. "In regard to movements we cannot judge here," Halleck wired. "You are the best judge." In the new electronic world, Washington was only seconds away from the front by wire. Halleck may not have been at the front, but the wire had given him a birds-eye view of events over a broad area, a physically detached perspective, and the ability to share his insights speedily. Yet, despite all this new capability, Henry Halleck, whose job as general-in-chief was to make decisions, refused to step forward and use the telegraph to take command.

• • •

Abraham Lincoln continued to suffer for want of leadership at the other end of the telegraph wire. In his ongoing quest for the right leader for the Army of the Potomac, Ambrose Burnside was removed and General Joseph Hooker became the fifth commander of Union forces in the east. The appointment began on a discordant note.

Joe Hooker was handsome, brave, aggressive, and had distinguished himself on the peninsula and at Antietam. The press had christened him "Fighting Joe." He had also distinguished himself for his arrogant attitude, including statements that the president was an "imbecile" and the national government had "played out." He had even gone so far as to suggest that perhaps the nation needed a dictator.

Lincoln needed a leader to replace Burnside. There was a clamor to bring back George McClellan, about the last thing in the world the president wanted. Joe Hooker, for all his arrogance, at least was a fighter. He also had the added benefit of never having been a part of McClellan's clique-y cabal.

Two days after his new appointment, General Hooker met with the president at the White House. During that meeting Lincoln handed his new commander a letter that put the general on notice about his arrogant ways, established expectations, and pledged support. It was the letter's reference to Hooker's suggestion of a dictator, however, that highlighted the challenge Lincoln faced in finding the right leader. "I have heard, in such a way as to believe it, of your recently saying that both the army and the government needed a dictator," Lincoln wrote. "Of course it was not for this, but in spite of it, that I have given you the command. Only those generals who gain success can set up dictators. What I now ask of you is military success, and I will risk the dictatorship."

As a term of the appointment, Hooker demanded that he report directly to Lincoln and not through Halleck. Such a bypassing of the general-in-chief was a reflection of many issues, including that Halleck and Hooker had been feuding for years and could barely abide each other. While it may have been personal with Hooker, however, such a reporting relationship was all business with Lincoln. The president had already lost confidence in Halleck as a result of the general's unwillingness to make decisions. Perhaps recalling the period when there was no general-in-chief and he dealt directly via telegraph with his field generals, Lincoln agreed to Hooker's demand. It was becoming a familiar pattern: Abraham Lincoln using electronic messages to step into the void created by the failings of those to whom he looked for military leadership.

The army that Hooker inherited was a dispirited force, shattered by too many defeats. Immediately the new commander took steps to remedy the situation. Food and sanitary conditions improved with a resulting reduction in camp illnesses. Furloughs were granted in units that had performed well. Whiskey was allotted to soldiers as they returned from picket duty. To instill unit pride, Hooker instituted distinctive insignia for each corps, a technique that has endured to the present time. Most important, the new general reorganized the army, purging the remaining McClellanites, and installing generals who had proven themselves beyond their political connections or sycophantic allegiance to the Young Napoleon.

Lincoln watched from the telegraph office as General Hooker put his imprint on the Army of the Potomac. Even though he had embraced electronic messages, the president still preferred face-to-face communications; thus he journeyed to Hooker's headquarters outside of Fredericksburg in early April. While there he continued the practice of memorializing the substance of his conversations in writing. The memorandum to himself reconfirmed the strategic reorientation from taking real estate to the destruction of the Rebel army: "Hence our prime objective is the enemies' army in front of us, and is not with, or about, Richmond." A few days later, having returned to Washington, the president received a hand-delivered report from Hooker that the plan the two of them had discussed was about to be implemented. "I hope Mr. President," Hooker wrote, "that this plan will receive your approval."

The president replied by telegram. Because the message was not in cipher, it was somewhat obtuse. "Your letter, by the hand of General Butterfield, is received, and will be conformed to. The thing you dispense with would have been ready by midday to-morrow." The "thing" to which the president referred was the first movement of the cavalry that would, in slightly over two weeks, result in the Battle of Chancellorsville.

General Hooker's plan for attacking the Confederates was inspired. The two forces remained essentially where winter had found them after the Battle of Fredericksburg, on opposite sides of the Rappahannock River. Hooker's plan called for feinting an attack below Fredericksburg while three Union corps delivered a swinging right hook to fall upon the Rebel rear.

Lincoln tried to use the telegraph to stay informed. The day after the maneuvering began he wired Hooker, "Would like to have a letter from you as soon as convenient." For two weeks the president patiently waited. Then, on April 27, he once again took to the wire. "How does it look now?" was the totality of the message to Hooker. The general replied 90 minutes later, "I am not sufficiently advanced to give an opinion. We are busy. Will tell you as soon as I can, and have it satisfactory."

The telegraph was exacerbating the natural tension between a general in the field and the commander-in-chief in the capital. Lincoln was, in his words, "anxious." He had been in this same position previously, waiting while his generals determined his fate, only to be disappointed. The lightning messages were a way of assuaging that anxiety. On the other end of the wire, Hooker's "We are busy" comment indicated how little the general appreciated the intrusion. Realizing, however, that he had a superior to keep happy, Hooker tried another line of reasoning designed to get the president out of his hair. In a masterful piece of bureaucratic sophistry, Hooker cautioned,

"You know that nothing would give me more pleasure than to keep you fully advised of every movement and every intended movement made and to be made by this Army, as is my duty to do so. But the country is so full of traitors, and there are so many whose desire is to see this Army with no success, that it almost makes me tremble to disclose a thing concerning it to anyone except yourself." Having thus positioned himself, hopefully, to have fewer telegraphic intrusions, Hooker relented and reported on "what I have done and what I propose to do."

Joe Hooker was a bullish man at this point. Robert E. Lee's Confederates had yet to discover his movements, and he was about to fall on their flank and rear. "The rebel army is now the legitimate property of the Army of the Potomac," he boasted. General Lee would have other thoughts.

The Union surprise on Lee's flank and rear had put the Rebel army between the hammer of the flanking forces and the anvil of the Fredericksburg troops that had once been his front. General Lee, however, refused to act as anticipated. Lee's actions continue to be studied today as one of history's finest examples of military leadership.

The logical action for a commander who discovers his outnumbered force trapped in this manner is to slip out the side to a more tactically feasible position. Lee, the ever-audacious commander, did nothing of the kind; he split his forces and attacked. It was a decision that violated one of the basic maxims of warfare to never divide your force in the face of superior numbers.

Lee's audacity caught Hooker by surprise. When the Confederates counterattacked, Hooker went on the defensive. Rather than continuing to drive forward, Hooker ordered his men to entrench. The initiative was lost, never to be regained.

General Hooker deliberately did not communicate with Washington during the fighting. He had little good to report anyway. Lee, the outnumbered and trapped underdog, split his troops again and continued to be the aggressor. Lincoln, having heard nothing from his commander, telegraphed General Daniel Butterfield, Hooker's chief of staff, on May 3, "Where is Gen. Hooker? Where is [Gen.] Sedgwick? Where is [Gen.] Stoneman?" Unfortunately for the Union cause, they were all being bested by Robert E. Lee.

On the morning of May 6 the president turned to the wire in search of information from his general. "We have nothing from your immediate whereabouts since your short despatch to me of the 4th, 4/20. P.M." Shortly thereafter the president wired General Hooker of reports in the Richmond paper "claiming that he [Lee] had beaten you." At 1:00 P.M. that afternoon General Butterfield wired the President, "the army has recrossed the river." The Richmond papers were correct; the president's forces were back where they started.

Butterfield's dispatch shocked the president. Noah Brooks, a newsman who happened to be visiting the White House that afternoon, wrote, "Had a thunderbolt fallen on the President he could not have been more overwhelmed." President Lincoln immediately departed to meet General Hooker at his headquarter. Again events conspired to require the kind of deep exchange than could only be accomplished face-to-face.

While at Hooker's camp, the president, as was his practice, put his thoughts in writing. Lincoln was looking to the next engagement and further reinforcing the strategic thinking about vanquishing the Rebel army. "What next?" Lincoln's letter inquired. "If possible I would be very glad of another movement . . . Have you already in your mind a plan wholly, or partially formed? If you have not, please inform me, so that I, incompetent as I may be, can try [to] assist in the formulation of some plan for the Army." Hooker replied, "I have decided in my own mind the plan to be adopted in our next effort—if it should be your wish to have one made." Then, as though ignorant of his own failings at Chancellorsville, Hooker added that his new plan "has this to recommend it—it will be one in which the operations of all the Corps . . . will be under my personal supervision."

The president decided to give Fighting Joe Hooker another chance. It was not a uniformly well-received decision. Six days later Lincoln telegraphed Hooker it was time for another meeting. "If it will not interfere with the service, nor personally incommode you, please come up and see me this evening." The general replied, "Will see you at Eight this Evening." It was the president's third face-to-face with Hooker in six weeks.

Again, Lincoln put his thoughts in writing to Hooker. "It does not now appear probable to me that you can gain anything by an early renewal of the attempt to cross the Rappahannock," the president wrote. Then Lincoln raised an issue that had been weighing on his mind: "I have some painful intimations that some of corps commanders and Division Commanders are not giving you their entire confidence." Having lost a battle he should have won through 2–to–1 numerical superiority alone, Hooker had lost the support of his generals.

While the Federals were worrying about what to do next, Robert E. Lee started north once again. This time it was Joe Hooker who did not read his adversary's movements. Knowing Lee was on the march, but not knowing where he was going, Hooker telegraphed the president on June 5 proposing to "pitch into his rear." Lincoln's reply disapproved of the suggestion on the grounds that dividing the army across the Rappahannock would make it like "an ox half over a fence."

Five days later, Hooker proposed a "rapid advance on Richmond." Lincoln's telegram reminded his general that Richmond wasn't the objective, Lee's army was. "If he [Lee] comes toward the Upper Potomac," Lincoln instructed, "follow on his flank, and on the inside track, shortening your lines, whilst he lengthens his. Fight him when oppertunity offers. If he stays where he is, fret him, and fret him."

Once again, those upon whom Lincoln relied were not meeting expectations. As Lee's Confederates moved northward, President

Lincoln not only studied the telegraph traffic "down to the raisins," but also reached out electronically to gather his own information. To Hooker on June 14 the president inquired as to events around Winchester, Virginia, at the mouth of the Shenandoah Valley and the entry to the Potomac and the northern states. "Do you consider it possible that 15,000 of [Confederate General] Ewell's men can now be at Winchester?" Only a few minutes later he wired General Benjamin Kelley at Harpers Ferry, 30 miles north of Winchester on the Potomac, "Are the forces at Winchester and Martinsburg making any effort to get to you?" Then to General Robert Schenck in Baltimore: "Get [Gen.] Milroy from Winchester to Harper's Ferry if possible. He will be gobbled up, if he remains, if he is not already past salvation."

As the picture became clearer, the tension mounted in the telegraph office. Indeed, Lee was emerging from the Shenandoah with Winchester and Martinsburg in his sites. To General Daniel Tyler, up the Potomac from Harpers Ferry at Martinsburg, the president queried, "Is Milroy invested, so that he cannot fall back on Harper's Ferry?" Tyler replied, "General Milroy is in a tight place. If he gets out, it will be by good luck and hard fighting . . . We are besieged here . . ." Lincoln fired back in a frustrated attempt to grasp just what was going on, "If you are besieged, how do you despatch me? Why did you not leave, before being besieged?"

All day the president had been using the telegraph to gather his own intelligence. Late in the afternoon he shared his information with General Hooker. "So far as we can make out here, the enemy have Milroy surrounded at Winchester, and Tyler at Martinsburg." Then Lincoln observed that Lee's long column "must be very slim somewhere," and asked, "Could you not break him?" Hooker replied at 11:15 P.M. with further queries about the situation at Winchester, and then added, "I do not feel like making a move for an enemy until I am satisfied as to his whereabouts." Still in the telegraph office at almost midnight, Lincoln replied that the information gathered that afternoon made it "quite certain that a considerable force of the enemy is thereabout."

The following evening, June 15, Lincoln wired Hooker that the troops at Winchester and Martinsburg had retreated to Harpers Ferry, conceding both towns to the Rebels. "I think the report is authentic that he [Lee] is crossing the Potomac at Williamsburg." Lincoln added, "I would like to hear from you." Hooker responded, "Your telegram of 8:30 received. It seems to disclose the intentions of the enemy to make an invasion, and, if so, it is not in my power to prevent it." At 10:00 P.M. Hooker telegraphed Lincoln again, "Your dispatch is more conclusive than any I have received. I now feel that invasion is his settled purpose."

Hooker's telegrams surely must have reinforced Lincoln's concern about his general's ability to command. In the first telegram, aside from stating he could not prevent an invasion into the northern states, Hooker had also discussed how he might be able to keep Lee from uniting his dispersed forces, then turned around and questioned his own suggestion, adding, "I am not prepared to say this is the wisest move, nor do I know that my opinion on the subject is wanted." The second telegram reiterated, "I do not know that my opinion as to the duty of this army in the case is wanted; if it should be, you know that I will be happy to give it."

These sentiments, from the general commanding a huge force on which the president and the nation had placed so much hope, could only have exacerbated Lincoln's worries. Hooker may have been responding in pique for having his previous proposals rejected, but the fact of the matter was the commanding general refused to act like one.

It might be argued that the telegraph's intrusion had sapped Hooker of his authority. Clearly he was frustrated, observing to a fellow general that dealing with Lee "had only occupied two hours of his time each day, Washington had required the remainder." Yet

"Fighting Joe" was hardly living up to his billing. Lincoln was in a box: Halleck refused to command, and Hooker was acting like a bureaucrat. Yet Lee's forces continued inexorably northward.

At 11:00 A.M. on June 16 Hooker wired the president with more bureaucratic moaning: "You have long been aware, Mr. President, that I have not enjoyed the confidence of the major-general commanding the army, and I can assure you that so long as this continues, we may look in vain for success . . ." Shortly after receiving this, Lincoln, sounding like a mediator, wrote General Hooker, "You do not lack his [Halleck's] confidence in any degree to do you any harm. On seeing him this morning, I found him more nearly agreeing with you than I was myself." The president almost pleaded, "I need and must have the professional skill of both [Hooker and Halleck], and yet these suspicions tend to deprive me of both."

With such a lack of support around him, Lincoln opened a window onto his own closely held feelings as to why he was so directly involved: "in the great responsibility resting upon me, I cannot be entirely silent." Then, in an effort once again to get his general focused, the president closed with: "Now, all I ask is that you will be in such mood that we can get into our action the best cordial judgment of yourself and General Halleck, with my poor mite added, if indeed he and you shall think it entitled to any consideration at all."

Hooker and Halleck, however, continued to skirmish. Halleck lectured Hooker on the need for cavalry to keep tabs on the enemy's movements. Hooker responded to Halleck's call to help Harpers Ferry by pointing out how the general-in-chief had not provided sufficient information about the situation at that point. The exchanges continued, often with only a half hour or so between one dispatch and the reply.

The to-and-fro may have demonstrated the power of instant messages to connect the command authority with the field, but their contents accomplished little. At 9:40 the evening of June 16, Hooker wired Lincoln that he had given orders "to march at 3 o'clock to-morrow morning." After observing all the electronic bickering, however, the news was almost anticlimactic. Twenty minutes later the president telegraphed Hooker that his special reporting relationship was no more. General Hooker was back in the chain of command: "To remove all misunderstanding, I now place you in the strict military relation to Gen. Halleck, of a commander of one of the armies, to the General-in-Chief of all the armies." The telegraph had drawn the president into the middle of bureaucratic battles from which he was now extracting himself.

Fifteen minutes after the president turned Hooker over to Halleck, the general-in-chief told Hooker not to look to him for guidance: "You are in command of the Army of the Potomac, and will make the particular dispositions as you deem proper. I shall only indicate the objects to be aimed at." The bickering, however, continued. Eleven days later, in the midst of another debate with Halleck, General Hooker telegraphed, "Earnestly request that I may at once be relieved from the position I occupy." It was an opening too good to pass up. Hooker's request was rapidly accepted.

The same day that General Hooker's request to be relieved was granted, General George Gordon Meade was placed in command of the Army of the Potomac. General Meade had been a corps commander under Hooker, but was virtually unknown to Northerners because of a conspiracy among reporters not to mention his name in retaliation for what they felt was the poor treatment they received from him. Indeed, Meade had challenges with interpersonal skill; within the army Meade's gaunt appearance, accentuated by his eyeglasses and his brisk manner, earned him the sobriquet "the goggle-eyed snapping turtle."

Only three days after Meade's promotion, the Confederate and Union armies converged around the small Pennsylvania farming community of Gettysburg for the greatest battle ever on North American soil.

• • •

DURING THE EVENTS LEADING up to Meade's assumption of command, Lincoln had continued to monitor telegraph traffic at the War Department, as well as to reach out electronically to gather his own information. Of General Darius Couch, commander of the Department of the Susquehanna in Pennsylvania, he inquired on June 24, "Have you any reports of the enemy moving into Pennsylvania?" The day Meade took command Lincoln again wired Couch, "What news now?" Couch replied the Rebels were burning bridges to slow the Union approach, that skirmishing was occurring, but that there had not yet been an attack in force.

The following evening Lincoln received a most ominous telegram from Simon Cameron, his former secretary of war now returned from being minister to Russia and a powerful force in Pennsylvania. "We have reliable and undoubted information from three distinct sources that General Lee now has nearly if not quite one hundred thousand (100000) men between Chambersburg on the Upper side of South Mountain and Gettysburg on the east side of the Mountain and the Susquehanna River . . . They have over two hundred fifty (250) pieces of Artillery by actual count—Within the next forty eight 48 hours Lee will cross the Susquehanna River for General Battle—Let me impress on you the absolute necessity of action by Meade tomorrow even if attended with great risk because if Lee gets his army across the Susquehanna and puts our armies on the defensive at that time you will readily comprehend the disastrous results that must follow to the Country."

The day the Cameron message arrived, the line to Meade's headquarters was cut by Confederate cavalry. President Lincoln was disconnected from his general in the field at the very time when the tension was thickest. The lines to others, however, remained open and Lincoln put them to work. "Short of getting into uniform," one historian observed, "Lincoln could not have been more involved in the buildup to battle." Seeking information from the Susquehanna, and hoping that no news was good news, he telegraphed General Couch, "I judge by the absence of news that the enemy is not crossing, or pressing up to the Susquehanna. Please tell me what you know of his movements."

In fact, less than an hour before Lincoln's "absence of news" telegram, General Couch had wired Secretary Stanton, but apparently the president had yet to see the report. "The best part of Chambersburg is in ashes," Couch reported, and, "Prisoners say that [Confederate General] Longstreet's Corps is to threaten Washington." Later in the day General Couch telegraphed the president with more information. "The rebel Infantry force left Carlisle early this morning on the Baltimore Pike . . . [Confederate general] Early with eight thousand left York this morning: went westerly, or north westerly."

The Rebels were on the march, not crossing the Susquehanna and not heading to Washington, but following the Pennsylvania road network to Gettysburg, the convergence point of 11 different thoroughfares. On July 1, 1863, just outside Gettysburg, Confederate troops ran into two Union cavalry brigades commanded by General John Buford. By the time the Battle of Gettysburg was over two days later more than 170,000 men had been engaged. The severed line repaired, "Lincoln was in the telegraph office hour after hour during those anxious days and nights," the manager of the office recalled. The telegraph not only kept Lincoln informed, but also assisted General Meade during the fighting. Unlike previous engagements, Meade had telegraphic communication with his corps and division commanders during the battle.

After three days of fighting, General Meade delivered something his predecessors had failed to accomplish: a decisive defeat of Robert E. Lee. The telegraph lines from the War Department carried the good news in a press bulletin on Independence Day 1863:

Washington City, July 4, 10. A.M. 1863

The President announces to the country that news from the Army of the Potomac, up to 10 P.M. of the 3rd, is such as to cover that Army with the highest honor, to promise a great success to the cause of the Union, and to claim the condolence of all for the many gallant fallen. And that for this, he especially desires that on this day, He whose will, not ours, should ever be done, be everywhere remembered and reverenced with profoundest gratitude.

Here was the message for which Abraham Lincoln had been longing. The challenge, now, was to bring into practice the goal of annihilating Lee's army before it could escape south. The forces of nature seemed to be cooperating as tremendous rains flooded the Potomac and blocked Lee's crossing. Bottled up against the river, the Rebel army had never been so exposed.

David Homer Bates, the manager of the telegraph office, told how "Lincoln began to realize that Meade was likely to lose much of the fruit of his hard-earned victory by allowing Lee's army to escape across the Potomac. So, he kept close to the telegraph instrument during the succeeding days." On July 4 General William French reported to General Halleck that his men had "entirely destroyed the [Confederate] pontoon bridge over the Potomac at Williamsport." The president stepped in and wired General Smith the following morning, "I see your despatch about destruction of pontoons. Cannot the enemy ford the river?" That evening General French answered the question in a telegram to Halleck: "Five hundred wagons (rebel), guarded by about 150 infantry, 150 cavalry, three pieces of inferior-looking artillery, and from 3,000 to 5,000 head of cattle passed through Hagerstown [Maryland] last night after 11 o-clock to about 4 o'clock. Could not cross the ford at Williamsport, the river being too high."

The following day, July 6, the president continued his monitoring of messages into and out of the War Department, increasingly incredulous that Meade was not administering the *coup de grace* to Lee's forces. That evening the president wrote from his summer cottage on the grounds of the Soldiers' Home, "I left the telegraph office a good deal dissatisfied." After recounting specific examples of dispatches he had read, the president observed, "These things all appear to me to be connected with a purpose to cover Baltimore and Washington, and to get the enemy across the river again without a further collision, and they do not appear connected with a purpose to prevent his crossing and to destroy him. I do fear the former purpose is acted upon and the latter is rejected."

Ever so gradually Meade increased the pressure on the Confederates. Union forces pushed closer to Lee's Rebels and skirmishing occurred at several points. Meade was preparing to attack, but when the appointed time came the Union advance discovered only abandoned trenches. The Confederates had been bottled up for 10 days with their backs against the Potomac. By the time Meade moved on their positions, however, the river had subsided and they were again back in Virginia. General Halleck delivered the president's displeasure in a July 14 wire to Meade: "the escape of Lee's army without another battle has created great dissatisfaction in the mind of the President, and it will require an active and energetic pursuit on your part to remove the impression that it has not been sufficiently active heretofore."

Meade did not take the message well. Ninety minutes after it was sent the general replied, "Having performed my duty conscientiously and to the best of my ability, the censure of the President conveyed in your dispatch of 1 p.m. this day, is, in my judgment, so undeserved that I feel compelled most respectfully to ask to be immediately relieved from command of this army." General Halleck replied, "My telegram, stating the disappointment of the President at the escape of Lee's army, was not intended as censure, but as a stimulus to an active pursuit. It is not deemed a sufficient cause for your application to be relieved."

But the fact of the matter was that Lincoln *was* sorely distressed. The president sat down and penned a letter to General Meade:

Executive Mansion
Washington, July 14, 1863

Major General Meade

I have just seen your despatch to Gen. Halleck, asking to be relieved of your command, because of a supposed censure of mine. I am very—very—*grateful to you for the magnificent success you gave the cause of the country at Gettysburg; and I am sorry now to be the author of the slightest pain to you . . . I have been oppressed nearly ever since the battles at Gettysburg, by what appeared to be evidences that yourself, and Gen. Couch and Gen. Smith, were not seeking a collision with the enemy, but were trying to get him across the river without another battle . . . You had at least twenty thousand veteran troops directly with you, and as many more raw ones within supporting distance, all in addition to those who fought at Gettysburg; while it was not possible that he had received a single recruit; and yet you stood and let the flood run down, bridges be built, and the enemy move away at his leisure . . . Again, my dear general, I do not believe you appreciate the magnitude of the misfortune involved in Lee's escape. He was within your easy grasp, and to have closed upon him would, in connection with our other late successes, have ended the war. As it is, the war will be prolonged indefinitely . . . Your golden opportunity is gone, and I am distressed immeasurably because of it.*

I beg you will not consider this a prossecution [sic], *or persecution of yourself. As you had learned that I was dissatisfied, I have thought it best to kindly tell you why.*

The telegraph had given the nation's leadership the ability to observe what was going on in distant places and insert themselves into the action. It also accelerated the pace of human reactions to its messages. One of Abraham Lincoln's continuing beliefs was that, while the telegraph was a valuable tool for short messages, the best communications were done in person (as illustrated by his repeated trips to see General Hooker), or if that was not possible by well-reasoned letter. Having expressed himself fully and completely in his letter to Meade, Lincoln then demonstrated another side of his leadership style. The letter to General Meade went into the desk drawer and stayed there. Just because something was written did not mean it should be sent.

CHAPTER EIGHT

EVEN WITH TECHNOLOGY, IT'S ALL ABOUT PEOPLE

The telegraph allowed Abraham Lincoln to monitor the activities of an army of several hundred thousand men across a large geographic area. In the Western Theater of the war—between the Appalachians and the Mississippi River—the power of lightning messages offered its greatest opportunity to the president.

The proximity of the eastern battlefields to Washington made it relatively easy to deliver a written message via courier or for the president or the commander of the Army of the Potomac to board a special train or boat to go meet with the other. Such communications were much more difficult with the nation's interior. No meetings between the president and a field commander ever took place in the Western Theater. The telegraph remained the most efficient means of communications, although there were problems at times due to the vast area and the activities of Rebel guerillas and raiders who took special pleasure in cutting the line.

On the day of General Meade's victory at Gettysburg another, even more important, victory was delivered by General Ulysses S. Grant at Vicksburg, Mississippi. Because the Confederate fortress at Vicksburg was (obviously) not on the Union telegraph line, the news had to travel via Union gunboat upriver to Cairo, Illinois, before it could be wired to Washington. When Lincoln walked into the telegraph office on the morning of July 7, there awaited a message that Vicksburg had surrendered.

Since Grant began his Vicksburg quest in December of the preceding year, Lincoln had been monitoring activities from the telegraph office. It was not as clean a connection as in the Eastern Theater, and most messages had to be routed through an intermediary point in the region such as Cairo or Memphis. Grant, however, was not much for communicating with the capital anyway. As the president described it, "Gen. Grant is a copious worker, and fighter, but a very meagre [*sic*] writer, or telegrapher."

As General Grant maneuvered around Vicksburg in March, Lincoln wired General Stephen Hurlbut in Memphis for information from the areas where Grant was operating, "What news have you? What news from Vicksburg? What news from Yazoo Pass? What from Lake Providence? What generally?" While he may have heard little from his general, the president had the capability to reach out electronically to fill the void. Earlier in Grant's campaign, Lincoln had even telegraphed Fortress Monroe, on the Hampton Roads in Virginia, for Vicksburg information: "Do Richmond papers of 6th say nothing about Vicksburg? or, if anything, what?"

Vicksburg, described as the nail that held the halves of the Confederacy together, was the most militarily important piece of real estate in North America. While Union gunboats controlled the river above and below the town, the Confederates controlled the river and its bridgehead to the west by refusing their passage.

Sitting at a hairpin in the Mississippi River, Vicksburg was a veritable Gibraltar. Posted on the city's western side atop 200-foot-high cliffs, Rebel artillery was capable of raining shot and shell on passing ships. These emplacements were impregnable to Union naval guns that could not elevate high enough to counter-fire. To the north Vicksburg was shielded by several thousand square miles of swamp. The only dry approaches were from the east and south through the heart of the Confederacy and far from any Union base of operations.

General Grant had been trying since December of 1862 to take the citadel. In six different attempts—ranging from an overland march from Memphis, to combined naval efforts through the swamp, to attempts to change the course of the Mississippi River—Grant had tried but failed to take Vicksburg. The president had been keeping track of these efforts by reading the dispatches sent to the War Department, and he was concerned.

The pressure was growing on Lincoln to relieve Grant. "This campaign is badly managed," wrote one of Grant's subordinate generals to his brother in Congress. "I fear a calamity before Vicksburg . . . all Grant's schemes have failed." Rumors that Grant was drinking heavily spread. The congressional delegation from Illinois warned Lincoln that leaving Grant in command of troops from that state imperiled Republican chances in the upcoming election. Under the guise of investigating paymaster accounts, Lincoln sent Assistant Secretary of War Charles Dana to scrutinize Grant.

Ulysses Grant, however, did something Abraham Lincoln longed for in his other generals: he persevered and stayed focused on the task before him. On his seventh attempt at Vicksburg, Grant struck out through the Rebel heartland. Leaving his wagons behind and living off the land, Grant mounted the Civil War's first blitzkrieg. The attack moved so far, so fast, that the Rebels were unable to sufficiently organize to counter the movement. It was everything Lincoln's generals in the east were not: bold, innovative, and decisive.

Grant's blitzkrieg proved successful. The army raced across Confederate soil, marching 180 miles in 17 days, fighting and winning five battles, and driving the Rebel defenders into Vicksburg. After unsuccessful attempts to break the Rebel's defensive positions, Grant settled into a siege. In the midst of this siege an anxious Lincoln sought information. Of General William Rosecrans, commanding in Tennessee, he queried, "Have you heard from Grant?" Rosecrans replied with a report that 20,000 Confederate troops were massing to counterattack. The following day the president again wired Rosecrans: "I would not push you to any rashness; but I am very anxious that you do your utmost, short of rashness, to keep [Confederate general] Bragg from getting off to help [Confederate general] Johnston against Grant."

After another week went by—a week where back in the east the president was struggling with Robert E. Lee's advance into the North and his concerns about General Hooker's ability to command—the president telegraphed Grant directly. The June 2 telegram was addressed to Grant "via Memphis," meaning that since Grant was not directly connected to the main Union telegraph line it took a circuitous route to reach the general. The president hoped that General Nathanial Banks's troops further down the Mississippi could unite with Grant to punch through the Vicksburg defenses. The president asked Grant, "Are you in communication with Gen. Banks? Is he coming towards you or going further off? Is there, or has there been any thing to hinder his coming directly to you by water from Alexandria?" Grant replied six days later that he would forward a letter from Banks. That letter was not what the president wanted to hear. Instead of the potential of linking the two forces, Banks wrote he would not be coming north: "It seems to me that I have no other course than to—carry my object here . . ."

The siege, however, was working. The residents of Vicksburg were living in caves to avoid the constant Union shelling, and their food supply was becoming exhausted. On the afternoon of July 3, while Gettysburg was concluding with Pickett's Charge, Confederate general John Pemberton met with Ulysses Grant to discuss terms for surrender. The following morning the Confederate Gibraltar was the property of General Ulysses Grant and the U.S. Army.

As previously noted, Abraham Lincoln was open and direct with his generals. On July 13, 1863, the president, using the fullness of a handwritten letter, expressed to Ulysses Grant his gratitude and growing respect for the general. It was the day before he wrote the stinging but never-sent letter to General Meade. The richness of the contrast, most surely, was not lost on the president.

In its many references to Grant's decisions that preceded the successful result, the letter exposed the degree to which Lincoln had been tracking Grant's activities from the telegraph office. Although the focus of this book is on Lincoln's telegrams, this letter is reproduced in its entirety because of the remarkable insight it gives into Abraham Lincoln, the close tabs he kept on activities, and how this man who placed such high expectations on his subordinates was personally humble in recognition of their achievements.

Executive Mansion
Washington, July 13, 1863

Major General Grant
My dear General

I do not remember that you and I ever met personally. I write this now as a grateful acknowledgement for the almost inestimable service you have done the country. I wish to say a word further. When you first reached the vicinity of Vicksburg, I thought you should do, what you finally did—march the troops across the neck, run the batteries with transports, and thus go below; and I never had any faith, except a general hope that you knew better than I, that the Yazoo Pass expedition, and the like, could succeed. When you got below, and took Port-Gibson, Grand Gulf, and vicinity, I thought you should go down river and join Gen. Banks; and when you turned Northward East of the Big Black, I feared it was a mistake. I now wish to make the personal acknowledgement that you were right, and I was wrong.

Yours very truly
A. Lincoln

How Ulysses Grant responded to the president's letter also speaks volumes about the general. After receiving such a powerful "you were right, and I was wrong" letter from the president of the United States, Ulysses Grant did not respond. The president, no doubt confused if not intrigued by the lack of response, waited three weeks before inquiring in another letter, "Did you receive a short letter from me, dated the 13th of July?" Another two weeks went by before General Grant, in a telegram to the president that discussed other topics, stated simply, "Your letter of the 13th of July was also duly received."

The telegram in which General Grant finally acknowledged the president's letter was responding to an earlier presidential message that had been triggered by Lincoln's reading the messages in the telegraph inbox, having an opinion about what he read, and sharing that with his general. "I see by a despatch of yours that you incline quite strongly towards an expedition against Mobile," the president wrote. "This would appear tempting to me also, were it not that in view of recent events in Mexico, I am greatly impressed with the importance of re-establishing the national authority in Western Texas as soon as possible."

As if the ongoing battlefield encounters and domestic political intrigue weren't enough, Abraham Lincoln had to concern himself with a pro-Confederate European government that had been installed in Mexico. Napoleon III, seeking to regain a foothold in the New World, attacked and defeated the Mexicans. In June of 1863 a French, pro-Confederate puppet government was installed in Mexico City. Lincoln wanted to show the flag and discourage any adventurous ideas Napoleon might have. General Grant understood the president's concerns and how they affected his operations. "After the fall of Vicksburg I did incline very much to an immediate move on Mobile," Grant explained. "I see however the importance of a movement into Texas just at this time." The Lincoln–Grant relationship had opened up. Two men who had never met were bonded by the desire for results. Increasingly they would also be tied together by the telegraph.

About 10 weeks after the fall of Vicksburg, September 19 and 20, the Union army in Tennessee, under the command of General William Rosecrans, was defeated at the Battle of Chickamauga. Lincoln, as at other critical periods, remained at the telegraph office monitoring the news. The advantages gained by victories at Gettysburg and Vicksburg could be offset if the Confederates controlled a wide swath in the middle of the country pushing up toward the Ohio River. "For three or four days the tension was very great, the President, Secretary Stanton, and General Halleck conferring together almost constantly," David Homer Bates, manager of the telegraph office, wrote.

The survivors fled to nearby Chattanooga. The Confederates occupied the high ground around the city and blocked the garrison from receiving supplies. There was but a single route open, winding on narrow trails through the mountains from the north, and it was insufficient to meet the city's needs. It looked like it could be the reverse of the siege at Vicksburg.

The day after the Battle of Chickamauga, the president was on the wire to General Ambrose Burnside, commanding at Knoxville: "Go to Rosecrans with your force, without a moments delay." An hour and a half later the president wired General Rosecrans, "Be of good cheer. We have unabated confidence in you, and in your soldiers and officers. In the main you must be the judge as to what is to be done. If I were to suggest, I would say, save your army, by taking strong positions, until Burnside joins you, when I hope you can turn the tide. I think you had better send a courier to Burnside to hurry him up. We can not reach him by Telegraph."

Picking up on the president's suggestion, Rosecrans sent a message to General Burnside: "Unless your troops can join us at once, it will not be practicable for them to come down on east side of river; the enemy will occupy that country. Come down on west side as rapidly as possible."

The following day, September 22, Lincoln kept on top of the telegraph traffic. As his anxiety mounted, the president wired Rosecrans

Washington City, D.C.
~~May~~ May 28. 1862. 8.40 P.M.

Maj. Gen. McClellan

I am very glad of Gen. F. J. Porter's victory— Still, if it was a total rout of the enemy, I am puzzled to know why the Richmond and Fredericksburg Railroad was not seized— Again, as you say you have all the Railroads but the Richmond and Fredericksburg, I am puzzled to see how, lacking that, you can have any, except the scrap from Richmond to West-Point— The scrap of the Virginia Central from Richmond to Hanover Junction, without more, is simply nothing—

That the whole force of the enemy is concentrating in Richmond, I think can not be certainly known to you or me— Saxton, at Harper's Ferry, informs us that a large force (supposed to be Jackson's and Ewell's) forced his advance from

2

Charlestown to-day— Gen. King telegraphs us from Fredericksburg that contrabands give certain information that fifteen thousand left Hanover Junction Monday morning to re-inforce Jackson. I am painfully impressed with the importance of the struggle before you; and I shall aid you all I can consistently with my view of due regard to all points. ~~and but I must be the judge as to the duty of the government in this respect~~

A. Lincoln

May 28, 1862, Lincoln to McClellan (previous page)
Lincoln's redirection of General McDowell's troops away from General George McClellan on the Peninsula below Richmond greatly upset McClellan, who wired the president, "It is the policy and duty of the Government to send me by water all the well-drilled troops available." Lincoln's reply illustrates his increasing frustration with McClellan, as well as his appreciation of the limitations of what could be said in an impersonal electronic message. After telling McClellan he was "painfully impressed" by the general's position, he added, "I shall aid you all I can consistently with my view of due regard to all points." The president's frustration then boiled over and he added, "and last I must be the Judge as to the duty of the government in this respect." Upon reflection Lincoln crossed out the last line. [Courtesy of Brown University Library]

Washington City, D.C.
Oct. 24. 1862
Majr. Genl. McClellan

I have just read your despatch about sore tongued and fatiegued horses— Will you pardon me for asking what the horses of your army have done since the battle of Antietam that fatigue anything?

A. Lincoln

October 24, 1862, Lincoln to McClellan
Following the Battle of Antietam (Sharpsburg) on September 17, 1862, Lincoln was frustrated by General George McClellan's unwillingness to pursue the Rebels. After McClellan wired the general-in-chief justifying the lack of advance by the poor condition of his army's horses, Lincoln stepped in. The president fired back "about sore-tongued and fatiegued [sic] horses," demanding to know "what the horses of your army have done since the battle of Antietam that fatigue anything?" [Courtesy of Abraham Lincoln Presidential Library and Museum]

Executive Mansion,

Washington, April 28, 1864.

Mrs A. Lincoln

Metropolitan Hotel

New-York.

The draft will go to you. Tell Tad the goats and father are very well—especially the goats.

A. Lincoln.

April 28, 1864, Lincoln to Mrs. Lincoln

Lincoln used the telegraph to communicate with his family, especially his wife, who traveled frequently. During the spring of 1864, while she and their son Tad were in New York, she sent a telegram to the president that perfunctorily inquired as to how he was, asked for $50 to be sent immediately, and in an afterthought added Tad's inquiry about his pet goats. Lincoln showed his sense of humor, as well as the pressure he was under, by responding that the check was on the way and she should tell Tad, "the goats and father are well—especially the goats." [Courtesy of National Archives]

51

Executive Mansion
Washington, May 14. 1864

Officer in Military Command at
Fort Monroe, Va.

If Thomas Doherty, or Welsh, is to be executed to-day, and it is not already done, suspend it till further order
A. Lincoln

May 14, 1864, Suspension of Execution

The largest number of telegrams Lincoln sent pertained to his review of military courts martial. This telegram, typical of his clemency decisions, did not pardon the individual but suspended carrying out of the sentence until further word from Lincoln (which was never forthcoming). [Courtesy of National Archives]

Time

Cypher.

6. P.M.

Office U. S. Military Telegraph,

WAR DEPARTMENT,

Washington, D. C., August 3, 1864.

Lieut. Genl. Grant
City-Point, Va.

I have seen your despatch in which you say "I want Sheridan put in command of all the troops in the field, with instructions to put himself South of the enemy, and follow him to the death. Wherever the enemy goes, let our troops go also." This, I think, is exactly right, as to how our forces should move. But please look over the despatches you may have received from here, even since you made that order, and discover, if you can, that there is any idea in the head of any one here, of "putting our army South of the enemy" or of "following him to the death" in any direction. I repeat to you it will neither be done, nor attempted, unless you watch it every day, and hour, and force it.

A. Lincoln

August 3, 1864, Lincoln to Grant

Lincoln did not impose himself on the activities of General Grant as much as he had on other generals. Nevertheless he was not shy about expressing his opinion. After he and Grant had differences regarding Grant's decision about the defense of Washington, Lincoln sent Grant a "Dutch Uncle" telegram. In it, the president reminds Grant that, while he approves of a recent appointment and Grant's plans, Grant needs to exercise vigilance "every day, and hour, and force it" if he is to achieve the desired results. [Courtesy of National Archives]

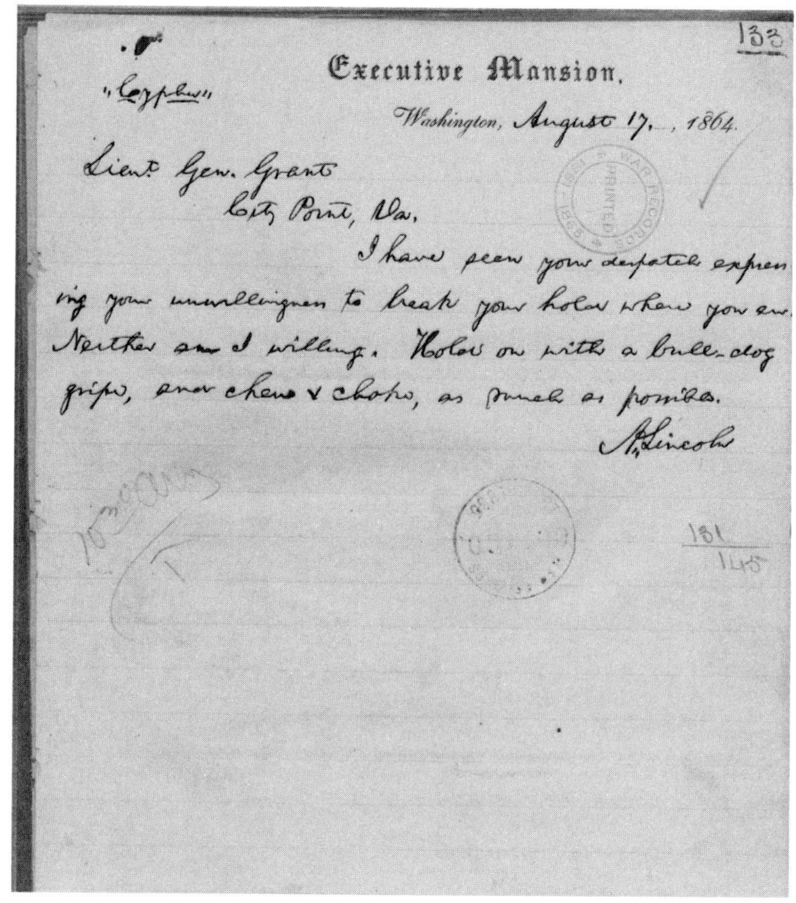

133

"Cypher"

Executive Mansion,

Washington, August 17, 1864.

Lieut. Gen. Grant

City Point, Va.

I have seen your despatch expressing your unwillingness to break your hold where you are. Neither am I willing. Hold on with a bull-dog grip, and chew & choke, as much as possible.

A. Lincoln

August 17, 1864, Lincoln to Grant

Three years into the war, with Confederate troops once again advancing northward and draft riots threatening major cities, Lincoln read a telegram from General Grant to the army chief-of-staff that worried about the effect these events might have on the depletion of his force attacking Richmond. Lincoln responded, telling Grant, "Hold on with a bull-dog grip, and chew and choke." When Grant received the message, he observed, "The President has more nerve than any of his advisors." [Courtesy of National Archives]

1991/2

Time ....

Office U. S. Military Telegraph,

WAR DEPARTMENT,

Washington, D. C., Oct. 12. 1864.

Lieut. Genl. Grant

City-Point, Va

Sec. of War not being in, I answer yours about election. Pennsylvania very close, and still in doubt on home vote. Ohio largely for us, with all the members of Congress but two or three. Indiana largely for us—Governor, it is said by 15.000, and 8. of the eleven members of Congress. Send us what you may know of your Army vote.

A. Lincoln

No 14

64 w chg WD

Recd 5 00

Sent 1135

By G

188
219

192

October 12, 1864, Lincoln to Grant

As the presidential elections of 1864 approached, Lincoln sent Grant this telegram outlining prospects for the outcome. The use of the phrase "for us" twice in such a message between a political leader and a military commander is particularly interesting. [Courtesy of National Archives]

3114

Time

Office U. S. Military Telegraph,
WAR DEPARTMENT,

"Cypher"

Washington, D. C., February 1. 1865

Lieut. Genl. Grant
City. Point.

Let nothing which is transpiring, change, hinder, or delay your Military movements, or plans.

A. Lincoln

312
320

9.30 A.M.

February 1, 1865, Lincoln to Grant

In early 1865, the Lincoln administration conducted clandestine peace discussions with representatives of the Confederate government. Lest there be any confusion in Grant's mind about military activities during this period, Lincoln instructed Grant, "Let nothing which is transpiring, change, hinder, or delay your Military movements or plans." [Courtesy of National Archives] at 8:30 in the morning. "We have not a word here as to the whereabouts or condition of your Army . . . Please relieve my anxiety as to the position & condition of your army up to the latest moment." Rosecrans replied at 5:40 P.M., "We are now in Chattanooga in line of battle . . . Whether they will attack to-day uncertain. General Burnside will be too late to help us. We are about 30,000 brave and determined men; but our fate is in the hands of God, in whom I hope."

The following morning General Burnside's reply to the president's request that he go to Rosecrans "without a moment's delay" arrived. Although it was sent two days after the president sent his telegram, the message was exactly what Lincoln wanted to hear: "Your despatch of the twenty first is recd & the order shall be obeyed at once. Every available man shall be concentrated at the point you direct & with as little delay as possible . . . I hope direct Telegraphic communication will be open with you tomorrow." That evening Lincoln met with Secretary Stanton and other cabinet members regarding the crisis at Chattanooga.

Burnside and his force were the best hope for the rapid reinforcement of Rosecrans. Lincoln's order to go to the aid of Rosecrans would be "obeyed at once," the general said. So why hadn't Burnside and his men been heard from in Chattanooga?

Despite his assurances, Burnside was not moving toward Chattanooga. When Lincoln saw a telegram indicating that Burnside's force was actually farther away than when he had been ordered to move "without a moment's delay" to Chattannooga, the president wrote Burnside a telegram expressing his frustration: "Yours of the 23rd just received, and it makes me doubt whether I am awake or dreaming. I have been struggling for ten days, first through Gen. Halleck, and then directly, to get you to go assist Gen. Rosecrans in an extremity, and you have repeatedly declared you would do it, and yet you steadily move the contrary way." Recounting three Burnside dispatches in which the general said he was moving to Chattanooga, Lincoln observed, "and now your dispatch of the 23rd comes from

Carter's Station, still farther away from Rosecrans, still saying you will assist him, but giving no account of any progress made towards assisting him." As with his Meade letter in July, the president subsequently thought better of the message and wrote on its back, "Not sent."

In the meantime General Burnside was using the telegraph to play bureaucratic rope-a-dope with the president. He wired Lincoln on the 27th, "I have just telegraphed General Halleck very fully, asking an explanation of your order, and anxiously await a reply." It was six days after Lincoln's explicit, "Go to Rosecrans with your force, without a moments delay," and Burnside's unequivocal, "the order shall be obeyed at once. Every available man shall be concentrated at the point you direct & with as little delay as possible." Now Burnside was asking for "explanation"?

This time the president's response went out. It was muffled furry: "My order to you meant simply that you should save Rosecrans from being crushed out." General Halleck's telegram to Burnside was less muffled: "Telegram after telegram has been sent to you to go to his assistance with all your available force . . . The substance of all telegrams from the President and from me is, you must go to General Rosecrans' assistance, with all your available force . . . The orders are very plain, and you cannot mistake their purport."

The telegraph had bridged the distances that in previous conflicts had kept wartime leaders from communicating, but success still came down to who was on the receiving end of the wire. Once again, Abraham Lincoln was failed by a subordinate. Finally, an exasperated Lincoln wired General Burnside to deal directly with General Rosecrans as to how he would help: "You can perhaps communicate with Gen. Rosecrans more rapidly by sending telegrams to him at Chattanooga. Think of it. I send a like dispatch to him."

Fortunately, at the evening cabinet meeting two days after the Chickamauga defeat, Secretary Stanton had put the wheels in motion to send other troops to Chattanooga. The movement would rely on the two civilian technologies that had redefined the nature of warfare: the telegraph and the railroad. Stanton proposed sending General Joseph Hooker and two corps from the Army of the Potomac to Chattanooga by rail. Halleck and Lincoln initially disagreed with the movement, but in the end Stanton prevailed. Via telegram, railroads were informed to make the engines and rolling stock available, the necessary rail lines were commandeered, and the subject corps were ordered to railheads.

It was the longest, largest, and fastest movement of men and material in the history of warfare. Twenty thousand soldiers, their supplies, 60 pieces of artillery, along with 3,000 horses and mules traveled 1,159 miles. Seven days after they set off the first reinforcements reached Rosecrans.

With the Herculean feat in progress, the president telegraphed General Rosecrans, asking a favor. "Unfortunately the relations between Generals Hooker and Slocum [one of the corps commanders now reporting to Hooker] are not such as to promise good, if their present relative positions remain. Therefore let me beg,—almost enjoin upon you—that on their reaching you, you will make a transposition by which Gen. Slocum with his corps, may pass from under command of Gen. Hooker, and Gen. Hooker, in turn receive some other equal force. It is important for this to be done, though we could not well arrange it here. Please do it."

Yet again, Lincoln was let down by the subordinate on the receiving end. In an amazing response from a general to his commander-in-chief's self-described begging, let alone from a general whose *in extremis* position was being rescued by the aforementioned troops, Rosecrans telegraphed the president, "Any attempt to mingle them [his troops] with Potomac troops by placing them under Potomac Generals would kindle a flame of jealously and dislike." He would not accede to the president's request.

Chattanooga hung by a thread and its commanding officer was worried about inter-unit jealousy! Lincoln knew it was time for a change. The president needed a no-nonsense general to reclaim the initiative. It was clear who that leader was. On October 16, 1863, the Military Division of the Mississippi, composing all the Union armies in the west, was created and General Ulysses Grant placed at its head.

Grant's first decision was to relieve General Rosecrans and place in command General George Thomas, who had distinguished himself at Chickamauga. General William Tecumseh Sherman was named to replace Grant as the head of the Army of the Tennessee. Grant's first telegram to his new commander was direct: "Hold Chattanooga at all hazards. I will be there as soon as possible." General Thomas' reply must have pleased his new boss: "I will hold the town till we starve."

Ulysses Grant rode into Chattanooga on October 23. Five days later he wired General Halleck, "General Thomas' plan for securing the river and south side road hence to Bridgeport has proven eminently successful. The question of supplies may now be regarded as settled. If the rebels give us one week more time I think all danger of losing territory now held by us will have passed away, and preparations may commence for offensive operations."

Less than a month later, resupplied and with his old command, now under General Sherman, further strengthening his force, Grant went on the offensive. The first day, Thomas took the Rebel picket outposts at the center of the Confederate line. The second day, Hooker took Lookout Mountain on the Confederate left while Sherman became bogged down assaulting the right. The third day's plan was for Hooker and Sherman to march toward each other, rolling up the Rebel positions atop Missionary Ridge; neither was successful. However, General Thomas, who was supposed to only threaten the center of the Rebel line in order to keep its troops from supporting the attacks against the wings, broke through quite unexpectedly. The Rebels fled for 30 miles.

On November 25, after the first two day's positive results, Lincoln telegraphed Grant, "Your dispatches as to fighting on Monday & Tuesday are here. Well done. Many thanks to all."

On December 7 the president issued another news bulletin and call for thanksgiving:

Executive Mansion, Washington D.C. Dec. 7—1863

Reliable information being received that the insurgent force is retreating from Eastern Tennessee, under circumstances rendering it probable that the Union forces can not hereafter be dislodged from that important position; and esteeming this to be of high national consequence, I recommend that all loyal people do, on receipt of this, informally assemble at their places of worship and tender special homage and gratitude to Almighty God, for this great advancement of the national cause.

A. Lincoln

The following day Abraham Lincoln telegraphed Ulysses Grant, "I wish to tender you, and all under your command, my more than thanks—my profoundest gratitude—for the skill, courage, and perseverance, with which you and they, over so great difficulties, have affected that important object. God bless you all."

THE TELEGRAPH HAD ALLOWED President Lincoln and the War Department to have unprecedented awareness of and access to commanders in the field. The technology had, without a doubt, changed the nature of the command relationship. Yet, while the technology was transformative, success still came down to the character of the person on the other end of the wire. Technology was important, but victory depended upon having the right people in command. Ulysses S. Grant's telegrams didn't whine like McClellan's, nor play bureaucrat like Hooker's and Rosecrans', nor procrastinate like Burnside's. In fact, Grant telegraphed as little as possible. He just delivered.

CHAPTER NINE

BUILDING THE MODERN LEADERSHIP MODEL

On February 29, 1864, Abraham Lincoln sent a handwritten message to the Senate of the United States: "I nominate Ulysses S. Grant, now a Major General in the Military service, to be Lieutenant General in the Army of the United States." The position of Lieutenant General had been recently revived by the Congress with Grant, the hero of Vicksburg and Chattanooga, specifically in mind. It was an act of poignant symbolism; the last person upon whom Congress had conferred this rank was George Washington. Accompanying the rank, Lincoln appointed Grant to replace Henry Halleck as general-in-chief.

Building around Grant, Lincoln created a tri-partite command structure. Once again he was walking an untrod path lacking the guideposts of historical precedent. Under the new structure the commander-in-chief established overall goals, approved strategy, and monitored performance. The general-in-chief would implement that policy, this time making the military decisions Halleck had been loath to make when he held the office. A new position, army chief of staff, was created as the chief administrative officer, the hub between the general-in-chief and his subordinates and the person responsible for the endless bureaucratic details.

Historically the military's broad geographic area of operations and lack of timely communications capability meant that authority was dispersed with a great deal of local autonomy. Prior to the Civil War, however, the telegraph began to change the management of civilian commercial institutions, ushering in the central supervision of dispersed manufacturing plants or railroad operations. As the civilian telegraph technology was put to work for military purposes, these commercial management concepts began to migrate to the War Department. Without being consciously aware of it, Lincoln's new command structure was applying the developing principles of industrial management to an electronically interconnected war machine.

The dispersed nature of the military was exacerbated by Ulysses Grant's decision not be a Washington-based general-in-chief but to command all of the armies of the United States while traveling with one of those armies in the field. After initially intending to remain in the West, Grant decided to make his headquarters with the Army of the Potomac as it sought to destroy the army of Robert E. Lee. General George Meade remained in command of the Army of the Potomac, but his boss would be traveling with him. General Halleck, who had let Lincoln down as a leader and decisionmaker, but who was, in the president's words, "a first rate clerk," was retained as army chief of staff. General Sherman took over Grant's old command as the head of the Western Theater. The vacuum created by Sherman's upward movement propelled proven (and just as important, Grant-trusted) generals up the chain of command in the west.

General Grant now held dominion over more than half a million men dispersed across two theaters totaling 800,000 square miles. His decision to operate from the field would not have been possible but for the army's central nervous system running over telegraph wires. As Grant wrote his father, "In these days of telegraph & steam I can command whilst traveling and visiting about."

General Sherman was quite specific in his *Memoirs* about the important role electronic messages played in allowing Grant to command: "the value of the magnetic telegraph in war cannot be exaggerated, as was illustrated by the perfect concert of action between the armies in Virginia, and Georgia during 1864. Hardly a day intervened when General Grant did not know the exact state of facts with me, more than fifteen hundred miles away as the wires ran." The same can be said for President Lincoln who saw all of the telegraph traffic between Grant and his generals.

Reliance on the telegraph was the culmination of a transformative process for both the president and General Grant. Such a transformation was proof positive how both men possessed the fundamental attribute of a great leader, and the absolute prerequisite for a wartime leader: the ability to grow and adapt in the job.

Lincoln's electronic evolution had progressed through two stages, as we have seen; now the president was entering his third electronic era. During the first 14 months in office he virtually ignored the telegraph, and then had his electronic breakout in May 1862. Eighteen sixty-four was the beginning of the third phase of Lincoln's electronic leadership because of the individual at the other end of the telegraph line. "Grant is the first general I have had," Lincoln observed wryly. The president began to adapt his use of the telegraph to reflect how he now had a general in command who was persistent in a single focus: destroying the enemy.

For General Grant, the embrace of the electronic instrument was also an interesting evolution. We have already seen Lincoln's description of Grant as "a copious worker, and fighter, but a very meagre writer, or telegrapher." From the outset of the war, the general had demonstrated his distain for the telegraph's ability to impose the will of others upon his activities. Following his first victory, the capture of Fort Henry, in February 1862, Grant, then a one-star general, wanted to push on; his superior, General Halleck, thought otherwise and told him via telegraph to dig in and prepare for a counterattack. Six days after capturing Fort Henry, however, Grant telegraphed Halleck that he was advancing on Fort Donelson, the next Rebel outpost. Immediately after dispatching the message, Grant ordered the telegraph line cut to prevent his decision from being countermanded.

As general-in-chief, however, the man, who as a general in the field wanted to be left alone, was now responsible for the activities of all other generals. As General Sherman's description supports, Grant began to use the telegraph as Lincoln did: as his eyes and ears on activities afar, and as the means to project his voice to those points. The telegraph also became the tool through which Grant "managed up," communicating crisply with Washington, principally through dispatches to General Halleck that he knew Lincoln would read.

The president and his general brought much in common to their telegraphic metamorphosis. As a result of their backgrounds, both were relatively unencumbered by the way things "should be" and, thus, were more receptive to change. Abraham Lincoln not only had no previous executive experience (let alone at such rarified heights), but was also bereft in military experience. Ulysses Grant, while a graduate of West Point, had finished near the bottom of his class in tactics and he claimed to have never read Jomini, the 18th-century military theorist whom Halleck had translated for his textbook and to whose now outdated theories so many other generals slavishly conformed. Most important, both men had grown as a result of their experiences. There can be no doubt that Lincoln grew as a leader as he became more familiar and comfortable with his office. Likewise, Grant had moved through the ranks of command, gaining experience with the nature of the new warfare at each point. The generals with whom Lincoln started the war were thrust into commands exceeding their experience; Grant assumed command because of his experience.

Lincoln's relationship with Grant appeared to be more hands-off than it had been with other generals. The president sent Grant only a dozen telegrams related to strategic management during a year in which his armies saw unprecedented fighting. Lincoln continued to actively review dispatches, and, as we will see, was not averse to inserting himself with a forceful message; but he refrained from the kind of micromanagement he had shown with Frémont, Banks, Shields, Hooker, Rosecrans, and Burnside.

The price Grant paid for such relative freedom was to buy off on the president's strategic grand design. So long as the general-in-chief was pursuing the president's plan, the manner in which he achieved those ends was subject to less intrusion than had been experienced by other generals. Abetting this shared strategic direction, General Grant simply stimulated more confidence; he was everything his predecessors had not been: stubborn and relentless, with a plan to accomplish the president's goals.

EARLY IN 1864, BEFORE Grant's promotion, General Halleck, still the titular general-in-chief, had urged him to lay out "freely and fully" his thoughts on a plan for "the coming campaign" in both the east and west. As an audition for his coming promotion, Grant's strategic proposal for the eastern theater must have been a cause of concern to the president. Grant proposed "an abandonment of all previously attended lines to Richmond." Instead, troops would be landed on the North Carolina coast to march northward, cutting off the supply lines from the south into Richmond. It smacked of McClellan in 1862; instead of going overland from Washington, protecting the capital by keeping the army between Lee and the city, Grant proposed that 60,000 men be moved to the other side of Lee's forces.

Perhaps a Union army slashing Lee's line of communications with the Confederate heartland made military sense, but it was a political risk that Lincoln was unwilling to take. Eighteen sixty-four was a presidential election year. The last thing that Lincoln needed was to open the door for another of Robert E. Lee's movements into Northern states. Nevertheless, Grant was going to be promoted to general-in-chief.

On March 8, 1864, Abraham Lincoln and Ulysses Grant met for the first time. The challenge now was to implement something heretofore unachieved in the war: a strategy that was a servant to, rather than dictator of, policy. For the first time since General Scott's short-lived plan of 1861, the Union war effort would be made by a coordinated, strategic political/military plan. In 1862 the absence of coordinated activities had helped drive Lincoln to step in and issue specific orders during Jackson's Valley Campaign. In 1863, with Halleck as an indecisive general-in-chief, Lincoln had been forced to improvise again by electronically monitoring affairs while keeping his generals on a tight leash. With a new general-in-chief and a new year of campaigning before him, the president sought a new model. It would begin with unanimity in strategic design.

From March 26, when he first took up residence with the Army of the Potomac, until May 4, when the force started moving, Grant came to Washington weekly to sit down with the president and discuss strategy. Grant's January plan was ash-canned. The new plan respected the political necessity of denying Lee the opportunity to move his troops into Union states. At the same time coordinated advances in the east and west would move like two pincers to converge on the south.

Among Abraham Lincoln's gifts as a political leader was his ability to guide the desired result while the other party believed it was his own idea. As Grant wrote in his *Memoirs:*

> *In my first interview with Mr. Lincoln alone he stated to me that he never professed to be a military man or to know how campaigns should be conducted, and never wanted to interfere with them; but that procrastination on the part of commanders, and the pressure from the people at the North and Congress, which was always with him, forced him . . . All he wanted or had ever wanted was some one who would take the responsibility and act, and call on him for all the assistance needed . . .*

Abraham Lincoln may have "never wanted to interfere" in military affairs, but his strategic vision would govern Grant's activities.

Politically, the war needed to be kept in the South and Lee kept from a third excursion across the Potomac. Militarily (which also had political ramifications) the Southern forces needed to be engaged and defeated. The president would be watchful from the telegraph office; if Grant's implementation of the strategy was successful it should be unnecessary to issue commands or second guess.

The general-in-chief communicated this strategy succinctly to his two army commanders. To General Sherman in the west, "It is my design . . . to work all parts of the army together, and somewhat towards a common center . . . You I propose to move against [Confederate general Joseph] Johnston's army, to break it up and to get into the interior of the enemy's country as far as you can, inflicting all the damage you can against their war resources . . . I do not propose to lay down for you a plan of campaign, but simply to lay down the work it is desirable to have done, and leave you free to execute it in your own way."

To General Meade in the east Grant was equally succinct. "So far as practicable all the armies are to move together, and towards one common center . . . Sherman will move at the same time you do . . . Joe Johnston's army being his objective point and the heart of Georgia his ultimate aim." Then, in an echo of Lincoln's admonition to General Hooker the previous year, Grant made Meade's objective clear, "Lee's army will be your objective point. Wherever Lee goes, there you will go also." Whereas Grant left Sherman to develop the details of the western campaign, he would be the father of what happened in the east. "The only point upon which I am now in doubt is whether it will be better to cross the Rapidan above or below him [Lee]," his instructions to Meade read, adding, "These advantages and options I will talk over with you more fully than I can write them."

At the end of April, just before Grant moved out with the Army of the Potomac, Lincoln sent his general a letter that exemplified both the president's political skills as well as his hope that circumstances had changed: "I wish to express, in this way, my entire satisfaction with what you have done up to this time, so far as I understand it." The grand strategy clearly bore Lincoln's hallmark and approval, yet the president wrote, "The particulars of your plans I neither know, or seek to know. You are vigilant and self-reliant; and pleased with this, I wish not to obtrude any constraints or restraints upon you." It was a combination of expectation and hope for a new plan and a new general, as well as a ritual kabuki dance, blessing his general while also distancing himself from any potential negative results by feigning noninvolvement. Continuing his part in the ritual, Grant replied that he had been given everything he had asked for and, "Should any success be less than I desire, and expect, the least I can say is, the fault is not with you."

Lincoln's letter to Grant may have been political and ritualistic posturing, but it was the optimal role for a commander-in-chief. The president had helped develop—indeed insisted on—key components of the overall strategy and now left the commander to worry about the details of the plan's implementation. As Grant, himself, had commented (and presumably mentioned at one of his weekly meetings with Lincoln), "When I have sufficient confidence in a general to leave him in command of an army, I have enough confidence in him to leave his plans to himself." It was Management 101, the combination of responsibility with authority, yet it was something Lincoln's previous deficit in generalship had not allowed him to successfully practice.

The telegraph would allow the president to observe whether his new management was delivering results. If necessary, it would also enable him to step in and provide the ultimate management decision making.

On May 4, 1864, the Army of the Potomac crossed the Rapidan River and proceeded against General Lee's Confederates. At the same time, at Hampton Roads, General Benjamin Butler put his

Army of the James on board ships to sail up the peninsula and pick up where George McClellan had left off. The following day Confederate president Davis sent word to General Lee that it appeared two major advances were heading towards Richmond. This time, however, Richmond was more the bait to bring the Rebel army into destructive battle in defense of its capital than the goal in and of itself.

The first challenge Meade's army faced was to traverse an area of untamed scrub brush and second-growth trees that the locals called the Wilderness. Only a few roads passed through the Wilderness, and its dense growth nullified the Union army's advantage in numbers and artillery by restricting maneuver and eliminating clear fields of fire. Grant's plan had been to sprint through the Wilderness in two days. Unfortunately, his new army wasn't made of sprinters.

Lee's Confederates, by comparison, were jackrabbits. The Rebels attacked the Union troops while they were still in the Wilderness. The fighting was bloody and hard, a hell compounded by the scrub brush igniting from the sparks of the weapons. For three days Grant could do nothing but watch and assess the caliber of the army he had inherited.

Lincoln knew there was a battle going on, but was disconnected from Grant since, for some reason, the field telegraph had not advanced with the army (a deficiency that was quickly corrected). The president monitored what telegraph traffic there was and devoured press accounts. Unlike when Lincoln had been cut off from his commanding general during the Second Battle of Manassas, this time there was no going around the chain of command to open new lines of communication.

The Union army lost the Battle of the Wilderness. The casualties were greater than Hooker's ignominious defeat the preceding year at nearby Chancellorsville. Unlike his predecessors, however, Grant saw the battle not as an end in itself but as the means to an end.

Since he did not yet have a telegraph in his camp, Grant grabbed a reporter who was heading to Washington to file his story. "If you see the President, tell him for me that whatever happens, there will be no turning back." When the reporter connected with the president and delivered the message, "Mr. Lincoln put his great, strong arms about me and, carried away by the exuberance of his gladness, imprinted a kiss on my forehead."

The battle over, the veterans in Grant's army assumed that history would repeat itself; another Union commander had led them into defeat against Robert E. Lee and would retreat to lick his wounds. Yet, as the head of the marching column came to a crossroads in the smoldering forest where one road led north in retreat while the other went deeper into Virginia, Grant turned his column south. The men cheered. For the first time in the war, the Army of the Potomac, having lost a battle, was advancing instead of retreating.

On May 9 presidential assistant John Hay recorded in his diary, "Received today the first despatches from Grant. The President thinks highly of what Grant has done. He was talking about it with me today and said 'How near we have been to this thing before and failed. I believe if any other General had been at the Head of that army it would not have been on this side of the Rapidan [i.e., it would have retreated]. It is the dogged pertinacity of Grant that wins.' "

For the next five weeks Grant attacked the Rebels. At Spotsylvania Court House, North Anna, Totopotomy Creek, and Cold Harbor the story line was the same: the Union troops were unable to overcome Lee's entrenched force. After each engagement Grant would roll to his left and proceed onward while Lee, taking advantage of his shorter interior lines, would fall back, race to get ahead of Grant, and entrench again.

Grant's tactics were horrific in their human cost. Constantly having to assault Rebel fortifications took a bloody toll. In Grant's first month of campaigning with the Army of the Potomac, he incurred a staggering 55,000 casualties . . . and there wasn't a single battlefield victory to show for it.

While Lee's army was the target, that force's movements were dictated by the need to defend Richmond. Every time Grant's army rolled left, it advanced closer to the Confederate capital. On June 14 General Grant, now in regular telegraphic dialog with Washington, informed Halleck of an even bolder movement. "Our forces will commence crossing the James [River] to-day. The enemy show no signs yet of having brought troops to the south side of Richmond. I will have Petersburg secured, if possible, before they get there in much force." This time, the tables would be turned; Grant would get his position established first and then allow Lee to waste himself in assaults.

For the first time since the campaign had begun five weeks earlier, President Lincoln telegraphed General Grant. The president had been reading the telegraph office inbox and saw the message to Halleck about crossing the James. "Have just read your despatch of 1 P.M. yesterday. I begin to see it. You will succeed. God bless you all."

What Lincoln was beginning to see was a dramatic end run by Grant. The army would cross the James River via the longest pontoon bridge ever built and then outrace Lee to Petersburg, south of the capital, where three railroad lines linked the Confederates to supplies from the southern heartland. Sever those connections and Grant's army would be at the doorstep of Richmond astride Lee's line of sustenance. Unfortunately, the president's prediction of success was not to be. After successfully crossing the James, Grant's generals failed to exploit their advantage to take Petersburg before Lee arrived. Lee's troops won the footrace and dug in. Unwilling to suffer the losses that would be required to break the Rebel's entrenched position, Grant settled into a siege.

Two days later, on June 20, the president boarded a ship to sail down the Potomac, through the Chesapeake, and up the James to meet with Grant. For five weeks he had patiently read the general's reports and refrained from second-guessing. It was time for a face-to-face meeting.

General Grant was direct and forthcoming with the president:

"You will never hear of me farther from Richmond than right now. I am just as sure of going into Richmond as I am of any future event. It may take a long summer day, as they say in the Rebel papers, but I will do it." This was clearly not McClellan. Although stymied so far, Grant told the president he would keep advancing to cut the railroads and draw Lee into decisive action. Lincoln returned to Washington reassured by Grant's resolve.

Then Robert E. Lee did what Abraham Lincoln worried about the most. Confederate troops began moving on the North. Just like the last time Union troops threatened Richmond, Rebel troops advanced up the Shenandoah Valley to threaten Washington. Lee had stripped the Richmond defenses of 14,000 troops, put them under the command of General Jubal Early, and sent them north. The thought that 14,000 Rebels could threaten Washington and sustain a Northern invasion was inconceivable to Grant. Yet Grant, himself, had stripped Washington of most of its defenders in support of his current campaigns. Fewer than 10,000 Union troops remained in the capital and many of these were men who because of wounds or sickness were judged unfit for the front lines. Washington was more thinly defended than during the great Lincoln–McClellan fracas of 1862.

The week before Lincoln sailed to meet with Grant, Early's men pushed off for the north. By Independence Day, augmented by troops under the command of Lincoln's 1860 presidential opponent John Breckinridge, the Rebels were approaching Harpers Ferry. During the following week they passed through Sharpsburg, site of the Battle of Antietam, and on through the same mountain passes where McClellan had defeated the Rebels in the lead-up to that battle.

His worst political and military fears now a reality, Abraham Lincoln began to revert to some of his old ways with the telegraph. During the Battle of the Wilderness the president had refrained from using the telegraph to develop his own sources of information. This time, however, with an invasion of the North at hand, Lincoln returned to using the telegraph to gather his own intelligence. The president of the Baltimore & Ohio Railroad had been wiring the War Department with the reports received from his outposts. The president had been reading these reports and on July 5 he inserted himself: "You say telegraphic communication is re-established with Sandy Hook [Maryland]. Well, what does Sandy Hook say about operations of the Enemy and of [Union general Fritz] Sigel, doing to-day?" The information received was not what he wanted to hear; Lincoln's troops were not stopping the advancing Confederates.

On July 9 a rapidly assembled band of 3,000 local militia, reinforced at the last minute by a like number sent from Grant, gave battle to Early's Confederates in Maryland, about 40 miles outside Washington along the Monocacy River. The day of the battle Lincoln wired the railroad president again, "What have you heard about a battle at Monocacy to-day? We have nothing about it here except what you say." The report came back, "Our troops at Monocacy have given way . . . General Wallace has been badly defeated." Union general Lew Wallace (who after the war would write *Ben Hur*) in fact had been defeated in a brave effort to stop the Rebel advance, but thanks to his strategic leadership, Early's force was delayed by a day in its march to Washington.

The situation had all the hallmarks of 1862 when Lincoln stepped in and began ordering troops around. Unlike General McClellan's dismissive arrogance, however, Grant sought to be a problem solver for the president. The same day as the Battle of Monocacy, General Grant telegraphed instructions to General Halleck: "Forces enough to defeat all that Early has with him should get in his rear south of him . . ." Then the general-in-chief offered, "If the President thinks it advisable that I should go to Washington in person I can start in an hour after receiving notice, leaving everything here on the defensive."

The next day President Lincoln sent his first substantive telegram to General Grant since the general's departure over two months earlier. "Your despatch to Gen. Halleck, referring to what I may think in the present emergency is shown to me. Gen. Halleck says we have absolutely no force here fit to go to the field . . . Now what I think is that you should provide to retain your hold where you are certainly, and bring the rest with you personally, and make a vigorous effort to destroy the enemie's [*sic*] force in this vicinity . . . This is what I think upon your suggestion, and is not an order."

It was a turning point in Lincoln's telegraphic relationship with Grant. For two months the president had been content to monitor Grant's activities. Now, as his worst fear was being visited upon him, Lincoln used the telegraph to reach out. The president needed not only troops in Washington, but also his general-in-chief. Like most of Lincoln's telegrams, Lincoln's message to Grant was presented as a "suggestion." Grant, however, missed the nuance that when your boss makes a "suggestion" it is best to view it as more than a gentle hint.

The following day Grant replied, "I have sent from here a whole corps commanded by an excellent officer, besides over three thousand other troops . . . They will probably reach Washington tomorrow night." Then Grant demonstrated his underappreciation for the president's "suggestion" that he "bring the rest with you personally." Stepping into a hole of his own making, Grant replied, "I think on reflection it would have a bad effect for me to leave here, and with Genl Ord at Baltimore and Hunter and Wright with the forces following the enemy up, would do no good." The telegraph may have connected the president with an ally who wanted to cooperate, but that ally had completely missed the message that his presence in Washington was not a purely military matter.

Lincoln also missed his chance to cut through the telegraph's lack of subtlety. The president responded the following morning, July 11, "Yours of 10.30 P.M. yesterday received, and very satisfactory . . . Some firing between Rockville [Maryland] and here now." Having sent the dispatch, the president in the words of John Hay's diary, "concluded to desert his tormentors . . . & travel around the defenses." A chain of earthenwork forts surrounded the capital and government clerks—including clerks from the telegraph office—were being armed and sent forward. Hay recorded that Lincoln was pleased by his tour: "The President is in very good feather this evening. He seems not in the least concerned about the safety of Washington."

The evening that Lincoln was "in very good feather," General Early learned that the troops sent by Grant had arrived. General Wallace's delaying action along the Monocacy had proven decisive; the Rebel force was now completely outmanned. On July 12 the Confederates skirmished in front of Fort Stevens but did not mount an assault. When night came, they withdrew. Grant had been correct militarily: the manpower was present to protect the capital. His misreading of the political and psychological impact of his absence, however, would come back to haunt him later.

The action at Fort Stevens produced a unique historical footnote. When the president returned a second time to Fort Stevens, on July 12, he strode around the parapet of the fort, stovepipe hat on his head, an appealing target for Rebel marksmen who were rising to the opportunity. One man standing next to Lincoln was hit by a Rebel round. Finally, an officer, some say Captain Oliver Wendell Holmes Jr., roared, "Get down, you fool, before you get shot!" Abraham Lincoln thus became the only sitting president to come under enemy fire in battle.

The difference between Abraham Lincoln's response to the 1862 threat to Washington and its 1864 clone could not have been more pronounced. In both instances, the telegraph connected the president with his general on the south side of Richmond. When that general was George McClellan, the message the president received was one of "get off my back," forcing Lincoln to take the reins. When that general was Ulysses Grant, the message was more supportive, troops were dispatched, and the military problem resolved.

Grant's misreading of the president's wishes, and Lincoln's missed opportunity to be explicit, however, illustrated how the men at both ends of the telegraph line still had a bit to learn about management by wire. In that regard it was a watershed in the Lincoln–Grant relationship. The president, who had been electronically uninvolved for over two months, henceforth did not hesitate to express himself, and in a manner that overcame the telegraph's inability to convey subtlety.

WHEN THE REBELS WITHDREW from Washington the night of July 12/13, they returned across the Potomac to the mouth of the Shenandoah Valley. Grant ordered one of the corps he had sent to defend the capital back to Petersburg.

General Grant telegraphed General Sherman, now moving on the Confederate heartland, to be on the lookout should Early's force come west to help the Rebel defense. Grant told his lieutenant he would try desperately to get the Petersburg situation to a point where he could hold his position with fewer men and send the others to help in the west.

Lincoln, who was reading all of Grant's telegraph traffic, not just those between the general-in-chief and the War Department, wired Grant the next day expressing concern about what he had seen. "In your despatch of yesterday to Gen. Sherman, I find the following, towit: 'I shall make a desparate [sic] effort to get a position here which will hold the enemy without the necessity of so many men.' " The president was concerned about what desperate plan Grant had in mind. Already, criticism of "Butcher Grant" and the high casualty rate he had sustained was causing a political firestorm. Lincoln sounded a note of caution: "I am glad to hear you say this; and yet I do hope you may find a way that the effort shall not be desparate [sic] in the sense of great loss of life."

Grant, however, had misjudged Lee's intentions. Jubal Early and his troops weren't going to Atlanta. Neither, however, were they going back to Richmond. Early's job was to help Lee's position by harassing Lincoln in the north. Once again, the Rebels crossed the Potomac. It had only been two weeks since Washington had recovered from Early's previous exploits. On July 30 Confederate troops burned Chambersburg, Pennsylvania, just down the road from Gettysburg. Lincoln's fear of Rebels marching through northern states was again alive.

Grant had turned the tide of Early's previous incursion by sending troops, but his decision to remain at Petersburg had estranged him from the nation's political leadership. Part of the president's previous desire for Grant to come to Washington was because Union forces in the area around Washington were under multiple commands and Lincoln had no one to look to for hands-on tactical coordination and decision making. Grant agreed: "It takes a long time for dispatches to come here and go back, during which conditions may change; consequently it is absolutely necessary that some one in Washington should give orders and make disposition of all the forces within reach of the line of the Potomac."

Grant's telegram was only logical; while he could provide strategic command, someone needed to be in tactical control. The comment, however, set him up for a coup. "[O]wing to the difficulties and delay of communications between his [Grant's] headquarters and Washington, it is necessary that in the present emergency military orders must be issued directly from Washington," Secretary Stanton wrote General Halleck. The president wanted Halleck put in command of all forces around Washington, extending from Pennsylvania to western Virginia.

Telegraphic communication had shown its weakness. First was Grant's failure to appreciate how the cold and dispassionate dots and dashes were delivering a message beyond pure military issues. The Confederate strategy had created a political problem for Abraham Lincoln. Such situations require physical presence, both as a show of support and as a means of picking up on and resolving concerns too subtle to survive electronic transmission. Second, as Grant's telegram explains, it is impossible for tactical decisions to be made from afar. Strategic command, like that exercised by Grant, could be communicated by telegraph, but someone had to be on the scene making the moment-to-moment decisions. The president already knew this and was moving to provide his own solution. Finally, the local command structure was too Balkanized; someone needed to have the mantle of authority and responsibility.

In his decision to give Halleck command, Lincoln was demonstrating both his understanding of management as well as just how desperately he required one person to whom he could look for guidance and supportive physical presence. Halleck had failed Lincoln previously precisely because of his unwillingness to make decisions; it was a measure of the president's frustration that he was now turning to the man who hated to make decisions in the expectation that he would do just that.

The president needed to communicate with his general-in-chief face-to-face. "Will meet you at Fort-Monroe at 8. P.M. on Saturday the 30th," Lincoln telegraphed Grant. They actually met a day later, for five hours, aboard the U.S.S. Baltimore. The fullness of Grant's failure to meet the president's needs was now well understood. The general-in-chief moved quickly to provide remedies. Halleck simply could not be given this important command authority; Grant wanted one of his trusted and successful subordinates from the west, 33-year-old General Philip Sheridan, calling the shots. On August 1, the day following his conversation with Lincoln, the general-in-chief telegraphed the chief of staff, "I want Sheridan put in command of all the troops in the field [around Washington], with instructions to put himself south of the enemy and follow him to the death."

As usual, the president was monitoring the telegraph traffic. It had been only three days since they had parted, presumably each understanding the other, but Lincoln wanted nothing left to chance. The president sent Grant a telegram in response to the general's order to Halleck. There was no subtlety in the president's message: "I have seen your despatch in which you say, 'I want Sheridan put in command of all the troops in the field, with instructions to put himself South of the enemy, and follow him to the death. Wherever the enemy goes, let our troops go also.' This, I think, is exactly right, as to how our forces should move." Having dispensed with his approval of Grant's military decision, however, Lincoln's telegram turned, in no uncertain terms, to management advice. "But please look over the despatches you may have received from here, even since you made that order, and discover, if you can, that there is any idea in the head of any one here, of 'putting our army *South* of the enemy' or of following him 'to the *death*' in any direction."

It was a "Dutch uncle" telegram, so direct as to overcome any potential for missing the point. Grant had not been exercising sufficient management vigilance regarding activities around the nation's capital and the president called him on the carpet. Just in case the importance of the message had somehow been missed, the president closed with, "I repeat to you it will neither be done nor attempted unless you watch it every day, and hour, and force it."

The message was not lost on its recipient. General Grant replied the same day, "Your dispatch of 6 P.M. just received. I will start in two hours for Washington . . ." Grant spent August 5 and 6 with the army in Maryland overseeing the transfer of command to General Sheridan. His instructions to Sheridan were succinct: Drive Early back to the Shenandoah, then drive him out of the Valley and into oblivion. In the process Grant told Sheridan to so completely destroy the breadbasket the Shenandoah represented to the Confederacy "that crows flying over it for the balance of this season will have to carry their own provender with them." Returning to Washington, Grant met with the president and Secretary Stanton and briefed them on his plan and instructions to General Sheridan. Having dealt with the military threat to his front as well as the threat to his political rear, Grant returned to his headquarters outside Petersburg.

Abraham Lincoln's handling of the second Early incursion was informative. He could have imposed himself as he had in 1862 and begun issuing orders by telegraph. Instead, he sought to bring in the necessary management, even if it meant Halleck. More important, however, the president's Management-By-Walking-Around instincts took him to meet face-to-face with Grant. Satisfied that he was now understood, the president stepped back from his Halleck plan, let his general-in-chief manage the situation, yet remained ever-vigilant.

General Sheridan chased Jubal Early back into the Shenandoah Valley. On September 12, two months to the day from Early's withdrawal from Washington and five weeks since Lincoln's "Dutch uncle" telegram, the president reinforced his prior admonition to General Grant in a new telegram. The message was more tactful than the earlier wire, but there was no missing Lincoln's thinking. "Sheridan and Early are facing each other as a dead lock. Could we not pick up a regiment here and there, to the number of say ten thousand men, and quietly, but suddenly concentrate them all at Sheridan's camp and enable him to make a strike?" The president had returned to his typical "This is but a suggestion," but Grant understood what was going on. Not missing any nuances this time, he wired back the very next day, "It has been my intention for a week back to start to-morrow, or the day following, to see Sheridan and arrange what was necessary to enable him to start Early out of the Valley. It seems to me it can be successfully done." The general-in-chief went to see Sheridan, was pleased with what he found, and returned to his headquarters.

A week later Sheridan telegraphed Grant, "I have the honor to report that I attacked the forces of Genl Early . . . and after a most stubborn and sanguinary engagement . . . completely defeated him." Lincoln telegraphed his congratulations directly to Sheridan, "Have just heard of your great victory. God bless you all, officers and men."

Then, belying his emotional desire to get hands-on, the president added, "Strongly inclined to come up and see you."

Lincoln, however, did not go to visit General Sheridan. The threat in the Shenandoah was almost vanquished, but how many times before had Lincoln been on the verge of victory only to see it slip through his fingers? Anxious that history not repeat itself, the president again telegraphed his thoughts to General Grant. It had been only ten days since Sheridan's victory, but the president was worried about what came next: "I hope it will lay no constraint on you, nor do harm any way, for me to say I am a little afraid lest Lee sends reenforcements to Early, and thus enable him to turn upon Sheridan." Grant replied immediately, "I am taking steps to prevent Lee sending reinforcements to Early by attacking him here. Our advance is now within six miles of Richmond . . ."

The president's fears were not unfounded. On October 19 a reinforced Early struck Sheridan at Cedar Creek. What appeared early in the struggle to be Confederate victory became a Union rout that afternoon as Sheridan counterattacked. The president again telegraphed Sheridan, "With great pleasure I tender you and your brave army, the thanks of the Nation, and my own personal admiration and gratitude, for the month's operations in the Shenandoah Valley; and especially for the splendid work of October 19, 1864." The threat in the Shenandoah Valley had been staunched. The pathway for invasion of the North was finally corked.

THE FIRST 10 MONTHS of 1864 found Abraham Lincoln constructing and maintaining, for the first time in the Civil War, a unified national command authority. That this was at all possible was attributable to the telegraph. The president, now blessed with a decisive general-in-chief, made the telegraph his tool for monitoring and verifying performance against plan, and when necessary, for interposing himself directly into the decision making.

It was significant that Lincoln, when faced with circumstances similar to those of 1862—a threat to Washington and the bulk of his army south of Richmond—did not respond as before and assume personal command. After some miscommunication-driven angst, the president relied upon the structure he had put in place. It was a structure whose usage evolved. Daily supervision via reading the telegraph traffic was its bedrock. After Jubal Early's first incursion, the president built on that bedrock to interact more frequently with his general-in-chief with no hesitancy to bring forth his own specific insights or proposals.

A new leadership model was under construction. The national command authority structure and the president's clear and direct messages through that structure produced successes in 1864 and, as we shall soon see, became the basis for ultimate success in 1865.

CHAPTER TEN

THE LAST LAP

THE PRESIDENT PASSED A NEATLY folded and securely sealed piece of paper around the table to his cabinet members. He asked that each of them sign the back of the document and return it to him unopened. It was August 23, 1864, two and a half months before the presidential election.

Abraham Lincoln expected to lose the upcoming election. Had the cabinet members been able to look inside the folded paper they had signed they would have found Lincoln's forecast for the coming referendum on his leadership. "This morning, as for some days past, it seems exceedingly probable that this Administration will not be re-elected. Then it will be my duty to so co-operate with the President elect, as to save the Union between the election and the inauguration; as he will have secured his election on such grounds that he can not possibly save it afterwards."

The election of 1864 was the first time in history that a popularly elected leader ever stood for re-election during a war. After almost four years of conflict, "The People are wild for Peace," New York's powerful Thurlow Weed had written Secretary of State Seward, adding, "I told Mr. Lincoln that his re-election was an impossibility." Republican leaders began an organized effort to convince Lincoln to withdraw and allow someone else to be the party's standard bearer.

The week after Lincoln passed the paper around his cabinet

meeting, the Democratic party nominated General George McClellan as their candidate for president. The Democrat's platform was decidedly antiwar and McClellan was presented as a man who could bring things to a close. "You think I don't know I am going to be beaten?" Lincoln confided to a friend, "but I do, and unless some great change takes place, badly beaten."

Keeping with custom, neither Lincoln nor McClellan campaigned directly. Their surrogates, however, left no brick untossed. Samuel F.B. Morse, upon whose device the president relied so heavily, was rabidly anti-Lincoln, anti-emancipation, and fervent in his efforts to remove from office "the present imbecile, & bloodthirsty administration." Morse distributed reams of pamphlets for the Peace Democrats; in his correspondence he labeled Lincoln "weak," "vacillating," "illiterate," and "a President without brains." Nothing about Lincoln's character or his politics avoided mockery, aspersion, or political slander. He was simultaneously a tyrant and a baboon more appropriate for a carnival sideshow than national leadership. The race card was played on the Great Emancipator when his opponents secretly produced a pamphlet promoting miscegenation and claimed it was from Lincoln supporters.

The president, however, was, in his own words, "more of a politician than anything else." As a result, he actively managed his own campaign to a point where one Republican senator observed, "The President is too busy looking after the election to think of anything else." Like any incumbent, Lincoln was not without tools to enhance his position. To please friends and avenge enemies, he freely dispensed political patronage. These appointees (as well as other Federal employees) were then expected to kick back a percentage of their salary to the Republican party. Friendly newspapers received sizable government printing contracts as their reward. Private firms providing services to the war effort were tapped for campaign contributions.

Added to these traditional political instruments was the ability to speedily coordinate activities and dispense favorable information via telegraph. Political information programs were initiated to take advantage of the newspapers' new telegraph-driven demand for fast-breaking news. The telegraph had created a new breed of journalist, the Washington correspondent. To feed the correspondents' insatiable demand for something to send home, government agencies, for the first time, began to put out news bulletins. Today we would call them press releases. President Lincoln himself sat down for one-on-one interviews and visits with journalists and editors to an unprecedented extent.

Lincoln also exploited the telegraph to talk politics with his generals. A telegram to General Grant reporting on the outcome in state elections less than a month before the 1864 presidential election sounded more like a message to a political operative than one from the commander-in-chief to his general-in-chief: "Pennsylvania very close, and still in doubt on home vote—Ohio largely for us . . . Indiana largely for us . . . Send what you may know of your army vote."

The repeated use of the term "us" in Lincoln's telegram to Grant is striking. The simple pronoun could either be a collective reference to his administration, or could be read to implicate Grant in an "us and them" political activity at the same time the general was leading citizen soldiers in battle.

The term "home vote" referenced in the president's telegram related to votes other than those cast absentee. Seventeen states had changed their procedures to allow soldiers to cast votes from the field. In five states—Indiana, Illinois, Delaware, New Jersey, and Oregon—soldiers could only vote in person at home. Thus, on September 19, Lincoln wrote General Sherman: "The State election of Indiana occurs on the 11th of October, and the loss of it to the friends of the government would go far towards losing the whole Union cause. The bad effect upon the November election, and especially the giving the State Government to those who will oppose the war in every possible way, are too much to risk . . . Indiana is the only important State, voting in October, whose soldiers cannot vote in the field.

Any thing you can safely do to let her soldiers, or any part of them, go home and vote at the State election, will be greatly in point."

Although Lincoln's request of Sherman specifically stated that the furloughed soldiers "need not remain for the Presidential election," Indiana governor Morton wired the president the day after the state election (and the governor's reelection), "I most earnestly ask that their furloughs be extended by a special order until after the Presidential Election." The president wired Morton in response that he had specifically told Sherman those furloughed did not have to remain for the November election. "I therefore can not press the General on this point." Then Lincoln, having established the record of being good to his word, deftly opened the door to granting the governor's wish: "All that the Sec. of War and Gen. Sherman feel they can safely do, I however, shall be glad of."

Governor Morton picked up on the opening, adding the spin that those furloughed were not fit for duty anyway. In a telegram to the president and secretary of war he observed, "It is my opinion that the vote of every soldier in Indiana will be required to carry this state for Mr. Lincoln in November. The most of them [the furloughed] are sick and wounded and in no condition to render service and it's better to let them remain while they are here." Similar exchanges were had with other governors, but the president largely stayed out of direct involvement, even when the telegrams were addressed directly to him.

It was not, however, just the matter of nonabsentee states that concerned the president. Thirteen of the 17 states that allowed voting from the field segregated those votes from the "home vote." Lincoln worried about the impact on the credibility of an election delivered by the "army vote" of men under his command, rather than by the noncombatants back home. Therefore, his administration worked to furlough soldiers in key electoral states so they could return home to cast a vote. That would be counted as a "home vote" rather than an "army vote."

The result of this furlough frenzy was illustrated by General

George Thomas's order, the week before the election: "By direction of the honorable Secretary of War you will grant furloughs to the 15th instant to all enlisted men belonging to regiments from the following States, who are in hospitals or otherwise unfit for field duty: Pennsylvania, Indiana, Illinois, Michigan, Wisconsin, Ohio, Connecticut, and Massachusetts . . . Transportation to be ordered to and from their homes." All told, thousands of soldiers were furloughed to return home to vote in swing states.

As it turned out, all these efforts were not necessary; Lincoln's victory was overwhelming. He carried 55 percent of the popular vote and all but three states. The Electoral College gave him a lopsided 212–21 margin.

On November 9, 1864, the day following the presidential election, General Grant sent a telegram to the secretary of war with the "official statement of the vote polled in the Army of the Potomac yesterday." The president had carried a majority of the army against their old commander, George McClellan. It was quite possibly the most decisive battle these soldiers and their civilian counterparts had ever fought. The decision at the ballot box put a spike in Confederate hopes that a new government might negotiate a peace in which the Southern states became an independent nation.

The last day of January in the new year 1865 brought a telegram from Ulysses Grant to Abraham Lincoln that was far different in its content from any of their previous exchanges. General Grant forwarded the text of a message received from three representatives from the Confederate government who desired admission to his lines, "to proceed to Washington to hold a conference with President Lincoln upon the subject of the existing war, and with a view of ascertaining upon what terms it may be terminated . . ." It was a high-level delegation: Confederate vice president Alexander Stevens, former U.S. senator R.M.T. Hunter, and assistant secretary of war and former U.S. supreme court justice J.A. Campbell. The president telegraphed instructions to General Grant: "A messenger is coming to you on the business contained in your despatch. Detain the gentlemen in comfortable quarters until he arrives and then act upon the message he brings."

The messenger was Major Thomas Eckert, the head of the War Department Telegraph Office. He carried Lincoln's carefully written instructions regarding what could or could not be said to the Confederate peace commissioners. Major Eckert was the advanceman, sent to ascertain the legitimacy of the Confederates' purpose. The secretary of state, William Seward, was dispatched to conduct the discussions, should Major Eckert's initial dialog prove fruitful.

Lest there be any confusion in the military ranks, the following day, February 1, the president sent the following 14-word telegram to General Grant: "Let nothing which is transpiring, change, hinder, or delay your Military movements, or plans." Grant replied, "Your dispatch received; there will be no armistice . . ."

Later on February 1, the president telegraphed Major Eckert that the secretary of state was on his way. "Call at Fortress Monroe & put yourself under direction of Mr S whom you will find there." Eckert reported in via telegraph at 10:00 that evening that he had told the Confederate commissioners that they should expect to be met "by some person or persons for the purpose of such informal conference." The commissioners' reply, however, was "not satisfactory," Eckert wired. He also reported that the commissioners had taken it upon themselves to contact General Grant with their insistence to proceed to Washington to meet with the president. "I notified them that they could not proceed further unless they complied with the terms expressed in my letter."

"On reading this despatch of Major Eckert I was about to recall him and the Secretary of State," Lincoln wrote in his report on the events to the House of Representatives, "when . . . [a] telegram of Gen Grant to the Secretary of War was shown me." Grant's telegram opined, "I am convinced . . . that their intentions are good and their desire sincere to restore peace and union." Then the military man ventured into political fields: "I fear now their going back without any expression from any one in authority will have a bad influence."

"This despatch of Gen. Grant changed my purpose," the president wrote. He wired Grant, "Say to the gentlemen I will meet them personally at Fortress Monroe as soon as I can get there."

"On the morning of the 3rd, the three gentlemen, Messrs Stephens, Hunter, and Campbell, came aboard of our Steamer and had an interview with the Secretary of State and myself of several hours duration." The president made clear a tri-partite position: (1) the restoration of the national authority, (2) no retreat on slavery and the Emancipation Proclamation, and (3) the disbanding of the Confederate armies. The Confederate representatives did not consent to these terms, nor, as Lincoln subsequently pointed out, did they "declare they *never* would so consent."

On February 4, Secretary of War Stanton wired General Grant, "The President desires me to repeat that nothing transpired, or transpiring with the three gentlemen from Richmond is to cause any change, hindrance or delay, of your Military plans or operations."

The telegraph had allowed Lincoln to coordinate an attempt at peace and reconciliation and to avoid any misunderstanding with his general-in-chief regarding the continuance of military activity during the discussions. Perhaps the telegraph's greatest role in this attempt at peace was how its lightning speed allowed for dialog between General Grant and the president, and how just as quickly Lincoln's reversal of position was communicated to his emissaries. That the telegraph was such an essential part of the whole process was made manifest when the House of Representatives asked for a report on the Hampton Roads peace conference. President Lincoln's report was essentially a cut-and-paste of the telegraph traffic during those important days.

Only a few weeks after the Hampton Roads meetings, the speed of the telegraph allowed Lincoln to once again inject himself into peace overtures from the Confederates. On March 3, during a conference to discuss an exchange of prisoners, Confederate General James Longstreet (who, coincidentally, before the war had been best man at Grant's wedding) indicated to Union general Edward Ord that General Lee was interested in meeting with General Grant to explore an end to the fighting. General Lee followed up with a personal note to General Grant in which Lee recounted Longstreet's description of Ord's comment "that if I desired to have an interview with you on the subject you would not decline, provided I had the authority to act. Sincerely desiring to leave nothing untried which may put an end to the calamities of war, I propose to meet you at such convenient time and place as you may designate with the hope that upon an interchange of views it may be found practicable to submit the subjects of controversy between belligerents to a convention . . ."

The response to General Grant was signed by the secretary of war but written in Lincoln's handwriting. In the telegram the president used a third party's voice to clip General Grant's wings insofar as political decisions are concerned and make it clear the general was to stick to matters military:

> *The President directs me to say to you that he wishes you to have no conference with General Lee unless it be for the capitulation of Gen. Lee's army, or on some minor, and purely, military matter. He instructs me to say that you are not to decide, discuss, or confer upon any political question. Such questions the President holds in his own hands; and will submit them to no military conferences or conventions. Meantime you are to press to the utmost, your military advantage.*

Lincoln's telegram to Grant was sent the day before he was reinaugurated president of the United States. In his inaugural address President Lincoln made clear his interpretation of why the war had occurred: "Both parties deprecated war; but one of them would *make* war rather than let the nation survive; and the other would *accept* war rather than let it perish." The president looked to the war's conclusion and an attitude that might soon prevail: "With malice toward none; with charity for all; with firmness in the right, as God gives us to see the right, let us strive on to finish the work we are in . . ."

TWENTY DAYS AFTER HIS re-inauguration Lincoln arrived at City Point, Virginia, Grant's headquarters along the James River about 10 miles northwest of Petersburg. It was an ersatz village, a massive military encampment with ships tied up at wharves unloading supplies, rough-hewn huts, and tents.

The president arrived in the evening, exchanged formal pleasantries with General Grant, and then retired on board the ship that had transported him from Washington. The first morning at City Point he climbed from the river up to the bluff where Grant had his headquarters. Reaching the headquarters, the president found things quite animated. That morning General Lee's Confederates had attacked the Union line at Fort Stedman in a last ditch attempt to open an escape route. The assault began well, taking Fort Stedman and progressing further, but withered under the Union counterattack.

"[T]here was a little rumpus up the line this morning," Lincoln wired Secretary Stanton at 8:30 that morning. The president went forward to see what the "rumpus" was about. From a hilltop he watched as his troops counterattacked. Shortly before 1:30 that afternoon the president sent a telegram to Stanton datelined "Meade's Hd. Qrs.": "I am here within five miles of the scene of this morning's action. I have nothing to add to what Gen. Meade reports, except that I have seen the prisoners myself." The secretary of war, concerned for the president's safety, admonished Lincoln via reply telegram: "I hope you will remember Gen. Harrison advice to his men at Tippecanoe [during the Indian Wars 50 years earlier], that they 'Can see as well a little further off.' "

The president's time at City Point and environs was spent visiting troops, making hospital calls, and meeting with generals. Much of the time he spent in the adjutant general's hut, the hub of Grant's telegraph operation. As with his time in the War Department telegraph office in Washington, Lincoln devoured the arriving dispatches. On March 29 those reports provided a running commentary of Grant's movement to destroy the Rebel army once and for all.

As Union forces moved on the Rebel's right flank, the telegraph wire moved forward as well. At 11:15 A.M. Grant wired Lincoln from the headquarters of the Second Corps, "Just arrived here 1112 A.M. Nothing heard from the front yet—No firing—I start [forward] in a few minutes. Sheridan got off at 3 this morning."

Another telegram followed: "The 2nd Corps are in the position designated for them today. No opposition has yet been met . . . Nothing heard from Sheridan yet Warren must be in the place laid down for him in orders." Around 5:00 P.M. another Grant telegram datelined "From Gravelley Creek" reported, "The enemy attacked Griffin Div 5" ac near where the Quaker road intersects the Boydtown road about 4 P.m. The enemy were repulsed leaving about 60 prisoners in our hands. There was some loss of life on both sides."

Lincoln responded, "Your three despatches received. From what direction did the enemy come that attacked Griffin? How do things look now?" Grant replied, "Griffin was attacked near where the Quaker road intersects the Boydtown Plank at 5.50 P.M. Warren reports the fighting pretty severe but the enemy repulsed leaving one hundred prisoners in our hands. Warren advanced to Attack at the hour named but found the enemy gone He thinks inside of his Main Works, Warren's Pickets on his left along the Boydtown Plank road reported the enemys [*sic*] Cavalry moving Northwest & they thought, Sheridan after them. Sheridan was in Dinwiddie this P.M."

The president, concerned about what might be happening at other points along the extended Union line, wired General Godfrey Weitzel, commanding the 25th Corps, "What, if any thing, have you observed, on your front to-day?" At 8:20 that evening General Weitzel responded that Confederate cavalry were heading toward Petersburg. Just after midnight he updated the report with information that deserters said there was no change in the Rebel line.

At 7:30 in the evening on March 30, the president reported in to the secretary of war. "I begin to feel that I ought to be at home, and yet I dislike to leave without seeing nearer to the end of General Grant's present movement."

"Gen. Grant's present movement" was heading toward a decisive battle at Five Forks two days later. At 12:50 P.M. on the last day of March, Grant wired Lincoln from his headquarters at Gravelley Run. There had been "much hard fighting this morning," as the result of a Rebel attack. "We are now about to take the offensive at that point, and I hope will more than recover the lost ground." That evening at 7:00 Grant, wiring this time from a more advanced position, announced the successful result of the counterattack, adding, "I will send you a rebel flag captured by Our troops in driving the Enemy back."

The president, acting as Washington's official reporter, telegraphed these messages to Secretary Stanton, adding, "Judging by the two points from which General Grant telegraphs, I infer that he moved his headquarters about a mile . . ." Later that day, at 9:30 P.M., Grant had a further report, this time datelined, "From Dabney Mills." "Sheridan has had hard fighting today—I can only communicate with him by courier at dark. He was hotly engaged at Dinwiddie. I am very anxious to hear the result. We'll let you know when I do hear. All else is apparently favorable at this time and I hope that will prove so also. Infantry has been sent down the Boydtown Road to his assistance."

The sentence about infantry being sent would prove decisive.

The calendar turned from March to April. Grant continued to keep Lincoln informed from the front; then at 5:50 P.M. on April 1, Grant forwarded a message from an aide who had been sent to determine Sheridan's activities: "Devins Div of Cavalry had just Carried the barricade at the five forks Held by Picketts Div . . . The whole 5" Corps is now moving from here to five forks & Gen S. will attack the enemy with every thing . . . Our men have never fought better." Five Forks not only was a critical intersection on a major artery feeding Richmond, but also was a key position for defending the Southside Railroad, an essential link with the world outside that was of special importance if Lee was to save his army and withdraw from Petersburg.

The morning of April 2 found Union forces out of their trenches and advancing all along the Confederate line protecting Petersburg. It was Sunday. A courier walked down the aisle during the service at St. Paul's Church in Richmond and handed Jefferson Davis a message. It was from Robert E. Lee; the lines had broken and the Southside Railroad was cut. An ashen Davis departed the church immediately. Subsequently he and other leaders of the Confederate government departed Richmond.

That same Sunday morning, at 7:45, the president telegraphed his wife and the secretary of war. "This morning Gen. Grant, having ordered an attack along the whole line telegraphs as follows 'Both Wright and Parke got through the enemies lines. The battle now rages furiously. Sheridan with his Cavalry, the 5th. Corps, & Miles Division of the 2nd. Corps . . . is now sweeping down from the West. All now looks highly favorable."

At 11:00 A.M. the president was back on the wire to Stanton: "Despatches frequently coming in. All going finely. Parke, Wright, and Ord . . . have all broken through the enemy's intrenched lines . . . Sheridan, with his own cavalry, Fifth Corps, and part of the Second, is coming in from the west on the enemy's flank, and Wright is already tearing up the South Side Railroad." One can only imagine the exuberance in the telegraph hut as reports from the many parts of the advancing army tumbled in. It had been 10 months ago that the Army of the Potomac had been dug in before Petersburg; now they were going into the city and beyond.

At 2:00 P.M. Lincoln wired Stanton, quoting a Grant telegram, "We are now closing around the works of the line immediately enveloping Petersburg. All looks remarkably well. I have not yet heard from Sheridan." For the rest of the day Lincoln read Grant's telegrams to others. That evening he wired his general-in-chief, "Allow me to tender to you, and all with you, the nation's grateful thanks for this additional, and magnificent success. At your kind suggestion, I think I will visit you to-morrow."

On the morning of April 3 the president boarded a special train to take him into Petersburg to meet with General Grant. While *en route* a telegram was received at Army Headquarters from General Weitzel: "We took Richmond at 8.15 this morning." Presumably, at their meeting Lincoln mentioned to Grant his desire to go into the former Confederate capital; for later that day the general telegraphed a staff officer, "Say to the President that an officer and escort will attend him, but as to myself I start toward the Danville road with the army. I want to cut off as much of Lee's army as possible."

The following morning the president boarded the ship that had brought him from Washington, and been his headquarters at City Point, and sailed up the James River to Richmond. On April 4, 1865—exactly one month after his re-inauguration—Abraham Lincoln, president of the United States, was sitting at the recently vacated desk of Confederate president Jefferson Davis. That evening he slept at Richmond aboard a ship anchored in the James River.

Back at Army Headquarters the following day, Lincoln and Grant stayed in telegraphic communication as the Union army pursued what remained of Lee's army. The morning of April 6, Grant forwarded a message from General Sheridan reporting that he had "routed them handsomely" and was "still pressing on with both cavalry and infantry." Sheridan closed his message with, "If the thing is pressed I think that Lee will surrender."

The reports continued to flow in from General Grant to the president. After one string of such messages describing Union successes, Lincoln wired his general-in-chief, "Gen. Sheridan says 'If the thing is pressed I think that Lee will surrender.' Let the *thing* be pressed."

With Richmond in hand and Robert E. Lee on the run, President Lincoln departed for Washington the evening of April 8. What he did not realize, and would not learn until he docked at the capital the following evening, was that about 14 hours later, on April 9, 1865, at around 1:00 in the afternoon, Ulysses S. Grant accepted the surrender of the Army of Northern Virginia from Robert E. Lee.

On the morning of April 14 Robert Lincoln arrived in Washington in time to have breakfast with his father at the White House. A captain on Grant's staff, Robert had been present at the Appomattox surrender (although not in the room). No doubt he regaled his father with a firsthand account of the fateful event.

Later that morning, as usual, the president went to the telegraph office. General Grant, who had arrived in town the preceding day, had begged off on the president's invitation to join him at the theater that evening. Secretary Stanton, who knew of rumored threats against the president's life, urged Lincoln to give up the theater outing. When he would not, Stanton urged that he should, at least, take someone along for security.

Standing in the telegraph office, Lincoln indicated that his choice for the security role was the head of its operations, Major Thomas Eckert. "I have seen Eckert break five pokers, one after another, over his arm, and I am thinking he would be the kind of man to go with me this evening," the president told Stanton. Knowing Stanton's displeasure with the president's outing, and determined not to be an enabler, Eckert declined on the grounds that he had work to do that evening. "Very well," Lincoln said to the telegraph man, "I shall take Major Rathbone along, because Stanton insists upon having some one to protect me; but I should much rather have you, Major, since I know you can break a poker over your arm."

At 10:20 that evening John Wilkes Booth entered the president's box at Ford's Theatre.

CHAPTER ELEVEN

"NOW HE BELONGS TO THE AGES"

THE WONDER OF THE STORIES we have just seen is how Abraham Lincoln, at a moment of such intense national and personal stress, seized upon telegraph technology and harnessed it to his purposes. Such awe is magnified by the total absence of any precedent in the use of electronic communications as a tool of national leadership.

We have seen Lincoln's application of the telegraph progress through three phases: from the first 14 months in office when sometimes an entire month would pass without a single telegram; to the next 22 months, beginning in May 1862, when the telegraph allowed the president to recast his leadership and become directly involved with military affairs; to the last 13 months of his life, when instinct combined with the experiences of the previous three years to build the model for electronic management. The story of Lincoln's experience with the telegraph is yet another example of his capacity for growth, including his ability to change as circumstances (including technology) warranted.

We are the beneficiaries of Lincoln's electronic evolution. The passage of time tends to dull the absolute miracle represented by the restoration of a *United* States and the simultaneous eradication of America's Original Sin of slavery. Beyond these miraculous achievements, however, Abraham Lincoln was also fighting for the ideal of a democratic republic—a concept, he would remind us, only a bit more than four score years old—that was still very much an experiment. Had Lincoln not prevailed, the ability of a minority to walk away from a government any time they lost an election would have been entrenched. Whatever government might have survived a Southern victory would have been prey to the next set of divisive issues.

That Lincoln had the magnetic telegraph to assist in his crucial crusade is one of the great blessings of historical Providence. Lincoln's embrace of electronic messages becomes even more poignant when compared to Confederate president Jefferson Davis, who also used the telegraph but never as effectively as Lincoln. Part of the difference, we know, lies in the self-inflicted wound administered by the prewar South's decisions to discourage industrialization and constrain the introduction of new technologies. Yet it was more than the total miles of wire that differentiated their electronic leadership.

The telegraph was simply one more item on a list of areas in which Abraham Lincoln outperformed the president of the Confederacy. Jefferson Davis, a graduate of West Point, former U.S. secretary of war and U.S. senator, seemed typecast to lead the rebellion's government. It was the frontier rail-splitter, however, who instinctively—and better—understood national leadership, including how a new technology could be utilized to enhance that leadership.

It is hard to overemphasize the stunning breakthrough represented by Lincoln's adoption of the telegraph as a bridge between civilian and military leadership. From a 21st-century perspective with over 150 years of electronic communications under our belts, Lincoln's actions appear logical and straightforward. President Lincoln, however, made his discoveries in a world where electricity was an abstract concept; at a time when the federal government was just advancing beyond clerks queuing up at Washington's central telegraph office; and when no national figure had ever used electronic messages in the exercise of his leadership. In that environment, Abraham Lincoln's embrace of the new technology was not just early adoption, it was inspired.

The telegraph was only a technology, however. The manner in which Lincoln adapted the raw capability of electronic messaging is what transformed the dots and dashes into an effective leadership tool. The outbound extension of his voice was the obvious application of a technology designed for the purpose of sending a message rapidly over great distances. It was how Lincoln used the traffic coming from the other direction—the inbound reports, including those not addressed to him—that broke new ground. By reviewing the contents of the telegraph clerk's drawer "down to the raisins," the president turned the telegraph into a window on activities spread over a vast geographic area and an insight into the thinking at his generals' headquarters.

Most important, however, is that once Lincoln placed himself at the information nexus, he acted on the knowledge thus garnered to participate in the distant events he was observing. When Lincoln inserted himself, whether invited or not, the leadership dynamic changed. "If I do not misunderstand Gen. Meade's last despatch," Lincoln wrote General-in-Chief Halleck in September 1863, "[he] desires your views and those of the government, as to what he shall do." The initial inquiry came from Meade to Halleck, yet Lincoln did not hesitate to insert himself. Who knows how the ever-reticent Halleck would have replied, but the president preempted him: "My opinion is that he should move upon Lee at once in a manner of general attack, leaving to developments, whether he will make a real attack," Lincoln told Halleck, who forwarded the instructions directly to General Meade.

The powers-that-be did not always appreciate Lincoln's evolution into more than a titular commander-in-chief. The generals lamented the loss of their field autonomy. Newspaper commentators criticized Lincoln's active engagement. "Some well-meaning newspapers advise the President to keep his fingers out of the military pie,"

Lincoln's secretary John Hay confided to his diary in September 1863. Then Hay countered that opinion with an observation that this investigation certainly bears out: "The truth is that if he did, the pie would be a sorry mess."

When it came to expressing himself, Abraham Lincoln had a hierarchy of communications. Just because it was possible to say something with lightning speed did not mean the electronic medium was the best means of communicating. The man who pioneered the use of electronic messages nonetheless placed them on the lowest rung of his communications ladder.

At the pinnacle of Lincoln's communications hierarchy was face-to-face dialog. Nothing was better than a personal meeting. The president made himself available for such sessions, and it was the heart of his Management-By-Walking-Around style.

The telegraph's information-gathering helped Lincoln determine when such face-to-face sessions might be necessary with his generals; then he used the device to set up the meetings. In July of 1862 he went to the peninsula. The following October he met with General McClellan at Antietam. The following month he journeyed to General Burnside's headquarters. Four times in April and May of 1863 the president met with General Hooker. Twice after the 1864 offensive began he sat down with General Grant; once going to Grant and the other time making it clear Grant needed to come to see him. Abraham Lincoln operated most comfortably at retail—exchanging ideas, reading nuances, and delivering messages as can only be done best in person.

Failing the ability to meet in person, the next highest tier in Lincoln's communications hierarchy was a letter.

"I write you more fully than I could communicate by the wires," he telegraphed General William Rosecrans in 1863.

"I will write on the subject within a day or two" said an 1864 telegram to Tennessee governor Andrew Johnson.

Lincoln realized that an electronic message was not always the appropriate medium for the fullness of what he wanted to say. If the message was not of timely importance, or if it required subtlety that normally could be conveyed through the dialog of a face-to-face meeting, then a thoughtful exposition written in his own hand was the next most acceptable alternative. While Lincoln's telegrams were short and to the point, his letters that substituted for meetings were more like legal briefs: cogent presentations that substituted rational organization for the kind of understanding that is possible in a person-to-person exchange.

The president also recognized the power of a personal note over the impersonal electronic message. His handwritten letter to General Grant upon the capture of Vicksburg is an example. Lincoln could have dashed off a telegram of congratulations to General Grant. Instead, he picked up a pen and wrote a gracious and humble letter that concluded, "I now wish to make the personal acknowledgement that you were right, and I was wrong." It was a message made all the more powerful by the fact that it was from Lincoln's pen directly to his general's hand and not transcribed by a telegraph clerk.

Lincoln did not jump to respond electronically, even when it was a telegraph message that triggered his desire to respond in the first place. The letter to General George Meade after the failure to pursue and destroy Lee's Rebel army post-Gettysburg illustrates both the hierarchy of communications—he could have zipped off a telegram—as well as his awareness that words written on paper can have a more powerful impact than the same things said verbally.

The instantaneous nature of the telegraph made such self-control even more important. An electronic message dashed off in pique contains the great potential to escalate the tension at both ends of the line. Thus, when the president drafted his "it makes me doubt whether I am awake or dreaming" telegram to General Burnside for failing to assist General Rosecrans at Chattanooga, he immediately thought better of it. Writing "Not sent" on the back of the telegraph form, the president filed away words that would not help him in the current situation. Lincoln had the technological capability to instantaneously dispatch his emotions, yet he recognized that just because a capability exists, it is not always necessary or wise to exercise it.

Abraham Lincoln's telegrams exploited the power of words. His messages were short, to the point, and used words that in themselves delivered a message.

Guiding and supporting General Grant in the tough summer of 1864: "Hold on with a bull-dog grip, and chew & choke."

Shutting down General Hooker's ill-conceived ideas in 1863: "I would not take any risk of being entangled upon the river, like an ox jumped over a fence, and liable to be torn by dogs, front and rear, without a fair chance to gore one way and kick the other."

Reminding Grant of his management issues as Early threatened the North: "Watch it every day, every hour, and force it."

Pushing to hasten the surrender of Robert E. Lee: "Gen. Sheridan says, 'If the thing is pressed I think Lee will surrender.' Let the *thing* be pressed."

The president seldom minced words with his generals, and he urged them to act likewise. While he was refereeing the June 1863 squabble between Hooker and Halleck, Lincoln wrote to General Hooker (again reinforcing the hierarchy of communications for such a sensitive message), "If you and he would use the same frankness to one another, and to me, that I use to both of you, there would be no difficulty."

Such frankness permeated the telegram that eventually was sent to General Burnside regarding the Chattanooga situation. When Burnside played bureaucratic games with Lincoln, the president responded, "My order to you meant simply that you should save Rosecrans from being crushed out."

Because words mattered to Lincoln, he responded positively when others exercised the same rhetorical discipline. Commenting on the telegraphic dialog with Colonel Herman Haupt during the Battle of Second Manassas (Bull Run), John Hay wrote that Lincoln was "struck with the business-like character of his [Haupt's] despatch, telling in the fewest words the information most sought for, which contrasted so strongly with the weak whiney vague and incorrect dispatches of the whilom General in chief [George McClellan]."

Ulysses Grant's relationship with the president was probably strengthened by the manner in which he composed his telegrams. General Grant's direct and firm communications reinforced the confidence his commander-in-chief had placed in him.

Lincoln's telegrams were seldom more than a handful of sentences. While some saw the blank telegram form as an invitation to an essay, for Lincoln it was all about getting down to business. Garry Wills, in his description of Lincoln's most immortal words, the Gettysburg Address, commented on their "telegraphic eloquence," devoid of excess words, staccato in rhythm, yet with a clear and unmistakable message. It was a style, Wills observed, which "did not come naturally, but had to be worked at."

One can easily envision the scene described by the telegraph office manager of Abraham Lincoln, seated at the desk next to the window overlooking Pennsylvania Avenue, taking up his pen or pencil, smoothing out the sheet of paper, and writing slowly and deliberately with an occasional thoughtful glance out the window in search of just the right way to convey his thoughts. He was communicating via an impersonal medium, yet Lincoln's careful use of words conveyed information beyond their black-letter definitions.

AS ABRAHAM LINCOLN DREW his last breath, Secretary Edwin Stanton observed, "Now he belongs to the ages." This immortality resulted in a never-ending examination of Abraham Lincoln; who he was, and just how he pulled off the miracle of saving the national union. For as long as such inquiries have been made, his telegrams have been scrutinized for the purpose of defining what happened. As we have just seen, however, Lincoln's telegrams themselves are a powerful story of a leader and a new technology coming together at precisely the appropriate moment.

All of these wonderful stories continue to live in their applicability to our on-line world of today. To repeat a thesis of this book, Abraham Lincoln developed the model for modern electronic leadership without text, tutor, or tradition for guidance. In the process of using the telegraph so that the Union might be preserved, however, Lincoln bequeathed to today's users of electronic communications precisely the kind of historical guidance he did not have. Abraham Lincoln in the telegraph office is the seminal story of electronic leadership, and a story that continues to echo today.

NOTES

Abbreviations Used in the Notes:

CW	Roy Basler, ed., *The Collected Works of Abraham Lincoln,* Rutgers University Press, 1953.
CWDBD	E. B. Long, *The Civil War Day by Day,* DaCapo Press reprint.
LDBD	Earl Schenck Miers, *Lincoln Day by Day,* Morningside edition, 1991.
LC	Library of Congress, *The Abraham Lincoln Papers,* transcribed and annotated by the Lincoln Studies Center, Knox College, Galesburg, Illinois. Available at http://memory.loc.gov/ammem/alhtml/alhome.html.
OR	*The War of Rebellion: A Compilation of the Official Records of the Union and Confederate Armies,* 128 vols., Government Printing Office, 1880–1901. Available at http://cdl.library.cornell.edu/moa/browse.monographs/waro.html.

Introduction

PAGE

xv The term "T-mail" was first introduced to me by Jim Walker in a 2000 letter. Seeing the telegrams several years later brought back that memory.

xvi As we will see, the Civil War was not the first wartime application of the telegraph, but it was the first time the telegraph played such a pervasive role.

xvii over 135 billion e-mails: The Radicati Group, cited in *New York Times,* "Got 2 Extra Hours for Your E-Mail?" November 10, 2005.

xix The first e-mail message: Ray Tomlinson, *The First Network Email,* http://openmap.bbn.cpm/~tomlinson/ray/firstemailmain.html.

xix CompuServe as first general public e-mail platform, see: http://www.livinginternet.com/e/ei.htm.

xxi The telegraph was an electronic network of binary on/off signals. While Internet Protocol (IP) networks have evolved far beyond this rudimentary application, they are at their core derivative electronic networks of binary on/off signals.

Chapter One: Electronic Leadership

PAGE

1 "What became . . .": *CW,* vol. V, p. 395.

3 General Scott taking a nap, see: Ernest B. Furguson, *Freedom Rising,* Knopf, 2004, p. 20.

3 "Lincoln hardly left his seat . . .": David Homer Bates, *Lincoln in the Telegraph Office,* University of Nebraska Press, 1995, p. 88.

3 The Telegraph Office as Situation Room, see: Eliot Cohen, *Supreme Command,* The Free Press, 2002, p. 28.

4 The French had used optical *télégraphé* (from which the word "telegraph" derives) at the time of the Revolution. The British used a magnetic telegraph in the Crimean War in 1857 as a means of connecting field headquarters. Never before, however, had there been such an ability to connect a military force in the field with the national government.

5 Extension of telegraph to government buildings, see: Bates, p. 35.

6 Patent no. 6469, May 22, 1849. A scale model of the invention is on display in the Smithsonian Institution in Washington, D.C.

6 "the completest change . . .": Jacques Barzun, *From Dawn to Decadence,* HarperCollins, 2000, p. 539.

6 The story of the Rock Island Bridge case, see: Sarah Gordon, *Passage to Union,* Elephant Paperback edition, 1997, p. 115.

7 "not to be kicked about . . .": *Hurd v. Rock Island Railroad Company,* U.S. Circuit Court, Northern District of Illinois, August 1857. The jury could not reach a verdict (an indication of the mixed emotions as-

sociated with the changes being imposed by the railroad). Fortunately for Lincoln's client, however, a hung jury was as good as a win.

7 "All creation . . .": *CW,* vol. II, pp. 437–39.

8 Lincoln's relationship with Baker began when they practiced law in Illinois. They grew so close that Lincoln's second son, who died in 1853, was named Edward Baker Lincoln. Baker had ridden with the president-elect to the inauguration where he introduced him prior to the oath of office.

8 McClellan's failure to discuss the Balls Bluff telegram with the president, see: Charles Ross, *Trial by Fire: Science, Technology and the Civil War,* White Mane Books, 2000, p. 151.

8–9 Under the blotter story, see: Bates, pp. 94–96.

9 Regarding the USMTC: Act of January 31, 1862, *Congressional Globe, 37th Congress, 2nd session,* 1862, vol. 32, pp. 334–35, and *OR,* Series 3, vol. 1, p. 889.

9–10 Equipment left at army headquarters, see: Ross, p. 152.

10 "His tall, homely form . . .": Bates, p. 7.

10 "There only was he comparatively free . . .": Bates, p. 137.

10 "take his pen . . .": Bates, p. 282.

11 "His thoughts by day . . .": Nicolay & Hay, cited in Bates, p. xiv.

11 Description of leaning over the telegraph clerk, see: Bates, Introduction by James Rawley, p. xiv.

11 "Lincoln's habit . . .": Bates, p. 41.

11–12 "So, when I reach the message . . .": Bates, p. 41.

12 "I have seen . . .": *CW,* vol. VII, p. 499.

13 "The President has more nerve . . .": Horace Porter, *Campaigning With Grant,* Bantam Books, 1991, p. 195.

13 Description of MBWA: Furguson, p. 106.

14 Hooker floating trial balloon, see: *OR,* Series 1, vol. 27 (Part I), p. 30.

14 "Yours of today . . .": *CW,* vol. VI, p. 249.

14 Hooker's deal with Lincoln, see: John F. Marszalek, *Commander of All Lincoln's Armies: A Life of General Henry W. Halleck,* Harvard University Press, 2004, p. 166.

14 "The foregoing . . .": *OR,* Series I, vol. 227 (Part II), pp. 31–32.

15 "His Excellency . . .": *OR,* Series I, vol. 27 (Part I), pp. 34–35.

15 "If left to me . . .": *CW,* vol. VI, p. 257.

15 "The President has just referred . . .": *OR,* Series I, vol. 27 (Part I), p. 35.

15 "This morning . . .": *CW,* vol. VIII, p. 384.

15–16 "I congratulate . . .": *LC.*
16 "I will take care . . .": *CW,* vol. VIII, p. 385.

Chapter Two: Messages by Lightning

PAGE

17 "I have the pleasure . . .": Thaddeus S.C. Lowe to Abraham Lincoln, June 16, 1861, *LC.*
17 Description of Joseph Henry, see: Ross, p. 144.
17 For a description of the early developments of the telegraph, see: Tom Standage, *The Victorian Internet,* Berkley Books, 1998; *Scots* magazine reference, p. 17.
18 Morse and Henry's relays, see: Harold Evans, *They Made America,* Little Brown & Company, 2004, p. 72.
18 Henry's failure to patent, see: Ross, p. 145.
18 Morse's pilgrimage: Evans, p. 74.
19 Morse's story is told well in: Kenneth Silverman, *Lightning Man,* Alfred A. Knopf, 2003, (his strong beliefs, p. 396), and Carleton Mabee, *The American Leonardo,* Purple Mountain Press reprint, 2000 (House Commerce Committee story, p. 210).
19 Regarding the shifting political winds, see: Paul Starr, *Creation of the Modern Media,* Basic Books, 2005, p. 161.
20 House vote, see: Silverman, p. 221.
20 The telegraph innovation less welcome in the South, see: Starr, p. 161.
20–21 Morse's return from Europe and "flash of Genius," see: Evans, p. 71; development of dots and dashes, see: Mabee, p. 149.
21 "4030" coding: http://speedwell.org/tel/tel.html.
21 Final passage of legislation, see: Mabee, p. 260.
22 Fifteen percent capacity, see: Starr, p. 162.
22 Warning about clergy, see: Robert Luther Thompson, *Wiring a Continent,* Princeton University Press, 1947, p. 26.
23 Telegraph line revenues, see: Thompson, p. 32.
23 "The use of an instrument so powerful . . .": *Report of the Postmaster General,* Ex. Doc. No. 2, 29th Cong., 1st session, 860. Cited in Thompson, p. 33.
23 Change in Congressional attitude, see: Starr, pp. 163–64.
23–24 Morse's growth plan, see: Thompson, p. 39.

24 Growth in telegraph mileage, see: Thompson, pp. 240–41 (chart). Although precise figures are unavailable, the 1852 Census Report states that an additional 10,000 miles were under construction.

24 "No invention of modern times . . .": Standage, p. 57.

25 "Of all the innovations . . .": Albro Martin, *Railroads Triumphant,* Oxford University Press, 1992, p. 23.

25 Charles Minot story, see: Martin, p. 24.

26 Living in the absence of information, see: Irwin Lebow, *Information Highways & Byways,* IEEE Press, 1995, p. xiii.

26 Time for news to travel, see: Menachem Blondheim, *News Over the Wires,* Harvard University Press, 1994. p. 17 (chart).

26 Founding Fathers' concerns, see: Sarah H. Gordon, *Passage to Union,* Ivan R. Dee Publisher, 1997, p. 4.

27 Southern response to railroads, see: Gordon, pgs. 5, 39.

28 John Calhoun opposition, see: Thompson, p. 51.

28 Northern vs. Southern telegraph infrastructure, see: Thompson, pp. 110–13.

29 "the right of each State to do as it pleases . . .": *CW,* vol. III, p. 323.

Chapter Three: The Telegraph Creates a President

PAGE

31 Lincoln's first exposure to telegraph, see: Bates, p. 4.

32 "The telegraph gives . . .": *New York Times,* September 9, 1859.

32–33 Lincoln speech at Cooper Union: Harold Holzer, *Lincoln at Cooper Union,* Simon & Schuster, 2004, pgs, 1, 5, 145.

34 "The difficulty . . .": *CW,* vol. III, p. 555.

34 "I authorize no bargains . . .": Carl Sandburg, *Abraham Lincoln: The Prairie Years and The War Years* (one volume edition), Harvest Books, 1982, p. 172.

34 "whole no 466 . . ." Benjamin P. Thomas, *Abraham Lincoln,* Barnes & Noble reprint, 1994, p. 214.

35 "We did it . . .": Sandburg, p. 174.

35 "for I then felt . . .": David Herbert Donald, *Lincoln,* Simon & Schuster, 1995, p. 255.

35 "telegraph me . . .": *CW,* vol. IV, p. 136.

36 "Telegraph, me instantly . . .": *CW,* vol. IV, p. 170.

36 Confederate commissioners using telegraph, see: Sandburg, p. 228.
37 "I am directed . . .": *CW,* vol. IV, p. 323.
37 "Positively determined . . .": *OR,* Series 1, vol. I, p. 187.
37 Jefferson Davis's decision, see: Sandburg, p. 229.
37–38 Organization of military telegraph, see: William R. Plum, *The Military Telegraph,* Ayer Publishers reprint, 2000, vol. I, p. 66.
39 "the first field telegraph that ever advanced . . .": Ross, p. 152.
39 "Win your spurs . . .": Steven W. Sears, ed., *The Civil War Papers of George B. McClellan,* DaCapo Press, 1992, p. 56.
39 "I think you should have attacked . . .": Sears, p. 58.
39 McClellan's ability to change plans, see: Edward Hagerman, *The American Civil War and the Origins of Modern Warfare,* Midland Books, 1992, p. 37.
39 "brief but brilliant campaign": Shelby Foote, *The Civil War: A Narrative,* Vantage Books, 11986, vol. I, p. 68.
39 "Our success is complete . . .": Sears, p. 56.
41 "The secession question had long since . . .": Foote, vol. I, p. 89.
41 "Will the President read my urgent dispatch . . .": Sandburg, p. 262.
41 "Been answering your messages . . .": *CW,* vol. IV, p. 484.
41 "Start your regiments . . .": *CW,* vol. IV, p. 485.
41 "Pardon us . . .": *CW,* vol. IV, p. 499.
42 Union telegraph mileage, see: Plum, vol. II, p. 374, *Annual Report of the US Military Telegraph Corps for the Fiscal Year Ending June 30, 1865.*
42 Confederate telegraph mileage, see: Thompson, p. 395 (footnote).
43 Jefferson Davis's use of telegraph, see: Ross, p. 164.
43 "all men as if they were idiotic insects": Foote, p. 393.
44 "I want the particulars . . ." and "It is impossible": *CW,* vol. IV, p. 560.

Chapter Four: Electronic Breakout

PAGE

46 "should not yet be disturbed . . .": *CW,* vol. V, pp. 86–87.
46 "I write you tonight": Ibid.
46 "Please do not lose time . . .": *CW,* vol. V, p. 87.
46 "Have arms gone forward . . . :" *CW,* vol. V, p. 90.
47 "I am not competent . . .": *CW,* vol. V, p. 91.
47 "Please name as early a day . . .": *CW,* vol. V, pp. 91–92.

47 "fearful that his command . . .": *CWDBD,* p. 160.
48 "leave said city entirely secure": *OR,* Series 1, vol. 5, p. 50.
49 "No one but McClellan . . .": Foote, p. 403.
50 "Is anything to be done?": *CW,* vol. V, p. 203.
51 "Our success is brilliant": Sears, p. 254.
51 Lincoln was livid, see: Thomas, p. 319.
52 *Merrimac* sallies forth: Ibid.
52 Lincoln reconnoiters, see: *LDBD,* p. 110.
52 "So has ended a brilliant week . . .": Thomas, p. 320.
52 "I beg that you will . . .": Sears, p. 264.
53 "I am still unwilling . . .": *CW,* p. 216.
53 "advance steadily & carefully . . .": Sears, p. 271.
53 "can reach you . . .": *CW,* p. 226.
53 "Whatever movement you make . . .": Foote, p. 423.
54 "The exposed position . . .": *CW,* vol. V, p. 230.
55 "Gen Fremont has been ordered . . .": *CW,* vol. V., p. 232.
55 "I have ordered General Shields . . .": *OR,* Series 1, vol. 12 (Part III), pp. 220–21.
55 "I am highly gratified . . .": *CW,* vol. V, p. 233.
55 "We have so thinned . . .": *CW,* vol. V, p. 231.
55 "In consequence of Gen. Banks' critical position . . .": *CW,* vol. V, p. 232.
56 "Please inform us . . .": *CW,* vol. V, p. 234.
56 "Could you send scouts . . .": *CW,* vol. V, p. 234.
56 "once more swung around . . .": Foote, vol. I, p. 435.
56 "I think the movement is a general . . ." ("defence" in original): *CW,* vol. V, p. 235.
57 "The object of the Enemys movements . . ." ("Enemys" in original): *LC*
57 "Can you get near enough . . .": *CW,* vol. V, pp. 239–40.
57 "Hope very soon . . .": *CW,* vol. V, p. 240.
57 "this movement . . .": *CW,* vol. V, p. 230.
57 "will move as ordered . . .": *LC*
57 "Do not lose a minute . . .": *CW,* vol. V, p. 231.
58 "I see you are at Moorefield . . .": *CW,* vol. V, p. 243.
58 "It is the policy and duty . . .": Sears, p. 279.
58 "and last I must be the Judge . . .": *CW,* vol. V, p. 245.
59 "I think the evidence now preponderates . . .": *CW,* vol. V, 246.
59 "Gen. McDowell's advance . . .": *CW,* vol. V, p. 247.
59 "Where *is* your force . . .": *CW,* vol. V, p. 250.
60 "For this additional reason . . .": *CW,* vol. V, p. 251.

60 "It seems the game is before you": *CW,* pgs. 250, 252.
60 "A circle of circumference . . .": *CW,* vol. V, p. 254.
60 "Shield's advance . . .": *CW,* vol. V, p. 255.
61 Jackson's 35-mile march, see: Foote, p. 453.
61 "Terrible storms . . .": Foote, p. 454.
61 "Anxious to know . . .": *CW,* vol. V, 258.
62 "Halt at Harrisonberg . . .": *CW,* vol. V, p. 264.
63 "I would be glad to have permission . . .": Sears, p. 304.
63 "I would be glad to have your views . . .": *CW,* vol. V, 279.
63 "I regret . . .": Sears, p. 310.
64 "The probability . . .": *CW,* vol. V, p. 286.
64 McClellan to Stanton telegram, see: Sears, p. 323.
64 "I am not responsible . . .": *CW,* vol. V, p. 289.

Chapter Five: After the Breakout

PAGE

68 "Any news . . .": *CW,* vol. V, p. 396.
69 "Do you hear anything . . .": *CW,* vol. V, p. 395.
69 "I was cut off . . .": Herman Haupt, *Reminiscences of General Herman Haupt,* Ayer reprint, 2000, p. 97.
69 "Two operators from Manassas . . .": *LC.*
70 "Intelligence received . . .": Ibid.
70 "What became . . .": *CW,* vol. V, p. 395.
70 "Our latest information . . .": *LC.*
71 "Is the railroad bridge . . .": *CW,* vol. V, p. 395.
71 "I reminded the General . . .": Haupt, p. 98.
71 "After sending this telegram . . .": Haupt, p. 99.
72 "I am much gratified . . .": *LC.*
72 "The President was in . . .": Haupt, p. 75.
72 "Yours received . . .": *CW,* vol. V, p. 397.
72–73 "One of Colonel Scammon's . . .": *LC.*
73 "The latest news . . .": Haupt, p. 110.
73 "What news . . .": *CW,* vol. V, p. 399.
73–74 "General Pope was . . .": *LC.*
74 "I am clear . . .": Sears, p. 416.
75 "I think your first alternative . . .": *CW,* vol. V, p. 399.

75 "The President was never so wrathful . . .": Michael Burlingame and John R. Turner Ettlinger, eds., *Inside Lincoln's White House: The Complete War Diary of John Hay,* Southern Illinois University Press, 1999, p. 37.
75 "What news?": *CW,* vol. V, p. 400.
75 "Firing this morning . . .": *LC.*
76 "Please send me . . .": *CW,* vol. V, p. 401.
76 "Our operator . . .": *LC.*
77 "Well, John . . .": Burlingame & Ettlinger, p. 38.
77 "What news?": *CW,* vol. V, p. 402.
77 "No news received yet . . .": Haupt, p. 124.
77 "It is due . . .": Burlingame & Ettlinger, p. 38.
78 "There is one man . . .": Burlingame & Ettlinger, p. 38.
78 "I was received . . .": Haupt, p. 135.
78 "We must use what tools we have": Burlingame & Ettlinger, p. 38.
79 "advancing up the Shenandoah . . .": *CW,* vol. V, p. 409.
79 "Where is Gen. Bragg?": *CW,* vol. V, p. 408–9.
79 "What degree of certainty . . .": *CW,* vol. V, p. 409.
79 "How certain . . .": *CW,* vol. V, p. 409.
79 "Do you know . . .": *CW,* vol. V, p. 410.
80 "How does it look now?": *CW,* vol. V, p. 412.
80 "all the troops . . .": *CW,* vol. V, p. 415.
80 "Please consider . . ." ("enemies" in original): Ibid.
80 "Your message . . .": Ibid.
80–81 "How does it look now?" ("advices" in original): *CW,* vol. V, p. 418.
81 "I have the whole rebel force . . .": Sears, p. 453.
81–82 "the Enemy . . .": *CW,* vol. V, p. 426.
82 "God bless you . . .": Ibid.
82 "I have the honor to report . . .": Sears, p. 470.
83 Potential march on Washington, see: Donald, p. 385.
83 "Already this Potomac Army clique . . .": Thomas, p. 346.
83 Rumor tied to Major John Key, see: Geoffrey Perret, *Lincoln's War,* Random House, 2004, p. 220.
83–84 "seemed wrung . . .": *CW,* vol. V, p. 486.
84 "The will of God prevails . . .": *CW,* vol. V, p. 403.
84–85 Emancipation Proclamation: *CW,* vol. V, p. 433.
85 "What I did . . .": *LDBD,* p. 141.
85 "would rapidly disintegrate . . .": Sears, p. 344.
85 "Hatch—Hatch . . .": *CWDBD,* p. 143.

85–86 "I am instructed . . .": *OR,* Series 1, vol. 19 (Part I), p. 10.
86 "I congratulate you . . .": *CW,* vol. V, p. 453.
86 "Cannot tell the number of dead yet . . .": *LC.*
86 "this division has done so much . . .": *LC.*
86–87 "You cannot have reflected seriously . . .": *CW,* vol. V, p. 452.
87 "Terrible battle yesterday . . .": *OR,* Series 1, vol. 16 (Part II), p. 602.
87 "Please send any news . . .": *CW,* vol. V, p. 457.
87 "We are very anxious . . .": *CW,* vol. V, p. 458.
87 "Battle was fought on Wednesday . . .": *LC.*
87–88 "You remember my speaking to you . . .": *CWs,* vol. V, p. 460.
88 "I have been unable to give your Excellency . . .": *LC.*
88 "I have just read . . .": *CW,* vol. V, p. 474.
88 "Yours in reply to mine . . .": *CW,* vol. V, p. 477.
89 "I cannot resist . . .": *OR,* Series 1, vol. 19 (Part II), p. 497.
89 "Most certainly . . .": *CW,* vol. V, p. 479.
89 "how necessary it is . . .": *OR,* Series 1, vol. 19 (Part II), p. 496.
89 "And now I ask . . .": *CW,* vol. V, p. 479.
90 "I commenced crossing . . .": *OR,* Series 1, vol. 19 (Part II), p. 497.
90 "I am much pleased . . .": *CW,* vol. V, p. 481.
91 "If I should be in a Boat . . ." ("wednesday" not capitalized in original): *CW,* vol. V, p. 511.
91 "The wounded and killed . . .": *LC* telegram from Anson Stager to Edwin Stanton.
91 "It is well . . .": Foote, vol. II, p. 37.
91–92 "I have good reason . . .": *CW,* vol. VI, p. 22.

Chapter Six: New Electronic Challenges

PAGE

93 "Washington is as near . . .": Blondheim, p. 190.
93–94 Information on Civil War publishing, see: James McPherson, *The Most Fearful Ordeal,* St. Martins Press, 2004, p. ix.
94 For a discussion of the price of a telegraph message, as well as of a newspaper, and the number and nature of special war correspondents, see: J. Cutler Andrews, *The North Reports the Civil War,* University of Pittsburgh Press, 1955, pgs. 24, 32, 60, 20.
95 "We must have . . .": McPherson, p. ix.

95 Newspaper reporting, see: Andrews, p. 6.
95 "Public sentiment . . .": *CW,* vol. III, p. 27.
96 First systematic censorship, see: Andrews, p. 649.
96 Reliance on patriotism, see: Andrews, p. 150.
96 "refrain from publishing . . .": House Report No. 64, 37th Congress, 2nd Session, 1862, p. 2.
96–97 Clearance of telegrams, see: Richard B. Kielbowicz, *The Telegraph, Censorship, and Politics at the Outset of the Civil War,* Civil War History 40, no. 2 (June, 1994), pp. 100–01.
97 Military possession of telegraph, see: *OR,* Series 3, vol. 1, p. 899.
97 "[A]ll telegraphic dispatches . . ."; House Report, pp. 2–3.
97 Limiting to official reports, see: Kielbowicz, p. 103.
97 "the Gov't wd . . .": Andrews, p. 103.
98 "A telegraphic censorship . . .": House Report, pp. 12–13.
98–99 Associated Press as preferred news provider with preferential access, see: Blondheim, pp. 130, 135.
99 "to prohibit all telegraphic despatches . . .": House Report, pp. 2–3.
99 "I take the associated press . . .": Kielbowicz, p. 110.
99 Use of General Dix, see: Gerald S. Henig and Eric Niderost, *Civil War Firsts,* Stackpole Books, 2001, p. 233.
99 "almost every Northern journalist . . .": Henig and Niderost, p. 260.
100 "as the telegraph is known . . .": Writers and Reporters of *The New York Times, The Most Fearful Ordeal,* St. Martins Press, 2004, p. 64.
100 "the bad quality of the mules . . .": John W. Thompson, Jr., *Jeb Stuart,* University of Nebraska Press, 1994, p. 351.
101 Dining on Union beef, see: *Encyclopedia of the Confederacy,* Simon & Schuster, 1993, vol. 4, p. 1573.
101 Coded telegram, see: Plum, vol. 1, p. 35.
102 Description of ciphers, see: Donald Markle, ed, *The Telegraph Goes to War,* Edmonston Publishing, 2003, p. 16.
102 Route system never broken, see: Ross, p. 165.
103 "Let execution of the death sentence . . .": *CW,* vol. VII, p. 122.
103 Description of "shot to death" and court martial proceeding, see: Thomas P. Lowry, *Don't Shoot that Boy!,* Savas Publishing Company, 1999, pgs. v, 11, 12.
104 "Today we spent 6 hours . . ." ("courtmartials" in original): Burlingame and Ettlinger, p. 64.
104 "This is the day . . .": Sandburg, p. 592.
104 Statistical analysis of executions, see: Lowry, p. iii.

105 "[Y]ou call [these cases] . . .": Richard Current, *The Lincoln Nobody Knows,* Hill and Wang, 1958, p. 166.
105 "I pray you do not . . .": Current, p. 166.
105 "I shot them first.": Sandburg, p. 592.
105 "I don't believe it will make . . .": Lowry, p. ii.
105 "With pardons as with patronage . . .": Current, p. 175.
105 "I have telegraphed to Chattanooga . . .": *CW,* vol. VII, p. 122.
106 "I see you are not very well acquainted . . .": Current, p. 166.
106 "Let execution in case of . . .": *CW,* vol. VIII, p. 159.
106 "The draft will go to you . . .": *CW,* vol. VII, p. 320.
107 "Mrs. Cuthbert & Aunt Mary . . .": *CW,* vol. V, p. 492.
107 "Dont be uneasy . . ." ("Dont" spelling in original): *CW,* vol. VI, p. 314. This message was not in Lincoln's hand but did have appended to it a note, "Please send at once."
107 "Come to Washington": *CW,* vol. VI, p. 323.
107 "Why do I hear no more . . .": *CW,* vol. VI, p. 327.
108 "The air is so clear . . .": *CW,* vol. VI, pp. 471–72.
108 "All is going well . . .": *CW,* vol. VI, pp. 34–35.
108 "All is very well . . .": *CW,* vol. VII, p. 106.
108 "We are all well . . .": *CW,* vol. VII, p. 112.
108 "I sent your draft . . .": *CW,* vol. VII, p. 121.
108 "All well, and very warm . . .": *CW,* vol. VII, p. 406.
109 "Tom is moving . . ." *CW,* vol. VII, p. 417.
109 Mrs. Lincoln's scolding, see: William C. Harris, *Lincoln's Last Months,* Belknap Press, 2004, p. 196.
109 "At 4:30 p.m. to-day . . .": *CW,* vol. VIII, p. 384.

Chapter Seven: Commanding Through the Inbox

PAGE

110–11 "It is not proposed . . .": K. Jack Bauer, *The Mexican War,* University of Nebraska Press, 1974, p. 237.
112 Description of Lincoln in telegraph office, see: Sandburg, p. 392.
112–13 Halleck and Jomini, see: Marszalek, p. 43.
113 "In regard to movements . . .": *OR,* Series I, vol. 51 (Part I), p. 958.
113 Halleck's refusal to make decisions, see: Marszalek, p. 158.
114 Hooker statements about Lincoln, see: Donald, p. 411.

114 "I have heard . . ." *CW,* vol. VI, p. 78.
115 Hooker's reorganization, see: Jeffrey W. Wert, *The Sword of Lincoln,* Simon & Schuster, 2005, p. 220.
115 "Hence our prime objective . . ." ("enemies' army" in original): *CW,* vol. VI, p. 164.
116 "I hope Mr. President . . .": *CW,* vol. VI, p. 169.
116 "Your letter . . .": *CW,* vol. VI, p. 169.
116 "Would like to have a letter . . .": *CW,* vol. VI, p. 173.
116 "How does it look . . .": *CW,* vol. VI, p. 188.
116 "I am not sufficiently advanced . . .": *CW,* vol. VI, p. 188.
117 "You know that nothing . . .": *CW,* vol. VI, p. 190.
117 "The rebel army . . .": Ernest B. Furguson, *Chancellorsville,* Alfred A. Knopf, 1992, p. 111.
117 Hooker's noncommunication with Washington, see: Wert, p. 253.
118 "Where is Gen. Hooker . . .": *CW,* vol. VI, p. 196.
118 "We have nothing . . .": *CW,* vol. VI, p. 198.
118 Richmond paper reports, see: *CW,* vol. VI, p. 199.
118 "the army has recrossed . . .": *OR,* Series 1, vol. 25 (Part III), p. 434.
118 "Had a thunderbolt fallen . . .": Wert, p. 253.
118 "What next?": *CW,* vol. VI, p. 201.
118 "I have decided . . .": *LC.*
119 "If it will not interfere . . .": *CW,* vol. VI, p. 215.
119 "It does not now appear . . .": *CW,* vol. VI, p. 217.
119 "pitch into his rear": *LC.*
119 "an ox half over . . .": *CW,* vol. VI, p. 249.
119 "rapid advance . . .": *CW,* vol. VI, p. 257.
119 "If he [Lee] comes . . ." ("oppertunity" in original): Ibid.
120 "Do you consider . . .": *CW,* vol. VI, p. 273.
120 "Are the forces . . .": *CW,* vol. VI, p. 274.
120 "Get Milroy . . .": Ibid.
120 "Is Milroy invested . . .": *CW,* vol. VI, p. 275.
120 "General Milroy is in a tight place . . .": *CW,* vol. VI, p. 275.
120 "So far as we can make out . . .": *CW,* vol. VI, p. 273.
120 "I do not feel like . . .": *CW,* vol. VI, p. 274.
121 "quite certain . . .": *CW,* vol. VI, p. 273.
121 "I think the report . . .": *CW,* vol. VI, p. 276.
121 "Your telegram of 8:30 . . .": *OR,* Series 1, vol. 25 (Part II), p. 43.
121 "Your dispatch is more conclusive . . .": *OR,* Series 1, vol. 25 (Part II), p. 44.

121 "I am not prepared . . .": *OR,* Series 1, vol. 25 (Part II), p. 43.
121 "I do not know . . .": *OR,* Series 1, vol. 25 (Part II), p. 44.
121 "had only occupied . . .": Wert, p. 268.
122 "You have long been aware . . .": *OR,* Series 1, vol. 25 (Part II), p. 45.
122 "Now, all I ask . . .": *CW,* vol. VI, p. 281.
122 Hooker-Halleck skirmishing, see: *OR,* Series 1, vol. 25, pp. 45–47.
123 "To remove all misunderstanding . . .": *CW,* vol. VI, p. 282.
123 "You are in command . . .": *OR,* Series 1, vol. 27 (Part I), p. 47.
123 "Earnestly request . . .": *OR,* Series 1, vol. 27 (Part I), p. 60.
123 Meade placed in command of Army of the Potomac, *OR,* Series 1, vol. 27 (Part I), p. 61.
123 Meade unknown because of press, see: Marszalek, 176.
124 "Have you any reports . . .": *CW,* vol. VI, p. 293.
124 "What news now?": *CW,* vol. VI, p. 299.
124 General Couch's reply, see: *OR,* Series 1, vol., 27 (Part III), p. 385.
124 "We have reliable . . .": *LC.*
124 Line to Meade's headquarters cut, see: Bates, p. 155.
124–25 "Short of getting into uniform . . .": Perret, p. 276.
125 "I judge by the absence . . .": *CW,* vol. VI, p. 310.
125 "The best part of Chambersburg . . .": *LC.*
125 "The rebel Infantry force . . .": *LC.*
125 "Lincoln was in the telegraph office . . .": Bates, p. 155.
126 Meade's use of telegraph at Gettysburg, see: Hagerman, p. 87.
126 "The President announces . . .": *CW,* vol. VI, p. 314.
126 "Lincoln began to realize . . .": Bates, p. 156.
126 "entirely destroyed . . .": *OR,* Series 1, vol. 27 (Part III), p. 524.
126 "I see your despatch . . .": *CW,* vol. VI, p. 317.
126 "Five hundred wagons . . .": *OR,* Series 1, vol. 27 (Part III), p. 546.
127 "I left the telegraph office . . .": *CW,* vol. VI, p. 318.
127 "the escape of Lee's army . . .": *OR,* Series 1, vol. 27 (Part I), p. 92.
127 "Having performed my duty . . .": *OR,* Series 1, vol. 27 (Part I), p. 93.
127–28 "My telegram, stating the disappointment . . .": *OR,* Series 1, vol. 27 (Part I), pp. 93–94.
128 "I have just seen your despatch . . .": *CW,* vol. VI, p. 328.

Chapter Eight: Even with Technology, It's All about People

PAGE

130 Problematic nature of telegraph in Western Theater, see: Plum, vol. I, pp. 325, 331.
130–31 Information from Vicksburg, see: Plum, vol. I, p. 321.
131 Arrival of Vicksburg message, see: Bates, p. 156.
131 "Gen. Grant is a copious worker . . .": *CW,* vol. VI, p. 350.
131 "What news have you?": *CW,* vol. VI, p. 142.
131 "Do Richmond papers . . .": *CW,* vol. VI, p. 43.
132 "I fear a calamity . . .": Foote, vol. II, p. 216.
132 Charles Dana sent to check on Grant, see: Jean Edward Smith, *Grant,* Simon & Schuster, 2001, p. 213.
132–33 "Have you heard from Grant?": *CW,* vol. VI, p. 233.
133 "I would not push . . .": *CW,* vol. VI, p. 236.
133 "Are you in communication . . .": *CW,* vol. VI, p. 244.
133 "It seems to me that . . .": *LC.*
134 "I do not remember that you and I ever met . . .": *CW,* vol. VI, p. 326.
135 "Did you receive . . .": *CW,* vol. VI, p. 374.
135 "Your letter of the 13th . . .": *LC.*
135 "I see by a despatch . . .": *CW,* vol. VI, p. 374.
135 "After the fall of Vicksburg . . .": *LC.*
136 Lincoln remaining in telegraph office, see: Bates, p. 158.
136 "For three or four days . . .": Bates, p. 158.
136 "Go to Rosecrans . . .": *CW,* vol. VI, p. 469.
136 "Be of good cheer . . .": *CW,* vol. VI, p. 472.
136 "Unless your troops . . .": *OR,* Series 1, vol. 30 (Part III), p. 149.
137 "We have not a word . . .": *OR,* Series 1, vol. 30 (Part III), p. 474.
137 "We are now in Chattanooga . . .": *OR,* Series 1, vol. 30 (Part I), p. 161.
137 "Your despatch of the twenty first . . .": *LC.*
137 "Yours of the 23rd . . .": *CW,* vol. VI., p. 480.
138 "I have just telegraphed . . .": *OR,* Series 1, vol. 30 (Part III), p. 940.
138 "My order to you meant simply . . .": *CW,* vol. VI, p. 483.
138 "Telegram after telegram . . .": *OR,* Series 1, vol. 30 (Part III), p. 906.
138 "You can perhaps communicate . . .": *CW,* vol. VI, p. 485.
138–39 Cabinet meeting, see: Marszalek, p. 186.
139 Informing railroads by telegram, see: *CWDBD,* p. 413.
139 Statistics on the movement, see: *CWDBD,* p. 417.

139 "Unfortunately, the relations . . .": *CW,* vol. VI, p. 486.
139 "Any attempt to mingle . . .": *LC.*
139–40 Lincoln needed a no-nonsense general, see: *CWDBD,* p. 423.
140 "Hold Chattanooga at all hazards . . .": *OR,* Series 1, vol. 30 (Part IV), p. 479.
140 "I will hold . . .": *OR,* Series 1, vol. 30 (Part IV), p. 479.
140 "General Thomas' plan . . .": *OR,* Series 1, vol. 31 (Part I), p. 56.
140 "Your dispatches as to fighting . . .": *CW,* vol. VII, p. 30.
141 "Reliable information being received . . .": *CW,* vol. VII, p. 35.
141 "I wish to tender . . .": *CW,* vol. VII, p. 53.

Chapter Nine: Building the Modern Leadership Model

PAGE

142 "I nominate Ulysses S. Grant . . .": Archives of the United States.
142 Revival of Lieutenant General, see: Smith, p. 284.
143 "first rate clerk": Burlingame & Ettlinger, p. 192.
143 "In these days . . .": *LC,* Grant Papers.
143–44 "the value of the magnetic telegraph . . .": William T. Sherman, *Memoirs of General W.T. Sherman,* The Library of America, 1990, p. 889.
144 Attributes of a great leader, see: Cohen, p. 32.
144 "Grant is the first general . . .": T. Harry Williams, *Lincoln and His Generals,* Alfred A. Knopf, 1952, p. 305. Williams gave voice to the theory that Lincoln and Grant had together developed the modern command structure.
144 "a copious worker . . .": *CW,* vol. VI, p. 350.
145 Grant never reading Jomini, see: Smith, p. 152.
146 Halleck's invitation to lay out a plan, see: *OR,* Series 1, vol. 32 (Part III), pp. 40–42.
146 "an abandonment of all . . .": *OR,* Series 1, vol. 33, pp. 394–95.
146 Lincoln unwilling to risk exposing Washington, see: MacGregor Knox and Williamson Murray, eds., *The Dynamics of Military Revolution,* Cambridge University Press, 2001, p. 82.
147 Strategy that was servant to policy, see: James Marshall-Cornwall, *Grant as Military Commander,* Barnes & Noble reprint, 1995, p. 132.
147 Grant's weekly meetings with Lincoln, see: Williams, p. 308.

147 "In my first interview . . .": Ulysses S. Grant, *The Personal Memoirs of Ulysses S. Grant,* Konecky & Konecky reprint, pp. 407–8.
148 "It is my design . . .": *OR,* Series 1, vol. 32 (Part III), pp. 40–42.
148 "So far as practicable . . .": *OR,* Series 1, vol. 33, pp. 827–29.
149 "The particulars of your plans . . .": *CW,* vol. VII, p. 324.
149 "Should any success . . .": *LC.*
149 "When I have sufficient confidence . . .": Marshall-Cornwall, p. 139.
150 Davis's message to Lee, see: *CWDBD,* pp. 490–93.
150 Field telegraph not advanced, see: Plum, vol. II, p. 132.
150–51 "If you see the President . . .": Smith, p. 334.
151 "Mr. Lincoln put his great . . .": Smith, p. 335n.
151 "Received today the first despatches . . ." Burlingame & Ettlinger, p. 195.
151 Grant's casualties, see: Wert, p. 366.
152 "Our forces will commence . . .": *OR,* Series 1, vol. 40 (Part I), p. 12.
152 "Have just read . . .": *CW,* vol. VII, p. 393.
153 "You will never hear . . .": *CW,* vol. VII, p. 406n.
154 "You say telegraphic communication . . .": *CW,* vol. VII, p. 424.
154 "What have you heard . . .": *CW,* vol. VII, p. 434.
154 "Our troops at Monocacy . . .": *CW,* vol. VII, p. 434n.
154 "Forces enough . . .": *OR,* Series 1, vol. 37 (Part II), p. 134.
154–55 "Your despatch to Gen. Halleck . . .": *CW,* vol. VII, p. 437.
155 "I have sent . . .": *OR,* Series 1, vol. 40 (Part III), p. 122.
155 "Yours of 10.30 . . .": *CW,* vol. VII, p. 438.
155 "concluded to desert his tormentors . . .": Burlingame & Ettlinger, p. 221.
156 Arming of clerks, see: Bates, p. 250n.
156 "The President is in very good feather . . .": Burlingame & Ettlinger, p. 221.
156 Man next to Lincoln hit, see: Burlingame & Ettlinger, p. 222.
156 "Get down . . .": *LDBD,* p. 272.
157 "In your despatch of yesterday . . .": *CW,* vol. VII, p. 444.
158 "It takes a long time . . .": *OR,* Series 1, vol. 40 (Part III), p. 457.
158 "[O]wing to the difficulties . . .": *OR,* Series 1, vol. 40 (Part III), p. 463.
159 "Will meet you at Fort-Monroe . . .": *CW,* vol. III, p. 469.
159 Lincoln-Grant meeting, see: *LDBD,* vol. II, p. 276.
159 "I want Sheridan . . .": *OR,* Series 1, vol. 37 (Part II), p. 558.
159–60 "I have seen your despatch . . .": *CW,* vol. VII, p. 476.

160 "Your dispatch of 6 P.M . . .": *OR,* Series 1, vol. 43 (Part I), p. 681.
160 "that crows flying over . . .": *OR,* Series 1, vol. 37 (Part II), pp. 300–1.
161 "Sheridan and Early . . .": *CW,* vol. VII, p. 548.
161 "It has been my intention . . .": *LC.*
161 "I have the honor to report . . .": *OR,* Series 1, vol. 43 (Part II), p. 110.
161–62 "Have just heard . . .": *CW,* vol. VIII, p. 13.
162 "I hope it will . . .": *CW,* vol. VIII, p. 29.
162 "I am taking steps . . .": *OR,* Series 1, vol. 42 (Part II), p. 1090.
162 "With great pleasure . . .": *CW,* vol. VIII, pp. 73–74.

Chapter Ten: The Last Lap

PAGE

164 "This morning . . .": *CW,* vol. VII, p. 514.
164 First popular election during a war, see: Henig & Niderost, p. 269. While James Madison ran for reelection in 1812, it was the outbreak of the War of 1812 and not the situation of an ongoing, multiyear conflict as was the election of 1864.
164 "The people are wild for peace . . .": *LC.*
165 "You think I don't know . . .": Donald, p. 529.
165 Morse's observations about Lincoln, see: Silverman, p. 411, and Sandburg, p. 372.
165 "more of a politician . . .": *CW,* vol. VII, p. 398.
165 "The President is too busy . . .": Donald. p. 538.
165 For description of political favors, see: Henig & Niderost, p. 271, and John C. Waugh, *Reelecting Lincoln,* DaCapo Press, 2001, p. 329–30.
166 "Pennsylvania very close . . .": *CW,* vol. VIII, p. 45.
166 Voting procedures, see: Waugh, p. 340.
166–67 "The State election . . .": *CW,* vol. VIII, p. 11.
167 "I most earnestly . . .": *LC.*
167 "I therefore can not press . . .": *CW,* vol. VIII, p. 46.
167 "It is my opinion . . .": *LC.*
167 For examples of Lincoln's staying out of direct involvement, see exchanges with Illinois governor Yates, *OR,* Series 3, vol. 4, pp. 871–72.
167 "Home vote" versus "army vote," see: Waugh, p. 340.
168 "By direction of the honorable . . .": *OR,* Series 1, vol. 39 (Part III), p. 603.

168 Electoral college vote, see: Waugh, p. 354.

168 "Official statement of the vote . . .": *OR,* Series I, vol. 42 (Part III), p. 570.

168–70 Quotes regarding Hampton Roads Peace Conference: Unless otherwise noted, all the quotes regarding this topic are from Lincoln's report to the House of Representatives, February 18, 1865 at the Library of Congress.

169 "Let nothing . . .": *CW,* vol. VIII, p. 252.

169 "Your dispatch received . . .": *OR,* Series 1, vol. 46 (Part II), p. 341.

170 "The President desires . . .": *LC.*

171 "that if I desired . . .": *LC.*

171 "The President directs me . . .": *CW,* vol. VIII, pp. 330–31.

172 "Both parties deprecated war . . .": *CW,* vol. VIII, pp. 332–33.

172 "There was a little rumpus . . .": *CW,* vol. VIII, p. 373.

172 Lincoln watching counterattack, see: Perret, p. 400.

172 "I am here within . . .": *CW,* vol. VIII, p. 374.

172–73 "I hope you will remember . . .": *LC.*

173 "Just arrived here . . ." (time expression in original): *LC.*

173 "The 2nd Corps . . .": *LC.*

173 "The enemy attacked . . .": *LC.*

173 "Your three despatches . . ." (form and words as in orginal): *CW,* vol. VIII, p. 376.

173 "Griffin was attacked . . ." (time expression and spelling in original): *LC.*

174 "What, if any thing . . .": *CW,* vol. VIII, p. 377.

174 "I begin to feel . . .": Ibid.

174 "much hard fighting . . ." (capitalization in original): *LC.*

174 "I will send you . . .": *LC.*

174 "Judging by the two points . . .": *CW,* vol. VIII, p. 378.

174 "Sheridan has . . .": *LC.*

175 "The whole 5" Corps . . ." (form in original): *LC*

175 "This morning . . ." ("enemies" in original): *CW,* vol. VIII, p. 381.

175 "Despatches frequently coming in . . ." ("intrenched" in original): *CW,* vol. VIII, p. 382.

176 "We are now closing . . .": *CW,* vol. VIII, p. 382–3.

176 "Allow me to tender . . .": *CW,* vol. VIII, p. 383.

176 Lincoln's trip to see Grant, see: *LDBD,* p. 324.

176 "We took Richmond . . .": *OR,* Series 1, vol. 46 (Part III), p. 509.

176 "Say to the President . . .": Ibid.

176–77 "routed them handsomely . . .": *OR,* Series 1, vol. 46 (Part III), p. 610.
177 "Gen. Sheridan says . . .": *CW,* vol. VIII, p. 392.
177 Robert Lincoln at White House, see: *LDBD,* p. 329.
177 "I have seen Eckert . . .": Bates, p. 367.
178 Description of Lincoln's decision to take Major Rathbone, instead of Eckert, with him to Ford's Theater, see: Bates, p. 368.

Chapter Eleven: "Now He Belongs to the Ages"

PAGE

181 "If I do not misunderstand . . .": *CW,* vol. VI, p. 450.
181–82 "The truth is . . .": Hay quoted in James A. Rawley Introduction to Bates, p. xxi.
182 "I write you more fully . . .": *CW,* vol. VI, p. 138.
182 "I will write . . .": *CW,* vol. VIII, p. 351.
183 "I now wish to . . .": *CW,* vol. VI, 326.
183 "it makes me doubt . . .": *CW,* vol. VI, p. 480–81.
184 "Hold on . . .": *CW,* vol. VIII, p. 499.
184 "I would not take . . .": *CW,* vol. VI, p. 249.
184 "Watch it every day . . .": *CW,* vol. VII, p. 476.
184 " 'If the thing' . . .": *CW,* vol. VIII, 392.
184 "If you and he . . .": *CW,* vol. VI, p. 281.
184 "My order . . .": *CW,* vol. VI, p. 483.
184–85 "struck with the business . . .": Burlingame & Ettlinger, p. 38.
185 Lincoln's relationship with Grant, see: Garry Wills, *Lincoln at Gettysburg,* Simon & Schuster, 1992, p. 170.
185 Description of Lincoln's "telegraphic eloquence," see: Wills, p. 161.
185 "Now he belongs to the ages,": Sandburg, p. 716.

BIBLIOGRAPHY

Alotta, Robert I. *Civil War Justice: Union Army Executions under Lincoln*. Shippensburg, PA: White Mane Publishing, 1989.

Ameigh, Michael. *The Vails of Speedwell,* paper presented at the Annual Symposium on Telecommunications History, Canadian Armed Forces Museum, Kingston, Ontario, September 1997. http://speedwell.org/Vail/Ameigh.html.

Andrews, J. Cutler. *The North Reports the Civil War.* Pittsburgh, PA: University of Pittsburgh Press, 1955.

Basler, Roy P. *The Collected Works of Abraham Lincoln.* Eight volumes. New Brunswick, NJ: Rutgers University Press, 1953.

Bates, David Homer. *Lincoln in the Telegraph Office: Recollections of the United States Military Telegraph Corps during the Civil War.* Lincoln, NE: University of Nebraska Press, 1955.

Bauer, Jack K. *The Mexican War 1846–1848.* Lincoln, NE: University of Nebraska Press, 1992.

Beringer, Richard E., Herman Hattaway, Archer Jones, and William N. Still, Jr. *Why the South Lost the Civil War.* Athens, GA: University of Georgia Press, 1986.

Bishop, Jim. *The Day Lincoln Was Shot.* New York, NY: Gramercy Books, 1955.

Black, Robert C., III. *The Railroads of the Confederacy.* Chapel Hill, NC: University of North Carolina Press, 1998.

Blondheim, Menahem. *News over the Wires.* Cambridge, MA: Harvard University Press, 1994.

Bruce, Robert V., *The Launching of Modern Science, 1846–1876.* New York, NY: Alfred A. Knopf, 1987.

———. *Lincoln and the Tools of War.* Urbana, IL: University of Illinois Press, 1989.

Burlingame, Michael. *The Inner World of Abraham Lincoln.* Urbana, IL: University of Chicago Press, 1994.

———, ed. *An Oral History of Abraham Lincoln: John G. Nicolay's Interviews and Essays.* Carbondale, IL: Southern Illinois University Press, 1996.

Burlingame, Michael, and John R. Turner Ettlinger, eds. *Inside Lincoln's White House: The Complete Civil War Diary of John Hay.* Carbondale, IL: Southern Illinois Press, 1997.

Carwardine, Richard. *Lincoln: A Life of Purpose and Power.* New York, NY: Alfred A. Knopf, 2006.

Coe, Lewis. *The Telegraph: A History of Morse's Invention and Its Predecessors in the United States.* Jefferson, NC: McFarland & Company, 1993.

Cohen, Eliot A. *Supreme Command.* New York, NY: Free Press, 2002

Coggins, Jack. *Arms and Equipment of the Civil War.* Mineola, NY: Dover Publications, 1962.

Cooling, Benjamin Franklin, III. *Symbol, Sword and Shield: Washington during the Civil War.* Shippensburg, PA: White Mane Publishing, 1991.

Cooper, William J., Jr. *Jefferson Davis, American.* New York, NY: Vintage Books, 2000.

Current, Richard N. *The Lincoln Nobody Knows.* New York, NY: Hill and Wang, 1958.

———, ed. *Encyclopedia of the Confederacy.* Four volumes. New York, NY: Simon & Schuster, 1993.

Davis, Burke. *Jeb Stuart, the Last Cavalier.* New York, NY: Rinehart & Company, 1957.

Davis, James. *Abraham Lincoln before the Presidency.* Illinois Periodicals Online. www.lib.niu.edu/ipo/ihy950225.html.

Davis, William C. *Jefferson Davis: The Man and His Hour.* Baton Rouge, LA: Louisiana State University Press, 1991.

Donald, David Herbert. *Lincoln.* New York, NY: Simon & Schuster, 1995.

———, ed. *Why the North Won the Civil War.* New York, NY: Simon & Schuster, 1960.

Donald, David Herbert, and Harold Holzer, eds. *Lincoln in the Times:*

The Life of Abraham Lincoln as Originally Reported in The New York Times. New York, NY: St. Martin's Press, 2005.

Eicher, John H. and David J. *Civil War High Commands.* Stanford, CA: Stanford University Press, 2001.

Evans, Harold. *They Made America: From the Steam Engine to the Search Engine: Two Centuries of Innovators.* New York, NY: Little Brown, 2004.

Foote, Shelby. *The Civil War, A Narrative.* New York, NY: Vintage Books, 1986.

Furguson, Ernest B. *Ashes of Glory: Richmond at War.* New York, NY: Vintage Books, 1996.

———. *Chancellorsville.* New York, NY: Alfred A. Knopf, 1992.

———. *Freedom Rising: Washington in the Civil War.* New York, NY: Alfred A. Knopf, 2004.

Goodwin, Doris Kearns. *Team of Rivals: The Political Genius of Abraham Lincoln.* New York, NY: Simon & Schuster, 2005.

Gordon, Sarah. *Passage to Union: How the Railroads Transformed American Life, 1829–1929.* Chicago, IL: Ivan R. Dee, 1998.

Grant, Ulysses S. *The Personal Memoirs of Ulysses S. Grant.* Old Saybrook, CT: Konecky & Konecky reprint.

Hagerman, Edward. *The American Civil War and the Origins of Modern Warfare: Ideas, Organization, and Field Command.* Bloomington, IN: Indiana University Press, 1992.

Harper, Robert S. *Lincoln and the Press.* New York, NY: McGraw Hill, 1951.

Harris, William G. *Lincoln's Last Months.* Cambridge, UK: Belknap Press, 2003.

Haupt, Herman. *Reminiscences of General Herman Haupt.* North Stratford, NH: Ayer Company Publishers reprint, 2000.

Henic, Gerard S., and Eric Niderost. *Civil War Firsts.* Mechanicsburg, PA: Stackpole Books, 2001.

Herzog, Melinda. *The Battle of Bull Run Railroad Bridge.* Hallowed Ground, Summer 2004.

Holzer, Harold. *Lincoln at Cooper Union: The Speech That Made Abraham Lincoln President.* New York, NY: Simon & Schuster, 2004.

Kahn, David. *The Codebreakers: The Story of Secret Writing.* London, UK: Weidenfeld and Nicolson, 1967.

Keegan, John. *The Mask of Command.* London, UK: Penguin Books, 1987.

Kielbowicz, Richard B. *The Telegraph, Censorship, and Politics at the Outset of the Civil War.* Civil War History, vol. 40, no. 2, June 1994.

Knox, MacGregor, and Williamson Murray. *The Dynamics of Military Revolution, 1300–2050.* Cambridge, UK. Cambridge University Press, 2001.

Kunhardt, Dorothy Meserve and Philip B. *Twenty Days: A Narrative in Text and Pictures of the Assassination of Abraham Lincoln and the Twenty Days and Nights That Followed—The Nation in Mourning, the Long Trip Home to Springfield.* Secaucus, NJ: Castle Books, 1993.

Lankford, Nelson. *Richmond Burning: The Last Days of the Confederate Capital.* London, UK: Penguin Books, 2002.

Lebow, Irwin. *Information Highways & Byways.* New York, NY: IEEE Press, 1995.

Leech, Margaret. *Reveille in Washington, 1860–1865.* New York, NY: Carroll & Graf reprint, 1986.

Leidner, Gordon. *Measuring the Presidents.* Columbiad, vol. 2, no. 1, Spring 1998.

Lesser, W. Hunter. *The First Campaign: War Begins in the Alleghenies.* Hallowed Ground Winter 2001.

Library of Congress, *The Abraham Lincoln Papers.* http://memory.loc.gov.

Long, E. B. *The True Believers: The Committee on the Conduct of the War.* Civil War Times Illustrated, August 1981.

Long, E. B. with Barbara. *The Civil War Day by Day.* Garden City, NJ: Doubleday, 1971.

Lowry, Thomas P. *Don't Shoot That Boy! Abraham Lincoln and Military Justice.* Mason City, IA: Savas Publishing, 1999.

Mabee, Carleton. *The American Leonardo: A Life of Samuel F. B. Morse.* Fleischmanns, NY: Purple Mountain Press edition, 2000.

Manber, Jeffrey, and Neil Dahlstrom. *Lincoln's Wrath: Fierce Mobs, Brilliant Scoundrels and a President's Mission to Destroy the Press.* Naperville, IL: Sourcebooks, 2005.

Markle, Donald E., ed. *The Telegraph Goes to War: The Personal Diary of David Homer Bates, Lincoln's Telegraph Operator.* Hamilton, NY: Edmonston Publishing, 2003.

Marszalek, John F. *Commander of All Lincoln's Armies: A Life of General Henry W. Halleck.* Cambridge, MA: Harvard University Press, 2004.

Martin, Albro. *Railroads Triumphant.* Oxford, UK: Oxford University Press, 1992.

Marvin, Carolyn. *When Old Technologies Were New: Thinking about Electric Communication in the Late Nineteenth Century.* Oxford, UK: Oxford University Press, 1988.

McEwen, Neal. *Morse Code or Vail Code? Did Samuel F. B. Morse Invent the Code as We Know it Today?* The Telegraph Office, 1997, www.metronet.com/~nmcewen/vail.html.

McPherson, James M. *Abraham Lincoln and the Second American Revolution.* Oxford, UK: Oxford University Press, 1991.

———. *The Most Fearful Ordeal: The Original Coverage of the Civil War by Writers and Reporters of The New York Times.* New York, NY: St. Martin's Press, 2004.

———, ed. *"We Cannot Escape History": Lincoln and the Last Best Hope of Earth.* Urbana, IL: University of Illinois Press, 1995.

Miers, Earl Schenck. *Lincoln Day by Day.* Dayton, OH: Morningside House, 1991.

Mitgang, Herbert, ed. *Abraham Lincoln: A Press Portrait.* Chicago, IL: Quadrangle Books, 1971.

National Archives, *Telegrams Collected by the Office of the Secretary of War,* Microfilm no. 473.

Neuman, Johanna. *Lights, Camera, War: Is Media Technology Driving International Politics?* New York, NY: St. Martin's Press, 1995.

Owens, Bill. *Lifting the Fog of War.* Baltimore, MD: The Johns Hopkins University Press, 2000.

Packard, Jerrold M. *The Lincolns in the White House: Four Years That Shattered a Family.* New York, NY: St. Martin's Press, 2005.

Perret, Geoffrey. *Lincoln's War: The Untold Story of America's Greatest President as Commander in Chief.* New York, NY: Random House, 2004.

———. *Ulysses S. Grant, Soldier & President.* New York, NY: Random House, 1997.

Peterson, Merrill, *Lincoln in American Memory.* Oxford, UK: Oxford University Press, 1994.

Phillips, Donald T. *Lincoln on Leadership.* New York, NY: Warner Books, 1992.

Pinsker, Matthew. *Lincoln's Sanctuary: Abraham Lincoln and the Soldiers' Home.* Oxford, UK: Oxford University Press, 2003.

Porter, Horace. *Campaigning with Grant.* New York, NY: Bantam Books, 1991.

Pritchard, Russ A., Jr. *Civil War Weapons and Equipment.* Guilford, CT: Salamander Books, 2003.

Plum, William R. *The Military Telegraph during the Civil War in the United States.* Two volumes. North Stratford, NH: Ayer Company reprint, 2000.

Reck, W. Emerson. *A. Lincoln: His Last 24 Hours.* Jefferson, NC: McFarland & Co., 1987.

Ross, Charles. *Trial by Fire: Science, Technology and the Civil War.* Shippensburg, PA: White Mane Books, 2000.

Roth, Mitchell P. *Historical Dictionary of War Journalism.* Westport, CT: Greenwood Press, 1997.

Rothman, Tony. *Everything's Relative and Other Fables from Science and Technology.* Hoboken, NJ: John Wiley & Sons, 2003.

Round, Harold F. *The Telegraph Road,* Civil War Times Illustrated, June 1967.

Royle, Trevor. *Crimea: The Great Crimean War, 1854–56.* New York, NY: Palgrave Macmillan, 2004.

Sandburg, Carl. *Abraham Lincoln.* Two volumes. Orlando, FL: Harcourt, 1954.

———. *Mary Lincoln: Wife and Widow.* Bedford, MA: Applewood reprint, 1995.

Sears, Stephen W. *Controversies & Commanders: Dispatches from the Army of the Potomac.* Boston, MA: Houghton Mifflin, 1999.

———. *To the Gates of Richmond: The Peninsula Campaign.* New York, NY. Ticknor & Fields, 1992.

———, ed. *The Civil War Papers of George B. McClellan.* New York, NY: Da Capo Press, 1992.

Sherman, William T. *Memoirs of General W. T. Sherman.* New York, NY: Literary Classics of the United States, 1990.

Shulz, Jay. *Hurd v. Rock Island Railroad Company: A Turning Point in Abraham Lincoln's Legal Career.* Illinois Periodicals Online, www.lib.niu.edu/ipo/ihy980236.html.

Silverman, Kenneth. *Lightning Man: The Accursed Life of Samuel F. B. Morse.* New York, NY: Alfred A. Knopf, 2003.

Standage, Tom. *The Victorian Internet.* New York, NY: Berkley Books, 1999.

Starr, Paul. *The Creation of the Media: Political Origins of Modern Communications.* New York, NY: Basic Books, 2004.

Smith, Jean Edward. *Grant.* New York, NY: Simon & Schuster, 2000.

Thomas, Benjamin P. *Abraham Lincoln: A Biography.* New York, NY: Barnes & Noble Books, 1994.

Thomason, John W. *Jeb Stuart.* Lincoln, NE: University of Nebraska Press, 1994.

Tomlinson, Ray. *The First Network Email.* http://openmap.bbn.com/~tomlinson/ray/firstemail.html.

Thompson, Robert Luther. *Wiring a Continent.* Princeton, NJ: Princeton University Press, 1947.

Van Creveld, Martin. *Technology and War from 2000 B.C. to the Present.* New York, NY: Free Press, 1989.

Waugh, John C. *Reelecting Lincoln: The Battle for the 1864 Presidency.* Cambridge Center, MA: Da Capo Press, 2001.

Weinstein, Allen, and David Rubel. *The Story of America: Freedom and Crisis from Settlement to Superpower.* New York, NY: DK Publishing, 2002.

Wert, Jeffrey. *The Sword of Lincoln: The Army of the Potomac.* New York, NY: Simon & Schuster, 2005.

White, Ronald C., Jr. *Lincoln's Greatest Speech: The Second Inaugural.* New York, NY: Simon & Schuster, 2002.

Williams, T. Harry. *Lincoln and His Generals.* New York, NY: Alfred A. Knopf, 1952.

Wills, Garry. *Lincoln at Gettysburg: The Words that Remade America.* New York, NY: Touchstone, 1992.

Winkler, H. Donald. *The Women in Lincoln's Life.* Nashville, TN: Rutledge Hill Press, 2001.

Wilson, Douglas L. *Honor's Voice: The Transformation of Abraham Lincoln.* New York, NY: Alfred A. Knopf, 1998.

INDEX

Page numbers beginning with 187 refer to endnotes.

INDEX